PASSING THE BUCK

JASMINE FARRIER

Passing the Buck

CONGRESS,
THE BUDGET,
AND DEFICITS

THE UNIVERSITY PRESS OF KENTUCKY

Publication of this volume was made possible in part
by a grant from the National Endowment for the Humanities.

Scholarly publisher for the Commonwealth,
serving Bellarmine University, Berea College, Centre
College of Kentucky, Eastern Kentucky University,
The Filson Historical Society, Georgetown College,
Kentucky Historical Society, Kentucky State University,
Morehead State University, Murray State University,
Northern Kentucky University, Transylvania University,
University of Kentucky, University of Louisville,
and Western Kentucky University.

Editorial and Sales Offices: The University Press of Kentucky
663 South Limestone Street, Lexington, Kentucky 40508-4008
www.kentuckypress.com

    08 07 06 05 04   5 4 3 2 1

Library of Congress Cataloging-in-Publication Data

Farrier, Jasmine, 1970–
    Passing the buck : Congress, the budget, and deficits / by Jasmine Farrier.
        p.   cm.
    Includes bibliographical references and index.
    ISBN 0-8131-2335-6 (hardcover : alk. paper)
    1. United States. Congress—Reform. 2. United States. Congress—Powers and
duties. 3. Budget—United States. 4. Budget process—United States. 5. Finance,
Public—United States. 6. Budget deficits—United States. I. Title.
    JK1021.F37   2004
    328.73'0778—dc22   2004010629

This book is printed on acid-free recycled paper meeting
the requirements of the American National Standard
for Permanence in Paper for Printed Library Materials.

Manufactured in the United States of America.

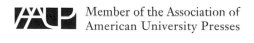

Member of the Association of
American University Presses

To my family

CONTENTS

LIST OF TABLES

ACKNOWLEDGMENTS

This book began as a graduate paper for a seminar on separation of powers taught by Jeffrey K. Tulis at the University of Texas at Austin, and I will always be deeply thankful for the many ways he helped to nurture and shape my ideas. I was also very fortunate to have been one of Walter Dean Burnham's last students before his retirement and thank him for his extraordinary wisdom and attention. My interest in institutional development was also influenced by three additional professors at Texas: Sanford Levinson, H. W. Perry Jr., and Gretchen Ritter.

The evolution of this project to its current state could not have happened without the guidance of many others. I am especially grateful for the careful reading and insightful criticism of Lawrence C. Dodd, Louis Fisher, and Daniel Palazzolo. For a fellowship year, I thank the Miller Center of Public Affairs at the University of Virginia and the Directors of their American Political Development Program, Sidney Milkis and Brian Balogh. For additional financial and institutional support, I also thank the Department of Political Science and the College of Arts and Sciences at the University of Louisville, where I am an assistant professor. Of course, the book would not have been possible without the suggestions and enthusiasm of Stephen M. Wrinn, director of the University Press of Kentucky, and his staff.

Finally, I must thank my immediate and extended family, to whom the book is dedicated, for the emotional, intellectual, and financial support that brought me to this moment.

CONGRESSIONAL DELEGATION OF POWER — NOW MORE THAN EVER

It is my own view that the people are protected in the Constitution, and that Congress could not knowingly turn the power of the purse over to the executive branch without surrendering the rights of the people and in my opinion abrogating a responsibility that I have as a representative of those people.

—*Representative Jamie Whitten (D-MS), 1973*[1]

Unfortunately, I think we have reached the point of "Stop us before we spend again." The power of the purse is already ours. It is a power we have abused too often, and too often, I might add, to the applause of our constituents. For too long, we have been rewarded for bringing home the bacon while condemning the presence and prevalence of trichinosis in the Congress. We cannot continue to have it both ways.

—*Senator William Cohen (R-ME), 1995*[2]

In numerous policy debates over recent decades Congress has openly questioned whether its powers are vital to advancing the national interest or, rather, serve to thwart it. Through such diverse delegations of power as fast-track presidential trade authority, military base–closing commissions, and the line-item veto, Congress tells the country that it is not suited to making tough decisions on major policy questions. In addition, Congress has not declared war (which it alone has the power to do) since the Second World War, opting instead to support undeclared presidential-led military actions from Korea to the Persian Gulf and to give the president enormous power and responsibility that

1

should be shared by both branches. Most recently, in the aftermath of the attacks on September 11, 2001, Congress delegated extensive powers to President George W. Bush to root out terrorism against the U.S. at home and abroad. Congress, with little dissent, approved dramatic legal and bureaucratic reform through the U.S.A. Patriot Act, almost immediately after the bill's introduction, and the creation of the Department of Homeland Security, the most dramatic overhaul of the federal bureaucracy in almost fifty years. With similar speed and limited deliberation, Congress approved broad resolutions in support of military force and reconstruction in Afghanistan and Iraq. And as the deficit soars to new heights, partly due to these actions, some Congress members have revived proposals to add balanced-budget and line–item veto amendments to the Constitution—the ultimate symbols of taking control of a problem through losing control over decision making. Through crises and more peaceful times and on many major issues, Congress has simply lacked institutional self-confidence.

Why does Congress repeatedly react to important policy challenges through delegation of power? By looking closely at the recent history of one major area of public policy making, we can get a sense of the institution's, and the nation's, most fundamental representation and legislative challenges. In this book, I examine the origins and significance of congressional delegation of power regarding the most important domestic function of any government: allocating resources and services in a budget. Although Congress is unique among legislatures in the world for its vast deliberative and procedural powers to shape the nation's fiscal policy, it does not consistently fight to retain its prerogatives and often works hard to reduce them when these powers are seen as an impediment to the nation's well-being. Just as delegation became a common tool in the fight against imbalanced budgets in the 1980s and 1990s, it has also become an important window on the uncertain place of Congress in the contemporary separation of powers system. Annual deficits have returned for the foreseeable future following a few years of surpluses, and, if past patterns are useful predictors, the next rounds of process reforms would come at the expense of Congress's budgeting powers more so than the president's, even though both share responsibility over the federal budget.

As the nation's battle against annual budget deficits escalated between the early 1970s and late 1990s, Congress's conception of its rightful budgeting powers changed dramatically. The goal of the landmark 1974 Congressional Budget and Impoundment Control Act was better budgeting through *increased* congressional power. The Congress created new committees, processes, and internal information sources to balance the pro-executive tilt of budget power of the previous fifty years. In the 1980s and 1990s, however, the goal behind budget process reform became the reduction of these congressional budgeting prerogatives, which were perceived to be a major cause of rather than the answer to high deficits and a public perception of fiscal irresponsibility in Washington. Gramm-Rudman-Hollings I (1985) and II (1987), the Budget Enforcement Act (1990), and the Line–Item Veto Act (1996) variously set annual deficit and spending caps, delegated enforcement of these and other budget rules to the president's Office of Management and Budget, required supermajorities to override the new limits and rules, and increased presidential rescission power to its pre-1974 level. Curiously, all of these reforms passed the Congress under conditions of divided government and over alternatives that would have preserved more power for the institution and future majorities.

This dramatic reduction of institutional ambition after the 1970s has fiscal, political, and institutional components. In all these budget reform cases, including 1974, years of deficits aggravated party differences on fiscal policy while also magnifying problematic institutional structures related to budgeting. What emerges through these decades of fiscal and partisan strife is an open admission of serious tensions in Congress related to its representative and lawmaking functions. Throughout all these reform histories, members of Congress repeatedly mentioned the difficulties of reconciling responsible national fiscal policy with insatiable spending desires of the public in a fragmented policy-making process.

But the crucial difference between the 1974 act and those occurring afterward is that these later reforms were centered on an anti-Congress movement, as the institution suffered a Republican-led crisis in confidence about the institution's ability to handle its fiscal responsibilities. While I am not the first to argue that Republicans and their fiscal allies used high deficits to wage an attack on federal spending and power in the 1980s and 1990s, this book takes a new approach to this history by emphasizing how these particular policy and political situations served to highlight Congress's larger, ongoing challenge to be a national representative institution composed of local voices and demands. In other words, while the general policy problem of the deficit and the specific political goals of the Republican Party both served to push congressional delegation of power in the 1980s and 1990s, an equally interesting *institutional story* emerges from these forces, one that in many ways transcends particular fiscal and political battles.

Budgetary delegation of power is at heart about the complexities and conflicts surrounding representation. In response to various fiscal pressures of the past thirty years, Congress has constantly wrestled with the representative duties and controversial legislative outcomes of its structures and procedures. To satisfy constituent demands and to get reelected, legislators often put spending pressures on the budget while resisting tax increases, even if their constituents criticized deficit spending in the abstract. In order to accommodate such representation and to give members opportunities to influence legislation and oversight, as well as to promote deliberation and policy expertise, the House and Senate are largely decentralized institutions composed of several layers of important and competing committees. Since the mid-twentieth century especially, these long-standing budgeting challenges have been strained by a growth in entitlements, indexed budgeting, and other kinds of "backdoor" spending that circumvent the annual appropriations process and further complicate the quest for balanced budgets. As a result of all these factors, the budget process is largely predisposed toward spending, but not tax, increases while Congress exerts real annual control over only a third of the budget known as discretionary spending and sometimes even less.

These tensions in congressional budgeting are well known to politicians and budget policy experts and have been the target of internal and external criticism since the late 1960s. However, those who called for significant delegation of power to resolve such problems were a small group until the early 1980s, when twelve-digit deficits became part of a conservative attack on the federal government, often symbolized as Congress. And enough Democrats joined the Congress-bashing bandwagon in 1985, 1987, and 1990 to allow the delegations to pass when their party controlled one or both chambers. Republicans continued the delegation pattern after taking control of Congress in 1995 by giving President Bill Clinton the line-item veto the following year, over the objections of his fellow Democrats in Congress.

These various alliances defended delegation of power by repeatedly arguing that Congress could not control the budget through normal legislative procedures. The very processes and structures that channeled constituent voices and demands into the system were ironically to blame for the deficits reviled in popular opinion. Supporters of reducing Congress's powers said that automatic caps and ceilings, internal rules requiring supermajorities to waive, and outside enforcement would all be useful to constraining Congress's budgetary vices. With these fetters in place, the budget process could be tilted toward balance or, at the very least, the president's "national" perspective on spending to counter Congress's more "parochial" wish lists. While the president's budget choices would be theoretically constrained by the Gramm-Rudman-Hollings and Budget Enforcement Act regulations as well, Congress's powers and prerogatives were under attack more explicitly in the legislative histories. And even as annual budget deficits began to decline around the mid-1990s, the Line–Item Veto Act and near success of two balanced budget amendment proposals further demonstrate an extraordinarily deep, almost pathological, anti-Congress mood within the majority party and the institution generally.

This dramatic shift away from institutional self-protectiveness in the early 1970s is seen in the epigraphs for this introduction. Such rhetoric can be dismissed as populist pretense related to partisan and electoral agendas, but that would ignore the complex institutional behavior underlying these events and the real reforms that resulted from it. Even assuming members and leaders had private reservations about the repercussions of enhancing executive power and fulfilling the various new budgeting restrictions, these reform movements are noteworthy because congressional rhetoric generally emphasized the flaws of the institution by repeatedly indicting *Congress* over any one party or fiscal philosophy. Although one could and should read between the lines of these self-diagnoses to see party differences on who was to blame for fiscal irresponsibility—and the floor votes on these delegations were often quite partisan—members such as Senator Cohen made "stop *us* before *we* spend again" arguments, rather than "stop *them* before *they* spend again." Along these lines, many members conveyed an image of institutional fear and self-loathing of Congress's most basic representative and legislative duties, in part because these duties were perceived as irreconcilable. By contrast, in the early 1970s Congress attempted to have it all in budgeting: representation, (relative) efficiency, and control. But while in the 1980s and 1990s members may have still coveted these political treasures behind the scenes, in public debate and law, the executive branch was seen as more worthy of them.

Important clues about why Congress delegates power come from an under-utilized source of legislative intent: the historical record. Thirty years of legislative action and rhetoric behind budget reform, under a variety of political and fiscal circumstances, yield an institutional history rich with debate over the structures and fundamental representative responsibilities of the Congress. These histories include the fiscal and political background of reform, the committee and floor action leading to the votes, and, the most interesting piece of the puzzle, how members of Congress publicly viewed their own representative powers and duties in light of the pressures of deficit reduction. This intriguing rhetoric of institutional self-diagnosis entails members' conceptions of the causes of unplanned deficit spending as well as their reasoning behind what institutional responses are appropriate. As the fiscal and political issues behind delegation of power in the 1980s and 1990s are generally well known, members' public ruminations on Congress's representational challenges and repeated rejection of more institutionally protective reforms will likely be the most surprising and interesting part of the story.

I bring these observations and other key aspects of reform history together to explain and assess Congress's institutional capacity and ambition for budgetary power. Of course, the notion that there is an entity called "Congress"—transcending more traditional units of analysis, such as individual legislators, committees, chambers, regional blocs, and parties—can raise scholarly hackles. But such challenges need not detract completely from this broader label's usefulness toward understanding the causes and consequences of delegation. One of this book's goals is to demonstrate the importance of institution-level analysis of congressional budgeting behavior over time to create a fuller explanation of why so many members seemed to view the reduction of congressional budgeting powers as a necessary part of deficit reduction, apart from short-term political goals. A heavy reliance on public legislative history brings the complex institutional nature of delegation to light by showing arguments and patterns that are deeper than short-term policy and electoral strategies, even as these latter calculations are integral to the moment's political fray.

This argument is developed throughout the book. In the two chapters of Part I, I analyze recent scholarly debates surrounding delegation of power and then present a brief history of congressional budgeting to put the past thirty years of reforms in context. In Part II, I begin the budget reform case studies with the pro-Congress outlier, the 1974 Congressional Budget and Impoundment Control Act (chapter 3), and then proceed to the delegation-based reforms: the Gramm-Rudman-Hollings Acts of the mid-1980s (chapter 4), the 1990 Budget Enforcement Act (chapter 5), and the 1996 Line–Item Veto Act (chapter 6). In the Conclusion, I offer some final thoughts and questions for further study.

Part I

DELEGATION OF POWER
AND REPRESENTATION

1

ORIGINS AND SIGNIFICANCE OF DELEGATION OF POWER

Ambition must be made to counteract ambition. The interest of the man must be connected to the constitutional rights of the place.

—Publius, Federalist 51[1]

This power over the purse may, in fact, be regarded as the most complete and effectual weapon with which any constitution can arm the immediate representatives of the people, for obtaining a redress of every grievance, and for carrying into effect every just and salutary measure.

—Publius, Federalist 58[2]

Congress was designed over two hundred years ago with the assumptions that members would fight for their institution and that budget powers would be especially dear to the hearts of legislators. When legislative behavior turns out differently on both counts in recent decades, it is important to investigate why and how these changes matter. In this chapter, I argue that strategic explanations of delegation do not appreciate its complex institutional origins and significance. Delegation of power should not be seen only as purposeful action by utility-maximizing political actors and organizations. While such micro-level strategies exist, they are sufficiently contradictory and risky to serve ultimately as evidence of something bigger: serious internal conflicts over the representative powers and place of Congress in the national government. In addition, delegation of power does not necessarily resolve these tensions and can easily exacerbate them.

11

Congress's constitutional charges include means (representation and deliberation) as well as ends (legislation). Delegation of power is an attack on all of these institutional responsibilities and is symptomatic of major, essentially permanent, institutional conflicts that flare up when the public wants contradictory things from the government: increased spending, lower taxes, and a balanced budget. While presidents can also be blamed for being too sanguine on the prospects of achieving all three goals, Congress also contributes to fiscal problems and paralysis because its multiple decision points breed too many sources of information and demands, all frustrating impediments to efficiency and coordination in lawmaking. At the same time, Congress is a unique place for a variety of perspectives to have their say, and the slow, deliberate pace of legislation can be healthy in the long run for public policy and maintaining a power balance between the branches.

Many of these challenges were sewn into the federal government and have been seriously aggravated by the growth of the administrative state. As national entities composed of locally elected members, the House of Representatives and Senate embody the tensions of reconciling representation from a variety of perspectives and were designed to clash with each other and with the other branches, as each institution holds a unique place in the process of deliberating over the national good. To make sure such conflicts occurred, the Constitution's designers gave the branches overlapping powers and different constituencies as well as different terms and timetables for public accountability. And as the federal government has grown dramatically in the past century to meet seemingly insatiable public demand for goods and services, these inherent representation challenges have grown too—but largely at the expense of Congress. Congress and the president are both under pressure to deliver high levels of entitlements and federal discretionary spending while trying not to raise taxes to pay for it all. But as Congress is often perceived as being more directly and openly responsive to local concerns than the president, it becomes the symbol of federal fiscal irresponsibility and out-of-control spending. Although both branches are technically responsible for all budget law and national spending, government dollars for such items as mohair cultivation and the Cowgirl Hall of Fame are derided as congressional "pork" while the president's directing of federal contracts, tax changes, and subsidies to key political and regional allies largely escapes that label because he is assumed to have the "national" interest in mind, despite the frequently uneven economic and geographic nature of his election support.

Through such different assessments of institutional fiscal responsibility, delegation of budgetary power in the 1980s and 1990s was driven by unpopular fiscal policies that were exploited by politicians, largely from the Republican side, who argued that reducing Congress's general fiscal powers would help end budget imbalances. Delegation was also supported by members of both parties who wanted to show their constituents they were serious about tackling the deficit problem, even though the public also bore some blame. But in a larger sense, delegation of budgetary power is a more nuanced and, in the long run, questionable response to planned constitutional conflicts. While power shifts away from Congress may appear to serve various member and party interests in the short-term, such action is risky enough to these very interests, as well as the institution overall, to make one wonder what the alternatives to delegation are and what such loss of power will do to the Congress, its members, and the nation.

Causes of Delegation of Power

Scholars from the rational choice approach to political research emphasize how members and parties act purposefully to obtain specific electoral and policy outcomes after assessing the costs and benefits of different paths. From this perspective, delegation of power is chosen because it serves specific member, party, and institutional ends related to reelection and policy preferences by overcoming information and collective action challenges that get in the way of these primary goals. By contrast, other scholars, largely from the American political development approach, emphasize how such strategies can cause and ultimately be constrained by broader institutional developments that have hurt Congress's capacity to maintain its coequal role with the other branches in recent decades.

In separating rational choice and American political development approaches to political behavior and history related to delegation of power I do not mean to imply that they are irreconcilable. Rather, each serves to show different kinds of tensions related to responsiveness and lawmaking that help us understand the complex nature of delegation.

Conflicts surrounding representation are present at every turn, from the narrow strategic perspective of looking over the shoulder of a member of Congress to broader trends in institutional development. Yet, I find the rational choice treatments of delegation inspire too many additional questions, even on their own terms, to conclude that delegation of power reflects simple strategic efficiency and to end the inquiry there without tracing this behavior to larger origins and consequences of institutional power loss.

Delegation as Electoral and Policy Strategy

Regarding member-level decisions to support delegation of power, it is not too controversial to relate almost all legislators' actions to their desire for reelection, credit, and blame avoidance. David R. Mayhew[3] famously writes that, as "single-minded reelection seekers," national legislators' behaviors are reflective of what they believe their constituencies will reward. Members may also wish to avoid electoral blame for unknown and unsavory outcomes, as others have argued is the case regarding power shifts to administrative agencies[4] and the president on foreign policy.[5] Applying these points to budget politics, legislators might want to shift the blame to automatic processes or outside institutions for spending cuts and/or tax increases their constituents may not favor, even if these are means to a popular end of deficit reduction. And if a legislator's constituency does not have a strong interest in an issue at the time of the vote, a legislator might support an act in anticipation that the issue will be raised by a challenger in the next election,[6] such as "incumbent X voted against fiscal responsibility in Washington by voting against the line-item veto." In addition, budget reform votes have powerful symbolic qualities when current processes and fiscal outcomes are unpopular.[7]

Even acknowledging such benefits, delegation of power can be a risky strategy for individual legislators. Delegation to external entities and automatic processes mitigate legislators' personal powers through committees and floor votes to protect or supply goods and services that could be rewarded by their electorates. The Line–Item Veto Act, for example, may have been supported by legislators whose constituencies and challengers thought it would help reduce unnecessary spending, but the reform was designed to reduce legislators' powers to act on targeted appropriations and tax benefits, which could have been rewarded by constituents as well. Affected legislators might respond that they can then shift the blame for any losses on another institution or that the likelihood of their projects being cut was minimal. Also, constituents have been shown to support "fiscal consistency," meaning they do not punish fiscal conservatives who fail to bring home large amounts of federal money.[8] Nevertheless, additional risks come into play since the item veto could have made *all members* vulnerable to virtual fiscal extortion by the president if party dominance of the White House changed.

Furthermore, members should be concerned with the long-term implications for the institution they bash as well as serve.[9] Regarding the institutional effects of members' reelection obsessions, David Mayhew makes a bold and very much under-appreciated statement about the significance of such individualism: "If members hope to spend careers in Congress, they have a stake in maintaining its prestige as an institution. They also have a stake in maintaining congressional control over resources that are useful in electoral quests. But if every member pursues only his own electoral goals, the prestige and power of Congress will drain away."[10] Such electoral individualism can negatively impact public sentiment about Congress[11] and traditional institutional norms.[12]

Such risks regarding delegation undermine the logic of partisan "principal-agent" strategies as well. D. Roderick Kiewiet and Matthew D. McCubbins[13] argue that various kinds of power shifts within and outside Congress can serve majority party interests if the party leaders maintain sanctioning power over the delegatees in a principal-agent relationship. Kiewiet and McCubbins do not differentiate between internal shifts of power to congressional committees and external delegation to the president and automatic processes so long as the principals can better pursue their policy objectives through either kind of delegation and the agents have "a comparative advantage in performing" the tasks. But Kiewiet and McCubbins acknowledge that maintaining a principal-agent relationship in external delegation might be more challenging for congressional party majorities, especially during times of divided government. Nevertheless, they assert that "the success of delegation has nothing to do with the appearance of power. Principals can be highly successful in using delegation to pursue their interests yet appear passive and ineffectual relative to their agents."[14] The evidence they use to support these arguments is the closeness of federal spending patterns to majority preferences of the Congress after the delegation has taken place. But they do not ponder whether even better outcomes were possible had the power been kept internally. This question becomes important because, as the following chapters' case studies show, in the 1980s and 1990s Congress explicitly rejected more power-saving alternatives on the table in favor of delegating greater powers to outside entities and automatic processes.

So why delegate externally if an internal agent is also available? The answer may lie in real or widely perceived limitations to Congress's institutional capacity to perform certain tasks in the first place. Synthesizing member-level reelection concerns with internal challenges related to information, oversight, and fragmentation, David Epstein and Sharyn O'Halloran[15] argue that the central question is why Congress chooses to delegate in certain areas but maintain control over policy details in others. They argue that congressional delegation boils down to a strategic institutional calculation—similar to a firm's "make or buy" decision—to give power in certain areas to the executive for political efficiency in light of Congress's structural disadvantages. My case studies confirm that members and leaders of Congress do indeed reflect on problems related to institutional capacity for responsible budgeting, especially regarding pork-barreling, logrolling, committee fragmentation, and other related tensions between being "effective" and "responsive," as Epstein and O'Halloran emphasize.[16] However, Epstein and O'Halloran underestimate the extent of the use of delegation and therefore do not fully assess the depth of institutional pathologies behind this "strategy." For example, they say Congress is unlikely to delegate power on distributive issues, especially during times of divided government, which is certainly not true of the 1980s' and 1990s' budget process delegations, as highlighted in the following chapters. While these delegations could also fulfill the low standard of "political efficiency,"[17] what do these actions say about Congress's conception of its more fundamental institutional responsibilities?

Precisely because delegation may not be "technically" or "economically efficient" it deserves scrutiny beyond its short-term political use. Bruce I. Oppenheimer[18] points out the irony of the Republican

Congress's delegating to the president at all for deficit control in the mid-1990s when the twentieth century shows the executive branch, under both Democrat and Republican control, has been the center of the federal government's efforts to expand. And budget experts Howard Shuman[19] and Louis Fisher[20] argue that the deficit explosion begun in the 1980s was a result of presidential exploitation of the budget process for risky fiscal calculations—not congressional irresponsibility. Delegation is thus not only a curious path, but Congress's harshest self-diagnoses might be wrong. While political efficiency is no doubt an important component of legislative action, it can ultimately separate members from their institution and harm Congress's long-term place in the political system and fiscal decision-making process when the executive branch is given disproportionate power.

Old and New Institutional Capacity Problems

These potential problems related to interbranch power shifts make delegation more deeply related to Congress's institutional and cultural developments in the twentieth century as it created and adjusted to new powers for the federal government. Congress has inherent institutional disadvantages relative to the executive branch that have been aggravated by legislative and enforcement pressures of the modern administrative state. Since the mid-twentieth century especially, congressional powers have been dispersed by committee fragmentation and individualistic members who weaken the institution against the president when such decentralization inadvertently, or by design, disadvantages party leaders. And as party leaders regained their centralizing strength in recent years, a political-cultural shift against the federal government's powers, often defined as "Congress," has been pushed by many Republicans, even those in control of the two chambers. Democratic leaders intermittently resist delegation of power to the president but then endure harsh public rebuke for being "obstructionist."

These recent trends may not be so surprising after all, as Congress was weakened from the very beginning precisely because the founders feared its potential strength. Lawrence C. Dodd[21] argues that the "institutional ambition" that the Federalists assumed was essential to healthy interbranch struggle was made purposefully weak in Congress, which was not endowed with institutionally cohesive features, in contrast to the executive branch and Supreme Court. Congress's bicameral nature, with each chamber being elected for different terms by different constituencies in (originally) different manners of selection, leads to internal dissimilarities that present a challenge to institutional thinking. The Federalists assumed legislators would be institutionally aggressive, so these structural handicaps were put in place to theoretically *equalize* the balance of power between the branches, as well as to foster different representative perspectives.[22] Despite these handicaps, Dodd argues, strong congressional leaders helped Congress generally maintain national dominance until the early twentieth century.

Afterward, as Dodd, Samuel P. Huntington,[23] and James L. Sundquist[24] agree, these inherent challenges to congressional cohesion were aggravated by the increasing desires of the general membership to control public policy and gain power in their chambers. As the federal government rapidly entered various aspects of the economy and citizens' lives, increasingly ambitious rank-and-file members began to pursue long-term congressional careers, which were greatly benefited by fragmented "committee government" but ultimately brought less legislator concern for the power of *Congress as Congress*: "[Members'] lives are also complicated by a cruel paradox, the ultimate incompatibility of widely dispersed power within Congress, on the one hand, and a strong role of Congress in national decision making, on the other."[25] Huntington similarly concludes, "Congress can assert its power or it can pass laws; but it cannot do both."[26]

In other words, decentralization in Congress took the place of centripetal, party-based hierarchy. Inroads on party leadership began with the revolt against Speaker Joseph Cannon in the House in 1910 and similar attacks on Senate leadership soon after. Although powerful congressional figures emerged subsequently, Huntington argues their successes were more functions of leadership style and political relationships than institutionalized strength.[27] In addition, various reforms of the committee system have further exacerbated these decentralizing trends, sometimes unintentionally. For example, the Legislative Reorganization Act of 1946 was passed to streamline congressional committees by reducing their numbers and eliminating overlapping jurisdictions. Ultimately, this reduction strengthened the surviving chairmen's powers and increased subcommittee proliferation. The 1970 Legislative Reorganization Act further contributed to fragmentation by reducing committee chair powers.[28]

Sundquist agrees with many of these diagnoses and adds another challenge to congressional power: rampant member individualism.[29] According to Sundquist, the members of the late 1960s and early 1970s reform era brought with them a new individualistic culture to the Congress. Without the institutional ties and incentives for loyalty in the traditional party system, members are freer to pursue policy initiatives and to vote independently. Individual members are also distracted by constituent service and reelection, and this parochialism can lead to episodes of intra-branch deadlock and immobilization that harm institutional power. In recent years, such individualism has become much more present in the Senate than in the House, but the House Republican leadership has not consistently translated its revived party powers into a defense of the institution.[30] In fact, majority leaders have used their renewed powers to attack certain congressional budgeting and other legislative prerogatives as part of an attempt to peel back various fiscal commitments of the federal government, even during the heightened interbranch tensions of the Clinton era.

But even with more institutionally defensive leaders, coordinating fiscal policy in annual budgets is fraught with representational tension because Congress will always have some measure of fragmentation and individualism to deal with high levels of constituent requests. Allen Schick makes two very important points on this fundamental issue of institutional budgeting capacity. First, coherent budgeting requires centralized processes and power to gather estimates, claims, revenues, and appropriations into a unified document. Congress has long resisted giving such powers to any one committee or leadership source. Second, it is inherently problematic for members to make claims on the budget in their representative capacity while also arbitrating between other members' desires. So Congress has reacted to all these pressures, especially since the mid-twentieth century, by creating new programs and entitlements, shielding many of them from annual review, and circumventing coordination with various other kinds of "backdoor" spending (discussed in greater detail in the following chapters). So the demands of budgeting in a modern administrative state ultimately lessened congressional controls over outcomes as more and more funds were already spoken for by the next budget cycle.[31]

It is easy to see how these tensions create serious fiscal policy problems as Congress translates public wishes into various budget bills that are ultimately criticized as irresponsible. Deficits are not popular even if the spending and tax programs fueling them are. Although part of the puzzle can be found in the two-thirds of the budget not easily controlled by Congress and the president annually, two sets of unrealistic expectations are also part of the story: citizens who love programs and hate taxes and deficits and members who want power to do good for their districts but avoid blame for everything else.[32] Again, these are fundamentally long-term problems of representation, as the public has high demands on Congress but sees the institution negatively as both too "professional" and too open to "special interests," even as these qualities help members stay responsive.[33] Delegation may be viewed by members and leaders of both parties as a solution to these fiscal and political dilemmas, but are these trends also evidence that Congress is permanently incapacitated?

Despite all these issues, Congress has repeatedly demonstrated that it can meet changing demands on it by *increasing its power and control* through the development of new internal processes. However, scholars disagree whether any particular congressional power advancements can last very long. Dodd argues that congressional attempts to reclaim various policy fronts from presidential domination are bound to be short-lived in the twentieth century (and probably beyond) due to the cycles related to congressional reform. Occasional bursts of institutional ambition are followed by a relatively calm period of interbranch cooperation, but congressional fragmentation ultimately resurfaces due to the distrust of centralized leadership within the institution and/or an influx of ambitious new members during the reform period. Renewed congressional fragmentation results in a similar cycle of executive usurpation, institutional crises, and reform.[34] But other scholars have argued that Congress's institutional development includes longer-term reorganization that enriches its powers.[35]

As Eric Schickler argues forcefully, institutional development is also beset by contradictions reflecting the many different interests driving it: incumbents of all stripes desiring reelection, broader institution-wide interests promoting one or both chambers of the Congress vis-à-vis the other braches, members who desire internal institutional power bases, power concerns of the majority and minority parties, and policy-based interests desiring new institutional processes to enhance specific outcomes. Through the confluence of a few or all of these interests, unintended consequences of reform can result, even institutional power loss.[36]

While Schickler does not focus on budget policy and delegation of power as an institutional movement, his study is useful to this history. The development of modern congressional budgeting has demonstrated that Congress sometimes works at cross purposes by not only making dramatic grabs for power in "reform eras," such as the early 1970s, but also by passing smaller-scale incremental improvements to internal processes—even while simultaneously delegating. Similar to the contradictory institutional behavior of the 104th Congress, which both defended its prerogatives against President Clinton and then attempted to give away various budgeting power, the same legislative changes that delegated power in Gramm-Rudman-Hollings I and II in the mid-1980s and the 1990 Budget Enforcement Act also strengthened various internal congressional procedures in response to problems in congressional budgeting raised by legislators, economists, and budget experts since the late 1970s.

Such complexities in institutional development are deeper than tensions between members' various motives, as Schickler argues, and reflect the evolving nature of representation, deliberation, and separation of powers in a local-national legislature. Although Schickler sees Congress's power losses largely as a by-product of different internal interests at odds with each other rather than an end unto itself, recent history has shown that delegation of power is a real institutional and partisan movement. While delegation can also be an inadvertent result of strategic inconsistencies, in recent budgeting history it is an explicit choice in the name of the national interest.

Significance of Delegation

Certain advantages to our separation of powers system are lost when Congress eagerly cedes its institutional prerogatives. While delegation of power can certainly streamline the policy-making process and help overcome intra- and interbranch paralysis, it can harm representation in three ways. First, delegation of decision making can significantly reduce deliberation and public debate.[37] Second, excessive power shifts cloud responsibility and accountability between the government and the people.[38] Third, related to both points, extraordinary power growth in one part of the government, usually the executive branch, can negatively affect the institutional virtues of the other branches.[39]

Of course, Congress's unique powers among the world's legislatures make it a planned source of irritation to those who desire an efficient and responsive, not just representative, democracy. Through the legislative process, individual members, coalitions, and parties channel constituent interests into the system, while also attempting to obstruct allegedly harmful measures through the use of committee and party membership, floor activity, and bargain-based compromises. Representation for local and national interests is therefore more than just promoting certain bills—it is also diluting, delaying, and blocking others. As is said repeatedly in the *Federalist Papers*, Congress and the separated federal system were meant to complicate easy translation of passionate and possibly ill-conceived popular will into governmental outcomes. The two-chambered Congress, each elected by different constituencies for different terms of office in (originally) different manners of selection, was an explicitly planned obstacle to national consensus, and still is,[40] as these structures were meant to encourage different constituent perspectives while keeping the entire federal structure relatively slow moving.

The founders of the U.S. government saw democracy as a process as the greatest impediment to democracy as a principle. Multiple layers of representation, deliberation, and power distribution among the branches thus become avenues for slowing down majority will and the potential for the tyranny of repressive, and simply bad, ideas. In addition to the more famous fears of majority factions found in Federalist 10, Federalist 42 says, "the mild voice of reason, pleading the cause of an enlarged and permanent interest, is but too often drowned, before public bodies as well as individuals, by the clamors of an impatient avidity for immediate and immoderate gain."[41] The Federalists' feelings about raw democracy are also apparent in Federalist 55: "Had every Athenian citizen been a Socrates, every Athenian assembly would still have been a mob."[42]

Deliberation then becomes the key mechanism to both promote

and thwart representation.[43] While the House largely represents local interests and the Senate largely represents state interests, the legislative process is by no means the simple amalgamation of these two perspectives topped off by the signature of the nation's executive. These three perspectives are ideally engaging each other from the beginning of the legislative process for personal and institutional gain. As Federalist 47 and 48 emphasize, the constitutional values of representation, deliberation, and avoidance of tyranny all require a vibrant system of inter-institutional checks rather than relying on mere "parchment barriers" between the branches. But such a complex government, designed with skepticism regarding human nature, was not meant to be wholly impotent, nor ineffective, as this chapter's epigraph from Federalist 58 shows. And in a larger sense, as Jeffrey K. Tulis argues, the system is designed to work not merely as a check and balance mechanism to thwart quick and ill-considered legislation but as a design based on other virtues related to institutional specialization in each branch that balances representation and deliberation in the Congress with energy in the executive and minority protection in the federal courts.[44] But if the requisite time, energy, and public patience for such extensive mulling over of legislation are too precious in the modern world, how fluid should separation of powers arrangements be to meet new demands while still retaining these various constitutional values?

Louis Fisher argues persuasively that not all delegation is inherently offensive to the Constitution. By definition, he says, delegation is necessary while abdication is not. Delegation and abdication differ on two counts: completeness (or reversibility) and the subject matter. Delegation to agencies over program administration and rule making is substantively different from "nondelegable legislative prerogatives: war and the power of the purse."[45] As Congress has repeatedly given power away on war, abdication in this issue area appears to be permanent. In budgeting, however, I argue that Congress generally retains more power to override or obstruct the president throughout the process than delegation of war-related power, and such budget power shifts might better be characterized as delegation with the looming possibility of abdication if legislators are lax in their oversight of executive powers or fail to utilize the powers they retained.

In other words, budgetary delegation can indeed coexist with deliberation, representation, and respect for Congress as an institution, but it should be suspect when it fails these constitutional values, especially if the results are, for lack of a better term, bad public policy. While deficits can be characterized as beneficial or harmful to the nation in the short- and long-term, depending upon one's economic school of thought, I argue that delegation can still be judged by a balancing test: achieving policy results along the lines of its objectives while retaining as much debate and oversight as possible for Congress in the reforms' provisions and use. Delegation is therefore irresponsible when the structures are unrealistic and specifically thwart deliberation in the process (as in the case of Gramm-Rudman-Hollings and the proposed balanced-budget amendments), responsible when it reduces deficits through more reasonable means and sensitivity to representation, deliberation, and power balance (as in the 1990 Budget Enforcement Act), or something in between when the potential for congressional abdication is high, but little actually changes (as in the Line–Item Veto Act).

Conclusion

By criticizing those who, explicitly or in effect, defend delegation as a rational electoral or policy strategy, I do not deny that delegation can entail tangible benefits for its supporters in Congress, nor that members and leaders engage in cost-benefit analyses when contemplating delegation. I accept these premises as true but add that the costs and benefits inextricably surround not only political efficiency and policy outcomes but the fundamental institutional responsibilities and place of the Congress in our political system. And institutional loss of power is not the only way to forge a balance between electoral and substantive policy goals. While it is true that Congress is very much aware of its collective action problems in budgeting and other legislative activities, the legislative histories of the reforms reveal that such challenges might be met with internally focused experiments and structures as a way of defending representation, deliberation, and compromise.

As delegation of power means delegation of these other constitutional values, the main puzzle is whether Congress can, with the president, satisfactorily respond to the demands of constituents, however contradictory or ill advised, while still forging good public policy. As the next chapter shows, budgeting was much simpler when we did not want much from the federal government. Since it is unlikely we will turn the clock back on our demands, if we conclude Congress cannot handle complex budgeting tasks it will be permanently stunted as a representative and power-balancing force. The recent history of institutionally protective budgeting reforms (although often rejected) shows how Congress might add to its capacity to make tough decisions rather than punting them to automatic processes and outside institutions. Such protectiveness is important to the fiscal, as well as constitutional, health of the system until it has been determined that faster, one-branch policy making always serves the nation better.

2

REFORMING THE REFORMS

A Brief History of Congressional Budgeting

> *Taken as a whole the federal budget is a representation in monetary*
> *terms of governmental activity. If politics is regarded in part as conflict*
> *over whose preferences shall prevail in the determination of national*
> *policy, then the budget records the outcome of this struggle.*
>
> —*Aaron Wildavsky*[1]

Although this book focuses on the past three decades of budget reform, an important question is how these recent cases fit, or not, with patterns evident in the overall evolution of the process. In this chapter, I argue that congressional budget reforms in the last thirty years continue a trend of ambivalence begun in the early twentieth century in which augmentation of executive budget powers is interspersed with more institutionally protective reforms. At the same time, the repeated success of delegation movements in light of the record deficits in the 1980s and 1990s shows how Congress has dramatically changed its view of its own institutional capacity to budget in a modern administrative state.

Congress dominated the annual budget process when federal government spending was very low and deficits were rare. In the nineteenth century, reforms of the budget process largely entailed taxation and spending territory shifts between congressional committees, not between the Congress and the president. While fiscal policy was certainly contentious prior to the twentieth century and the executive branch enjoyed moments of dominance in domestic and foreign affairs, there was no successful congressional movement to augment executive budgeting power. Congress alternately centralized and decentralized its budgeting processes to meet various political and structural challenges. Problems with congressional fragmentation and capacity to budget in a modern state became apparent at the turn of the century, and delegation-based reforms began to dominate budget-process changes. From the Progressive Era through the 1990s, during both unified and divided government, Congress granted major formal powers to the president regarding annual budget making and other aspects of fiscal policy. But not all twentieth-century congressional delegations were to the executive. In the early part of the century, the Federal Reserve banking system and General Accounting Office were created to ease various legislative and executive burdens, and, in the late twentieth century, automatic spending and deficit caps and restrictive new procedures, which theoretically constrain the president as well as the Congress, were included in almost all reform movements.

It is also noteworthy that Congress made two major attempts to recapture various parts of its spending powers and to rein in executive budgeting in the twentieth century. The budget reforms of 1946 and 1974 attempted to establish a congressional budget to rival the president's, and both occurred during times of high conflict between the legislative and executive branches. Both reforms were also hampered by institutional complexities that undermined their congressional power potential. The almost immediate failure of the 1946 congressional budget process and the widespread criticism of the 1974 reform ten years after its passage can also be seen as evidence that larger institutional constraints on congressional budgeting exist.[2]

Throughout all these reforms, institutional issues in federal budgeting history surround whether Congress's multifaceted challenges of local and national responsiveness through a fragmented policy process—usually under conditions of fiscal constraint—must lead to external delegation of power, or whether Congress should attempt to reconcile conflicting claims on the budget in more internally protective processes. During the 1974 budget process (as is detailed in the next chapter), pro-Congress reformers were determined to avoid the pitfalls of the doomed 1946 budget changes. But the 1974 reforms ultimately came under attack too as deficits grew dramatically a decade later. So is Congress destined to be blamed for budgeting failures while presidents escape unscathed and even stronger?

Two relatively recent reform movements that have not yet succeeded, the balanced-budget constitutional amendment and biennial budgeting, do not fully settle this question. The near-passage (twice) of the balanced-budget amendment through Congress shows that more than a majority of members of both chambers lost confidence in their (and possibly the president's) basic ability to balance the budget through normal legislative processes and electoral controls. And the amendment movement has very recently regained some life as deficits have climbed to nearly $400 billion after a few years of budget surpluses. There are also lingering controversies over the merits of biennial budgeting, which differs from the amendment premise as both supporters and opponents argue from a base of institutional protectiveness. Again, these inconsistencies demonstrate that Congress is more fundamentally ambivalent about using its budgeting powers than abdicating them.

As mentioned in the last chapter, these developmental contradictions can serve to highlight layered and various motives for institutional change[3] as well as cycles of Congress-President power struggles,[4] but they should also be seen as lenses on the changeable value of Congress's particular kind of local-national representation. Some reforms were founded in organizational theories of centralization to enhance presidential power (as in the 1921 Budget and Accounting Act). Others were based on renewing Congress's representative prerogatives (such as the 1974 Congressional Budget and Impoundment Control Act). And most recent reforms centered on the deficit as a national policy problem that the pro-Congress 1974 process was not able to address (for example, the two Gramm-Rudman-Hollings laws, the 1990 Budget Enforcement Act, and the Line–Item Veto Act). The tensions behind all these changes are how best to balance representation and effective legislation with limited money to pay for everything we want. When the federal government became more directly important to the economic lives of citizens, institutional conflicts emerged as a permanent debate over which branch truly has the national interest at heart.

1789–1920: Congress in Control of the Federal Budget Process

With a relatively weak executive branch, a small federal budget, and generally ample revenue from customs activities, it was relatively easy for Congress to maintain its responsibility in budgeting matters before the Civil War.[5] Although there were notable skirmishes between the president and Congress on appropriations issues, Congress had a lot of oversight power regarding annual outlays since agencies brought their requests directly to congressional committees in what was called a "Book of Estimates." One early conflict was whether the budget should contain line-item or lump-sum appropriations. Presidents generally preferred the latter so as to have more discretion to transfer funds from one category to another. Congress, however, generally insisted on line-item appropriations so that it could control individual expenditures. Congress could maintain this attention to detail because total spending was low. With the House Ways and Means Committee and the Senate Finance Committee legislating both revenues and most appropriations, the process was not terribly complicated, and Congress could focus on budgeting at the item-level without losing sight of the overall totals.

Congressional concern with spending control increased after the Civil War, as did fragmentation of the budget process. To cope with postwar budget activity and spending, Congress created the Appropriations Committee in the House in 1865 (and a Banking and Currency Committee in the same year) and then in the Senate in 1867. Ways and Means and Finance became responsible for taxation and other revenues exclusively. Two decades later, jurisdiction over some money bills was transferred from the Appropriations Committee to authorizing committees, which are the standing committees responsible for that area of legislation. This "Divestiture of 1885" is generally argued to have increased expenditures because the new fragmentation gave a wider variety of committee members a say over spending with fewer centralized controls.[6]

In the new budget-making process, spending pressures also came from the executive branch. Agencies could take advantage of the new and more fragmented appropriations process by asking one set of committees for annual funding and another for supplements to cover deficiencies arising from overspending early in the year or in light of a change in needs. At the same time Congress started to get away from strict line-item appropriations toward larger lumps with increased agency discretion, members passed the Anti-Deficiency Acts of 1905 and 1906 to better control agencies' spending habits. These acts mandated agencies to apportion their funds over a full year to avoid spending abuses requiring emergency or deficiency funds, and

later amendments to the Anti-Deficiency Acts gave the president power
to impound agency funds for various reasons.[7]

Less than a decade later, Congress began to make its first delegations to other institutions to help handle an increasingly complex
economy. In 1913, the power to coin and regulate the value of money
was transferred to the new Federal Reserve System in the Federal Reserve Act. The power to pay debts and borrow money on the United
States' credit was delegated to the Treasury Department under the Lib-
erty Bond Act of 1917. Before 1917, Congress authorized the Treasury
to borrow specific amounts each time it requested funds. The change
occurred to make financing of World War I more efficient, as Congress would grant the Treasury a wider power to borrow up to a certain
limit and would review the debt ceilings periodically.

In light of more complicated federal commitments at home and
abroad and general concerns about government spending, presidential
budgeting was born. President Taft sent two executive budgets to Congress and, although they were ignored, set up a Commission on
Economy and Efficiency, which in 1912 released a report on "The Need
for a National Budget." This proposal was rejected, but spending increases continued into the Wilson administration, as did presidential
support of new budgeting powers for the executive branch. Activities
surrounding World War I escalated federal outlays from about $700
million in 1916 to $18.5 billion in 1919, and the federal debt increased
from $1 billion to $25 billion during the same time. Wholesale prices
more than doubled between 1913 and 1919. These economic concerns
were not new. In the decades prior to the war, deficits and spending
increased due to the costs of the Spanish–American War, the Panama
Canal project, increased pensions, and other new federal duties. These
costs, as well as bouts of economic recessions, brought the perceived
need for budget-process reforms to a head. Drawing a parallel between
congressional budgeting problems in the early twentieth century and
several decades later, in 1973 the Senate Government Operations
Committee's characterization of congressional budget control in the
Progressive Era was grim: "Congress could not cope with this drasti-
cally altered situation. It still possessed supremacy in budget matters,
but it was by now unable to wield effective control. Appropriations
responsibility was scattered among a dozen or more committees, none

of which had concern for total spending. The situation was chaotic as each executive agency trafficked with its favorite legislative committee, disregarding the consequences for the budget as a whole."[8]

1921–1974: Presidential Control Increasing with Intermittent Congressional Resistance

In 1921, Congress passed the monumental Budget and Accounting Act, which created the annual executive budget, the Bureau of the Budget (now the Office of Management and Budget) to analyze and submit agency estimates and requests under a president-appointed director, and the General Accounting Office to oversee and audit agency spending.[9] The president's budget was to be a unified recommendation based on agency requests to ensure better control over spending totals. Although the 1921 act ostensibly gave Congress more power to understand and control the budget in terms of total spending, the overall result was a dramatic shift in budget-making power to the president. The executive branch was now enhanced with new offices for information gathering and budget implementation, and Congress was not. Although the act ultimately prompted both branches to centralize their budget-making processes, James L. Sundquist argues that "the modern presidency, judged in terms of institutional responsibilities, began . . . the day that President Harding signed the Budget and Accounting Act."[10]

In the decades following the 1921 act, administrative regulations increased the Budget Bureau's control over federal spending levels. The first Budget director, Charles G. Dawes, established procedures in which "appropriations from Congress were to be treated as a mere ceiling on expenditures rather than as a directive or invitation to spend the full amount."[11] Dawes also created the practice of "central clearance," in which the Budget Office reviews agency proposals prior to their going to Congress, coordinates departmental recommendations on proposed and pending legislation, and gives advice to the president on signing and vetoing enrolled bills. The New Deal further increased presidential power over budgeting through new acts, agencies, and executive orders giving the president more power over budgets and the economy. In addition, the executive branch reorganization in 1939 increased the staff of the Budget Bureau and moved it to the new Executive Office of the President.[12]

Domestic and war-related spending increases in the 1940s prompted a new round of budget process reforms attempts. Federal spending went from $9 billion in 1940 to $98 billion in 1945. In 1946, Congress passed the Employment Act, which officially recognized the need for federal government intervention to promote employment, specifically, and economic stability and growth generally. The president became responsible for studying the nation's economic health and proposing corrective and stabilizing action, if necessary, in an annual Economic Report. The 1946 act also created the president's Council of Economic Advisers and the congressional Joint Economic Committee to help him in these efforts, although the congressional committee received much less funding. Nevertheless, the Republican-dominated Congress controlled much of fiscal policy in these years and pushed a potentially dramatic structural shift in budgetary balance of power.[13]

In 1946, Congress passed the Legislative Reorganization Act to overhaul legislative practices generally and authorize the creation of an annual congressional budget. This act created a joint budget committee to examine the president's budget and then report its own recommendations, accompanied by a concurrent resolution (not presented to the president for signature) by February 15 regarding maximum appropriations for the year. The new committee had an unwieldy one hundred and two members because it was composed of all the members of the two appropriations committees, as well as Ways and Means and Finance, but it was broken into several subcommittees to perform various functions. The legislative budget was tried in 1947, but Congress was unable to adopt a ceiling. In 1948, Congress did adopt a ceiling but ignored it in later appropriations. No legislative budget emerged in 1949, even after the deadline was extended to May 1. The legislative budget was then ignored and ultimately repealed in the next Legislative Reorganization Act in 1970.

Why did this experiment in congressional budgeting fail? Separate House Rules and Senate Government Operations Committee reports touching on the subject prior to the 1974 act both concluded that a period of divided government in the Truman years was not the only challenge to the law's use, and both deserve to be quoted at length.

The fate of this [1946] provision conclusively demonstrates that a true legislative budget process cannot come into being without a full marshaling of congressional resources and the construction of special procedures to link the legislative budget with other congressional processes related to spending decisions. The 1946 initiative was based on the expectation that statutory authorization alone would suffice to successfully launch the difficult and complex legislative budget. No staff was provided, no permanent committee arrangement, no capability for fixing an appropriate level of expenditures, no adjustment in the authorizations process, no means of keeping score of appropriations actions in Congress.[14]

The lessons [of the 1946 act] are quite clear, and they must be paid heed if the current drive for budgetary improvement is not to be stillborn. Responsibility for adopting a legislative budget must be coupled with time, staff, and informational resources. The process must be nonpartisan, and have available expert analytic and information handling capability. The total spending level must be based on a careful determination of program needs and priorities, and it must be sensitive to economic conditions and other factors. Finally, rules must be applied to preserve compliance with the legislative budget, but ways should be open for Congress to revise its spending ceilings as conditions and events warrant.[15]

After the congressional budget failure, new reforms surfaced in the 1950s. In 1950, Congress adopted a single appropriation act covering all the regular bills that had been previously handled separately. The omnibus bill successfully passed that year, but it was not used in subsequent years because there was concern by members of the appropriations committees and others that it did not allow sufficient opportunity for the consideration of program merits and needs. In other words, too much was being packed into a single bill, and the appropriations subcommittees did not like to cede power over their policy specialties to the whole committee.[16] Then, another effort to create a joint budget committee began in 1951 in the Senate, but the House did not pass the proposal for fear that such a committee would weaken the House's prerogative to initiate appropriations. In 1955, the Hoover Commission argued that one way to control spending is to authorize appropriations that will be spent only in the upcoming fiscal year. As will be discussed in more depth in the following chapters, a major problem with the modern budget is that authorizations for spending do not necessarily translate into outlays in the next fiscal year. When agencies and departments act on their authorized funds in years after the original congressional action, those later Congresses have no power to stop the expenditures. This problem of huge carry-over balances is one of the longer-standing issues in congressional budget control. Nevertheless, future contract authority is needed for many kinds of government projects that do not require all related costs to be paid in one year (like construction). Therefore, the Hoover Commission's recommendation was to give agencies independent ability to contract for future needs without a formal appropriation until the agency had to make payments, but this solution was perceived as another example of "backdoor" spending, and the proposals were not enacted. However, statutes in 1956 and 1958 mandated that agencies maintain their accounts on an accrual basis and authorized the president to propose limitations on annual accrued expenditures.

In the late 1960s and early 1970s, Congress again addressed pressing issues concerning national spending. In 1968, based on an executive commission's recommendation the previous year, Congress created a new "unified" budget, combining federal funds and trusts into one document to get a more truthful overall fiscal picture. In 1970, the Bureau of the Budget was renamed the Office of Management and Budget (OMB) and given new powers over economic and budgetary analysis not overtly subject to congressional review and control. This reorganization passed because it was widely perceived that the president required more centralization and control over agency estimates and spending to conduct his economic and managerial duties properly. But perhaps not surprisingly under conditions of divided government, the new OMB immediately brought conflicts with Congress over presidential budgetary prerogatives. In 1973, Congress demanded to share appointment power for the director and deputy director of the agency.[17]

In an especially interesting display of institutional ambivalence at a time of interbranch tension, Congress also flirted with reining itself in through spending ceilings, in response to spending and deficit pressures related to the Vietnam War and domestic spending in the late 1960s and early 1970s. Unlike the 1946 experiment, though, these ceilings were imposed in an *ad hoc* manner from budget to budget, rather than by a regular concurrent resolution from within Congress. All of these ceilings were considered to have failed because they either resulted in no real budgetary changes or because increases in exempt programs offset decreases in areas subject to the ceiling's limits. So as problems with economic policy, deficits, foreign and domestic spending, and presidential budgeting powers continued, cries for major reform of the budget process grew again. The Senate Government Operations Committee report on proposals for change in 1973 asserts a strong cautionary note that is very prescient regarding the issues that would surround the following decades of budget reform:

The budget improvement efforts of the past 25 years have left their mark on contemporary practices, but not to the extent that their proponents had hoped. Each innovation had its own problems or obstacles, but together they leave one clear message for those who would offer a new package of budgetary improvements. The new proposals must be in harmony with the traditions and procedures of Congress. It is not sufficient that the concept be attractive in terms of the national interest: it also has to be workable without undue change in the ways Congress is accustomed to doing business.[18]

The landmark 1974 reforms were designed to give Congress better support to research and execute a congressional budget while not upsetting current intra-institutional balances of power too much. New budget processes such as annual resolutions and reconciliations would be coordinated by the budget committees in the House and Senate, but these committees would have members in common with the traditional budget power brokers such as Appropriations, Ways and Means, and Finance. The budget committees would draw up various budget totals, which would be approved by the chambers, and then instruct committees to comply with these totals. At the same time that the new process was designed to impose internal discipline on Congress, the 1974 Congress explicitly rejected complete centralization, set spending ceilings, and restrictive rules to curtail majority preferences.

Related to this rejection of rules and processes that would restrict the spending prerogatives of the Congress was another means of increasing institutional control over annual budget outcomes—impoundment reform. For years, President Richard Nixon claimed authority from the Anti-Deficiency Acts' goals of managing agency spending practices and the 1946 economic policy delegations to the president to repeatedly impound congressionally approved appropriations. The 1974 reform's impoundment controls continued to allow presidential deferrals and rescissions, but gave Congress explicit oversight procedures to stop these withholdings if Congress wished to do so. After 1974, if

Congress wanted to stop a spending deferral, it would have to pass a disapproval bill. But if Congress wanted to stop a rescission, it did not have to do anything because each rescission under the 1974 act required a bill of congressional approval within forty-five days or the funds in question would be released.

Post-1974: Anti-Congress Backlash

Despite stagflation throughout the 1970s, the 1974 budget reforms were successful when measured by levels of deficit and debt until the early to mid-1980s, when huge deficits brought the public's wrath down on Congress. In the wake of Congress's passage of President Reagan's controversial supply-side spending and tax proposals and the recession that followed the Federal Reserve's tight-money policies to rein in inflation, the annual deficit rose from $74 billion in fiscal year 1980 to $221 billion in fiscal 1986. In the same years, the debt as a percentage of gross domestic product rose from 26 percent to 40 percent. And between the mid-1970s and mid-1980s, the annual percentage of "controllable" spending decreased from roughly one-third of the budget to one-quarter.

Fiscal and political pressures related to these budgetary issues brought a new wave of reform, but one that was not protective of congressional spending prerogatives as in 1974. The two Gramm-Rudman-Hollings reforms of 1985 and 1987 (officially called the Balanced Budget and Emergency Deficit Control Acts) attempted to decrease deficits by reducing congressional spending powers in two ways. First, each of these acts set five-year deficit-reduction schedules that were supposed to be unalterable by future Congresses except in emergency situations. Second, these ceilings were to be enforced internally through restrictive rules requiring supermajorities to waive and externally through a novel budget "sequestration" procedure. If the Congressional Budget Office and the Office of Management and Budget estimated during the annual budget-making cycle that the deficit would exceed that year's cap, eligible defense and nondefense discretionary accounts could be cut across the board.

The executor of the sequestration report was designated to be the Comptroller General of the Government Accounting Office in the original 1985 act but was changed to the Office of Management and Budget in the 1987 version. This alteration was designed to comply with the 1986 Supreme Court ruling *Bowsher v. Synar*, which said the Comptroller General was an agent of the legislative branch and therefore could not perform executive functions. Nevertheless, this second choice of agent was curious in light of the OMB's partisan reputation during the Reagan administration and the fact that the 1986 off-year election returned a Democrat majority to both chambers. Notably, in the legislative history of both the 1985 and 1987 acts, an internal alternative to external sequestration was proposed and rejected in which a temporary congressional committee performed the end-of-cycle budget cuts to comply with the deficit ceiling. The 1987 act also readjusted the deficit ceilings to reflect higher deficit projections and delayed the projection year of balance from 1991 to 1993.

Despite this alteration to the deficit-reduction schedule in Gramm-Rudman-Hollings II, the deficit far exceeded the caps each year after the law went into effect. A new round of budget process reforms emerged in 1990, as the anticipated $64 billion deficit for fiscal year 1991 became $269 billion. In the famous summer budget summit in 1990, President Bush abandoned his "no new taxes" pledge, and he and the Democrat-dominated Congress agreed to a five-year budget deal that included reform provisions entailing extraordinary changes to the annual budget process and that significantly reduced Congress's budgeting powers. Although the 1990 Budget Enforcement Act included new overall annual deficit-reduction targets, the reform emphasized a schedule of annual discretionary spending caps and strict pay-as-you-go rules for new spending and taxation proposals. OMB retained the power to execute an overall budget sequester and was granted two additional sequestration duties related to the discretionary spending caps and PAYGO rules while also receiving power to "score" congressional spending during the budget process. The Congressional Budget Office (CBO) was given an advisory role in the new process, but the conference committee noted that if OMB abused its new powers, the CBO might be utilized for scoring in the future. Along with the booming U.S. economy, this budget agreement of 1990 and the others forged under the new processes (in 1993 and 1997 especially) were given credit for the recent, but short-lived, elimination of the deficit. Notably, many of its most restrictive provisions have been allowed to expire without renewal in 2002 as the deficit began to climb again, but some members have revived the notion of self-imposed PAYGO rules in 2004.

Even as the deficit was declining in the mid-1990s, an extremely curious delegation of power was passed by Congress: the so-called line-item veto. The Republican Party pushed the line-item veto in the 1980s and early 1990s, when the White House was controlled by Republicans but Congress was not, and the party continued to do so even after it gained the majority in Congress in the 1994 off-year elections and the president was a Democrat. The 1996 Line–Item Veto Act was actually a reform of the 1974 impoundment provisions rather than a "true" item veto. The item veto that most state governors have grants them the ability to delete lines from a budget while still signing the rest of the bill into law. The presidential equivalent of this power was widely considered to require a constitutional amendment and was abandoned in favor of various statutory alternatives that enhanced the president's rescission powers. Rescission allows the president to permanently withhold spending after the budget bills are signed into law in their entirety.

The main institutional criticism behind the line–item veto movement was the pro-Congress bent of the 1974 impoundment provisions, so the 1996 act attempted to alter this balance of power. Although Congress allowed almost $93 billion in rescissions between 1974 and 1995, presidents had varying success with their proposals and often argued that they needed more power to control pork-barrel spending included in appropriations bills and packages. The "enhanced rescission" provisions of the 1996 act turned the 1974 procedure on its head: congressional inaction on a presidential rescission proposal would automatically allow the rescission rather than disallow it. If the Congress wished to stop a rescission after this change, it could propose and pass a disapproval bill, which the president could then veto. A supermajority was then needed in both chambers to override this veto. What is notable in the legislative history of the Line–Item Veto Act is that Congress explicitly rejected a more pro-Congress alternative to the 1974 procedures. The "expedited rescission" proposals also reduced Congress's power to stop a presidential rescission proposal by merely ignoring it, but it allowed a simple majority, rather than a supermajority, to override the president's request. Two years after its passage, the Supreme Court struck down the 1996 act in *Clinton v. City of New York* for violating the presentment clause of Article I of the Constitution.

Recent Unsuccessful Budget Reform Initiatives

The two most prominent failed budget reform initiatives in recent decades are the balanced budget constitutional amendment and biennial budgeting. The amendment proposal gained much public attention between the early 1980s and the late 1990s but largely disappeared once the deficit was brought under control. Various biennial budgeting proposals have received repeated attention in several congressional committees over the past decade, but none has gone to the floor of both chambers for a full vote. Although the balanced budget amendment and biennial budgeting proposals are very different from each other, both share the premise of other post-1974 reform: for the federal government to have a more responsible fiscal policy, Congress needs to have fewer controls over budgeting.

The main difference between the biennial and amendment proposals is that biennial budgeting is seen by some as ultimately being an avenue for greater congressional budgeting and oversight power, while there is no question that the purpose of the balanced budget amendment was to curtail majority control over annual spending. In both cases, the executive branch would also have to change dramatically its budgeting procedures. With biennial budgeting, the entire executive branch would have to change its estimation and testimony schedules, but that could likely increase its independence from Congress. However, the balanced budget amendment would severely reduce presidential power to propose deficits as well as shrink Congress's power of the purse. Yet, there is little evidence that widespread institutional protectiveness in Congress has prevented the success of these reforms. Even though the balanced budget amendment proposal was ultimately defeated twice, most members supported various incarnations of the proposal for over a decade. Likewise, internal surveys and experiment mandates within Congress show continuing and considerable support for the concept of biennial budgeting. So a determined minority of lawmakers has successfully stopped these proposals, which if passed would alter intra- and interbranch relations on the scale of the 1921 and 1974 acts.

Balanced Budget Constitutional Amendment

The balanced budget amendment is very worthy of attention for its dramatic possibilities and high levels of support in Congress in the mid-1990s, especially in the House. It was prevented from going to the states for ratification by a razor-thin margin in the Senate. Over previous decades, balanced budget proposals took different guises, but all essentially required a supermajority in both chambers for deficit spending. Various proposals also called for tracking budget outlays and increases to the GNP, allowing targeted presidential cuts to achieve balance, various rules for waiving the requirements for domestic emergencies and war, and new specifications regarding how Congress could raise taxes and the debt ceiling. Enforcement of the amendment by special rules, annual legislation, and/or the courts was especially contentious and not fully resolved, even as the amendment almost went to the states in 1995 and 1997.

Despite periodic battles with deficits in U.S. history, little sustained interest in balanced budget amendments was visible until the early 1980s.[19] A few amendments on the issue were proposed between 1936 and 1956, and all died in committee.[20] Beginning in 1980, the Republican-dominated Senate showed repeated support for the issue in committee and on the floor, but the Democratic-dominated House did not. The states also took a keen interest in federal balanced budget amendments beginning in the 1970s and thirty-two passed petitions to convene a constitutional convention, two shy of what is necessary to do so. Of course, the issue peaked after House Republicans added the amendment to the Contract with America election pledge in 1994 and won control of both chambers.

The first near success of the amendment proposal came at the very start of the 104th Congress, in January 1995 but the momentum fizzled out two years later. The necessary House supermajority of two-thirds passed a version of the amendment in early 1995 that mandated three-fifths votes for deficit spending and raising the limit on the national debt. Although the Contract with America provided for the same level to approve tax increases, the House proposal allowed for a simple majority to do so. That March, the Senate voted for the amendment 65 to 35, failing by two votes, but it was in reality only one vote shy of pas-

sage as Majority Leader Bob Dole (R-KS) was in favor of the amendment but voted against it to preserve his ability to call up the measure
again. A year later, in June 1996, a second Senate vote yielded 66 to 34
for the amendment and it was declared dead for the 104th Congress.
In the 105th Congress, the balanced budget amendment proposal was
again defeated in the Senate by one vote in March 1997, and the House
neglected to act that year.[21]

As the balanced budget amendment would severely restrict presidential budgeting practices too, the supporting rhetoric was less anti-
Congress than anti-"Washington," but the opposition argument was
fundamentally protective of both the president's and the Congress's
budgeting powers. These different perspectives are seen in a Senate
Judiciary Committee report: "Washington has not balanced the Federal budget since 1969. . . . Just as one would do with an out-of-control
credit-card shopper, America needs to limit Washington's access to
credit and force it to confront the budget problems it has disregarded
for too long. Hundreds of economists agree that Washington has lost
its moral sense of fiscal responsibility and, while we cannot legislate a
change in political morality, Congress can put a formal constitutional
restraint into place by passing the Balanced-Budget Amendment."[22]
Opponents argued that this amendment would harm majority rule,
separation of powers, entitlements, and the fiscal health of the country.
By the time the amendment was debated in early 1997, opponents also
noted the important deficit-reducing steps the Congress and president
had realized through their difficult decisions and tough votes. Senators Patrick Leahy (D-VT), Edward Kennedy (D-MA), and Russell
Feingold (D-WI) defended their institution's (and party's) record in
their arguments against the amendment:

We cannot legislate political courage and responsibility. No amendment to
the Constitution can supply the people's representatives with these essential
attributes. . . . Political courage has been an essential ingredient that has
helped us achieve remarkable deficit reduction over the past four years—
recent history the majority report ignores.[23]

In matters of substantive policy making within the jurisdiction of
Congress, our constitutional democracy has from its inception been
predicated upon the concept of majority rule. Federal legislative power is
nowhere in the Constitution subjected to a supermajority requirement.[24]

But, overall, such arguments demonstrated a concern for institutional power apparently not shared by most members at that time. By contrast, debates over biennial budgeting have blurred the lines over institutional protectiveness, as both sides have argued their intentions to maintain and even augment congressional power vis-à-vis the executive branch.

Biennial Budgeting

Biennial (two-year) budgeting is considered by some to be more efficient than annual budgeting and its use could positively or negatively affect congressional powers regarding representation and oversight. Two different kinds of biennial proposals have been on the table for the last two decades. One would allow Congress to create a two-year budget over a period of two years, essentially stretching the current process to ensure more time for oversight and careful budget preparation. Another model would allow the Congress to prepare a biennial budget in one session and devote the other to oversight, nonbudgetary activities, and supplemental appropriations. This "split" model is more common in reform proposals, with the idea that Congress needs to devote less, not more, time to budgeting.

Post-1974, Congress has had three separate annual budget processes: authorizations, budget resolutions and reconciliations, and appropriations. Although these fragmented annual processes provide members with ample ability to give input to the process in ways that will help advance their districts' interests, the budget process requires an extraordinary amount of time each session for balancing attention on taxation, spending, and oversight. Appropriations were always annual, but prior to the 1974 act, most authorizations were routinely multiyear or permanent. Despite the fact that the framers of the 1974 act were not supportive of annual authorizations, they did become more common afterward.[25]

The 1974 act also stipulated a study of biennial budgeting by the Congressional Budget Office, and the CBO laid out its recommendations in a study three years later, advocating that the House and Senate Appropriations Committees assess programs amenable to a two-year cycle. A separate report the same year by OMB also advocated multiyear budgeting. These reports led to Representative Leon Panetta's (D-CA) introduction of the first biennial budgeting bill in the Ninety-fifth

Congress. But the first hearings were not held until the early 1980s during the Ninety-seventh and Ninety-eighth Congresses.[26] In 1983, two separate Senate studies recommended biennial budget and appropriations cycles.[27] In the Ninety-ninth Congress, the Senate and House Armed Services committees' fiscal year 1986 authorization for the Department of Defense included an amendment to require the president to submit two-year budget proposals for Defense beginning in fiscal year 1988, although the authorization process has remained annual.

Biennial Budgeting continued to receive attention in hearings and favorable committee recommendations in both chambers in the 100th, 101st, and 103rd Congresses. The 1987 Gramm-Rudman-Hollings II legislation and that year's reconciliation bill included support for experiments with two-year appropriations and multiyear authorizations.[28] The Senate in 1990 and the House in 1995 began to fund their committees on a biennial basis.[29] In the 103rd Congress, the Vice President's National Performance Review (Gore Report) strongly advocated biennial budgeting. Related proposals received a lot of attention in both chambers through extensive hearings in several committees, including the Joint Committee on the Organization of Congress. The Joint Committee recommended a two-year cycle for presidential budget submissions, budget resolutions, reconciliation, and general appropriations bills. The Joint Committee's recommendations were reported in a bill by the House Rules Committee, and Senator Pete Domenici (R-NM) attempted to add biennial budgeting as an amendment to the District of Columbia's appropriations. Senator Robert Byrd (D-WV), a staunch supporter of Appropriations and congressional powers generally, stopped the amendment with a successful point of order.[30] But biennial budgeting has been a quiet, but steadily popular, plan among some budget-watchers.

According to many critics of the current budget process, annual authorizations and appropriations have not increased overall congressional control over the budget. As the Senate Rules and Administration Committee puts it: "Instead, it has created pressure for committees to act too quickly on some authorizations, with an attendant decline in oversight. . . . Proponents of biennial budgeting have long contended that multiyear authorizations would help relieve Congress's heavy workload by better distributing it."[31] The complex annual budgeting process also often pushes other legislative priorities to the back burner and usually concludes later than law mandates, resulting in continuing resolutions to keep the government operating after the new fiscal year begins. Budget summit meetings between the president and Congress are often the only way to get the budget passed on time.[32] Although congressional budget-related committees, the CBO, and the OMB are mandated to perform multiyear projections and estimations, their figures do not have the same force of law that biennial budgeting would. Likewise, multiyear budgeting agreements between presidents and Congresses in 1987, 1990, 1993, and 1997 show some supporters of this reform that such binding actions can be hammered out in relatively short time frames. One House Rules Committee report in favor of biennial budgeting put it bluntly: "The current budget process is overly repetitive, inefficient, and bureaucratic, and filled with time-consuming budget votes. Effective oversight gets crowded out."[33]

Recent congressional surveys of members and executive agencies show general agreement on the positive potential of such reform, but not on the precise nature of what "biennial" should entail. A recent survey by the Senate Committee on Governmental Affairs showed various agencies favoring biennial appropriations for both short- and long-term goals. Agency budget requests are sent to Congress eight months before the new fiscal year, but appropriations are signed into law at the last minute, if even then. Agencies therefore spend weeks into the new fiscal year sorting out their budget, and year-to-year fluctuations can make continuity and long-term planning difficult.[34] But a prior survey of Senators cited by the Senate Rules and Administration Committee showed stronger and more consistent support among members of both parties for a two-year resolution and multiyear authorizations than biennial appropriations legislation. This Senate committee report also questioned whether long-term agency estimations could avoid overstatement of need.[35]

Support for biennial budgeting was also evident through committee reports and favorable recommendations in the 105th and 107th Congresses, but there has not been a vote on either chamber's floor. Despite seemingly strong support in both parties—although support is weaker among members of the appropriations committees—biennial budgeting is controversial because it would be a dramatic departure from Congress's current practices. But, intriguingly, there is a lot of explicit institutional ambition in both sides' arguments. Unlike the previous major budget reforms from 1974 onward, there is uncertainty about whether biennial budgeting would strengthen or weaken congressional control of spending. The 1974 reforms were decidedly pro-Congress, with the following reforms decidedly attempting to handicap congressional prerogatives. Debates on biennial budgeting show both sides claim pro-Congress intent.

The following two quotations from the House and Senate Rules committees sum up the lukewarm support of this reform over the past decade.

While it is not a panacea for all the perceived shortcomings of the budget process, two year budgeting, in the Committee's view, can be an important tool for assisting both Congress and the executive branch in more efficiently managing the budget. A biennial cycle can give Congress a better time frame for budgetary action and help avoid decisions made in haste, with inadequate consideration of the need or consequences.[36]

There is concern that if Congress were to adopt biennial appropriations, that valuable oversight contributed by the Appropriations Committee could be diminished. . . . Annual appropriations action allows Congress to closely monitor the various departments and agencies of the Federal Government, and to determine whether or not they are indeed carrying out the will and intent of the Congress. The requirement of having to return to Congress each year for funding helps to ensure that congressional intent is implemented.[37]

But current challenges to oversight and deliberation give supporters of biennial budgeting fuel too. The House Rules Committee in the 107th Congress cited a CBO report identifying $112 billion in appropriations for federal programs whose authorizations had expired, presumably due to committees' inability to attend to their proper oversight. The fact that the annual appropriations process is so time-consuming has led to neglect of the authorization process, where most programmatic oversight is conducted. As a result, large portions of the discretionary federal budget are left unauthorized each year. According to the Rules report, many programs receiving taxpayers' dollars to function each year are not receiving the careful scrutiny that they should from the committees in Congress with the greatest expertise.[38]

However, dissenters on the current Rules Committee, Martin Frost (D-TX), Louise Slaughter (D-NY) and Alcee Hastings (D-FL) explain their opposition to biennial budgeting with the same end goals of its proponents. Citing the sudden need to adjust spending and economic assumptions after September 11, 2001, the abrupt elimination of the budget surplus, and a dramatic lowering of interest rates by the Fed, these critics of biennial budgeting argue Congress cannot and should not attempt to legislate for twenty-eight months into the future: "We heartily concur with proponents of biennial budgeting that committees other than . . . Appropriations . . . must strive to fully examine programs under their jurisdiction in order to hold the Executive accountable. But we do not understand how giving the Executive branch a biennial pass on answering questions posed to them by the very committees who write their checks will ensure that the programs and activities administered by the self-same Executive are 'fully and faithfully executed.' . . . Congress has a Constitutional responsibility to ask questions about money, management, and administration on a regular, ongoing basis."[39]

Conclusion

As this brief summary indicates, congressional delegation of power to executive and other outside authorities was not consistently pursued in the twentieth century, but overall Congress has ceded many of its fiscal prerogatives to the president and ultimately abandoned or diluted the two main attempts at reclaiming power in the reforms of 1946 and 1974. Most recently, complete budget power abdication was averted by the narrow loss of the balanced budget constitutional amendment proposals of the mid-1990s, and there is evidence that both supporters and opponents of biennial budgeting reform claim to be looking out for Congress's power. In other words, reports of the death of institutional ambition in Congress may have been exaggerated, but there was some foundation to the rumors, as seen in the reforms of Gramm-Rudman-Hollings and the line-item veto. And while procedural reforms of the budget process have become less of a priority for both the Congress and president since the turn of the new century, the Congress has deferred to the George W. Bush administration in a more direct way: supporting much of the president's tax and spending proposals in floor votes.

By contrast, delegation of power in recent decades was much more nuanced through complex procedural reforms. The next four chapters explore the details of the fiscal, political, and institutional issues behind the process changes of 1974, 1985, 1987, 1990, and 1996, including the legislative action and rhetoric surrounding various alternatives and the principles and structures of the passed acts. Although 1974 is an important pro-Congress outlier to the century-long pattern of delegation, the long-standing institutional capacity issues raised in this case shed light on the nature of both the preceding and subsequent movements to decrease legislative budgeting power.

Part II

INSTITUTIONAL SELF-DIAGNOSIS AND BUDGET REFORM, 1974–1996

3

1974 BUDGET ACT

Congress Takes Control

It is essential that Congress develop ways of making its own decisions on budget priorities so that realistic control over the purse can be regained by the Congress, as intended by the Constitution.
—*Joint Study Committee on Budget Control, 1973*[1]

I, myself, am impatient with this idea that Congress has lost control of the power of the purse. . . . Congress demonstrates its power of the purse when it delivers it to some modified degree to the Executive. It can give or it can take away, demonstrating that it does have control.
—*Representative George H. Mahon (D-TX), 1973*[2]

Budget reform must not become an instrument for preventing Congress from expressing its will on spending policy.
—*House Rules Committee, 1973*[3]

The 1974 Budget Act is a rare example of Congress viewing its own power as crucial to budget control. In this way, the 1974 reform is a stark contrast to subsequent episodes of congressional budget process changes in the 1980s and 1990s, which emphasized reduction of congressional power through external delegation and automatic spending-reduction procedures.

For its scope and longevity, the 1974 Congressional Budget and Impoundment Control Act was the most important bundle of budget process changes since the 1921 Budget and Accounting Act, which created the annual executive budget. The new Congressional Budget Of-

fice, House and Senate Budget Committees, and annual budget resolution and reconciliation processes were all created to enhance congressional control and coordination of annual budget and appropriations
decisions. And, unlike the short-lived experiment with congressional
budgeting in the late 1940s, the 1974 act's processes are still the core of
annual budget-making today.

At the same time, the 1974 act's background and results show important institutional challenges to congressional budgeting, which are
echoed in each subsequent reform. The Budget Act was an institutional response to two significant and persistent institutional challenges
to congressional budgeting highlighted again and again through the
reforms of the 1980s and 1990s. First, and most generally, structural
problems related to Congress's representative and legislative processes
make balanced budgeting inherently difficult. The district-based representative viewpoint of legislators is translated into spending pressures that are difficult to control and coordinate in the fragmented
division of labor in Congress that has long separated revenue and appropriations processes. Second, and related to the first challenge, growing entitlements and other kinds of "backdoor" spending circumvent
the annual appropriations process and leave only a minority of the budget truly controllable each year.

Despite an overwhelming indictment of congressional budgeting
practices based on these problems, delegation of power, automatic
mechanisms, and restrictive rules were explicitly rejected by Congress
in 1974. This conscious burst of institutional ambition stems from the
unusual political and institutional contexts of the reform period. The
Budget Act is often compared to the 1974 War Powers Resolution for
being emblematic of congressional retaliation against the "imperial
presidency" generally, and President Richard Nixon specifically. Important policy differences between congressional Democrats and the
president were illustrated by Nixon's extensive use of his impoundment powers to alter the disbursement of congressionally approved
funds. These budget battles were also intertwined with larger interbranch conflicts involving Watergate and the Vietnam War. Congress's
reassertion of budgetary power was also tied to internal changes in the
institution, which ultimately complicated the design and use of the 1974
reforms. The late 1960s and early 1970s were marked by a revolt of
more liberal junior members against powerful committee chairmen,

and new budgeting entities within Congress could satisfy some of these demands for wider institutional power. The act attempted to forge a balance between these forces of decentralization and an attempt to emulate, rather than rely upon, the centralized budgeting structures of the executive branch.

In different ways, this legislative action confirms important aspects of "strategic delegation" models' assumption of congressional behavior. Kiewiet and McCubbins's principal-agent delegation theory does not differentiate between Congress's use of internal and external agents—both are logical as long as the majority party principals retain power. But they imply that external agents will be more likely to go astray, so perhaps such a delegation would be strategic only if Congress could not find a suitable internal one. The 1974 act is rife with new internal agents through the budget committees and the CBO. The impoundment reforms also show how the majority attempted to rein in an agent who did not use previously delegated power to the principal's liking. Epstein and O'Halloran's argument about delegation are also borne out. They say Congress is unlikely to delegate distributive powers under conditions of divided government, and this is certainly the case in 1974. Congress carefully examined how different delegation alternatives would suit its budgetary preferences. However, as the subsequent case studies show, neither approach to delegation retains the same explanatory power. The 1974 reform is unique among modern budgeting changes, and its "strategic" components are more easily found. At the same time, party differences are harder to discern than institutional ones. The extraordinarily bipartisan support for the 1974 reform shows it was fundamentally a Congress–versus–the executive moment, which made delegation unattractive to most congressional Republicans too.[4]

The dominant argument of the reform's legislative history was that Congress had ceded far too much budgetary power to other institutions over the course of the century. However, a few vocal opponents of the reforms were Republicans who blamed the majority Democrats for deficits and advocated giving more budgeting power to the president and OMB. But the end vote shows how solidly the institution supported itself. The House passed the Budget Act 401 to 6, and the Senate's vote was 75 to 0. The bipartisan nature of the 1974 act undoubtedly shows that both parties saw the reform as being in their

political and policy interests at the time. The question of whether these
new entities were useful in spending and deficit control became much
more controversial in the 1980s and 1990s. The fact that so many of
these new structures and procedures themselves became the target of
criticism under both parties' leadership further illuminates the long-
standing institutional issues behind delegation movements and sets the
stage for anti-Congress sentiment.

In the following description of the background of the act, I highlight important fiscal, political, and institutional issues behind the reform movement. This format is used in each of the case studies to
demonstrate how all three repeatedly led to indictments of Congress's
budgeting capacity—but only in 1974 did Congress see its power as
the means to better budgeting control.

Background of the 1974 Act

The telling origin of the 1974 Congressional Budget and Impoundment
Act was a congressional debate regarding whether the Republican
President should be given extraordinary budget powers by the
Democrat-dominated Congress. In July 1972, Nixon proposed that
Congress cap the next fiscal year's budget at $250 billion and give him
the power to enforce that limit through various kinds of unilateral action
if Congress exceeded it. Later in the year, when expenditures seemed
likely to surpass the cap, Nixon asked for explicit powers to perform
the cuts. In an odd action in light of what was to come, the House
passed such a bill over criticism by majority leaders. The Senate Finance
Committee recommended passage, but the bill lost on the floor over
concerns for institutional power loss if the delegation was enacted.[5]
Various compromises to delegate more limited powers to the president
died in the conference committee, but Congress resolved to examine
its spending behavior and budgeting practices. The Joint Study
Committee on Budget Control (JSC) was commissioned in this 1972
budget agreement.[6] Although the JSC's two reports are important
components of the reform's legislative history, the 1974 act was also
the culmination of what Allen Schick calls "The Seven Year Budget
War," which began in 1966.[7] Like most prolonged budget conflicts,
this war was the result of interconnected fiscal, partisan, and institutional

issues, all of which entailed severe criticism of congressional budget practices.

Fiscal Issues

The most pressing fiscal matters prior to the 1974 act were deficits and steady uncontrollable increases in annual federal outlays. Dramatic overall spending increases after World War II contributed to both problems, and were exacerbated by the guns-and-butter policies of the Johnson administration and stagflation in the early 1970s. After low unemployment and low inflation in the mid-1960s, many economists and legislators assumed that economic growth could compensate for incremental federal spending growth. But by the early 1970s, this scenario did not occur, as total outlays more than doubled between fiscal years 1965 and 1974, inflation was increasing rapidly, and annual deficits became commonplace.[8]

Increases in raw spending numbers were not the only justification for changing the way the annual budget was produced. Congress found itself without the ability to act on its budgetary priorities. The fiscal component of this problem was the increased percentage of spending that was unalterable except by changing the basic authorizing statute, which was politically risky in the case of entitlements. By the time of the 1974 reforms, less than half the budget was subject to annual appropriations votes and almost 75 percent was considered essentially uncontrollable under existing law.[9] Federal entitlements were the largest percentage of uncontrollable spending. Before 1964, 25 percent of the budget went to transfer payments, and ten years later it was 40 percent. These transfer payments include entitlements, various other kinds of public assistance, and unemployment compensation, all of which are sensitive to varying annual enrollment numbers and economic conditions related to unemployment, which was relatively high in the early 1970s. In addition, most transfer programs are adjusted with the consumer price index, so relatively high rates of inflation, which were also present in the early 1970s, increased expenditures further.[10] Partially due to these issues, the federal deficit and debt rose, although the debt actually declined as a percentage of annual gross domestic product, as seen in Table 3.1.

Table 3.1: Federal Budget Deficit and Debt, Fiscal Years 1960–1975

Fiscal Year	Deficit (in billions)	Deficit as % of GDP	Total Public Debt (in billions)	Debt as % of GDP
1960	surplus (+.5)	0%	$237	45.6%
1961	3	0.6	238	45.0
1962	7	1.3	248	43.7
1963	5	0.8	254	42.4
1964	6	0.9	257	40.1
1965	1	0.2	261	38.0
1966	4	0.5	264	34.9
1967	9	1.1	267	32.9
1968	25	2.9	290	33.3
1969	surplus (+3)	0	278	29.3
1970	3	0.3	283	28.1
1971	23	2.1	303	28.1
1972	23	2.0	322	27.4
1973	15	1.1	341	26.0
1974	6	0.4	344	23.9
1975	53	3.4	395	25.4

Source: Congressional Budget Office Historical Tables; www.cbo.gov

Although deficit spending was not consistently increasing each year between 1964 and 1975, and even the largest amounts do not seem very high by today's standards, deficits were a pressing issue leading up to the 1974 act. But notably, the Joint Study Committee's discussion of the deficit problem is largely in institutional terms. The JSC argued that a lack of centralizing structure in Congress to reconcile spending and revenues is a major contributing factor to the need for Congress "to obtain better control over the budget."[11] Although the JSC argued that deficits demonstrated spending problems in Congress, it did not recommend a strict balanced-budget policy. Rather, when a deficit or surplus occurs it should be, as much as possible, "the result of planned rather than an unplanned congressional policy."[12] But planned or not, deficit spending was also an important component to the interbranch struggles over President Nixon's impoundments.

Partisan Issues

President Nixon justified his repeated impoundment of congressionally authorized funds as a necessary tool for spending and deficit reduction. Nixon argued that Congress was incapable of reining in its spending, for both ideological and institutional reasons.[13] Among other budget process criticisms, Nixon disagreed with the prevailing incremental budgeting strategy of continuing programs previously approved and arguing only about new increases, not the budgetary bases. Acting on this argument, he attempted to reduce or eliminate the bases of several agriculture, health, education, housing, and economic development programs. Although several previous presidents had taken advantage of presidential impoundment power, the ensuing clashes with Congress were unprecedented, partially because of other simmering political conflicts between the branches, ranging from the secret bombings of Cambodia to the Watergate investigation.

The impoundment controversy began in 1971 and continued until Nixon resigned and beyond (due to related agency litigation).[14] In his fiscal 1972 budget, President Nixon proposed that fifty-seven programs be terminated, reduced, or restructured for an immediate savings of over $2 billion. In his fiscal 1973 budget, Nixon listed thirty-six cuts he could make unilaterally and fifteen more that Congress could cut through substantive legislation, for a reduction of almost $3 billion. The fiscal 1974 budget contained an eight-page table listing program reductions Nixon was planning to make for a targeted savings of $17 billion. Only 6 of the 109 items were listed as needing congressional approval. Examination a year later demonstrated that the president was able to achieve most of his desired reductions despite congressional and federal court disapproval of some reductions.[15]

Nixon justified his actions through related partisan and institutional criticisms. He repeatedly emphasized congressional inability to examine budget totals and specifically drew attention to the Democratic majority's inability to adhere to congressional spending ceilings passed in 1968, 1969, and 1970.[16] The precedents for these impoundments were based on various and, in some cases, vaguely worded directives and budgetary statutes (such as the Anti-Deficiency Acts), which ordered the executive branch to save money when changes in circumstances after appropriations warranted. Nixon and his administration also argued that economic stabilization language in the 1946 Employment Act indirectly allowed the president to make adjustments in spending to combat inflation and to reduce the need for new tax revenues. And Nixon's administration used constitutional arguments related to the "take care" and executive power clauses in Article II to defend impoundments.[17]

Nixon's actions were indirectly supported by Arthur Burns, the chairman of the Board of Governors of the Federal Reserve System, during the 1973 Joint Study Committee hearings. Burns argued, "procedures that produce deficits that the Congress itself does not desire invite corrective actions by the Executive."[18] Representative Claude Pepper (D-FL) disagreed, as he argued presidential impoundments are violations of the oath of office and the Constitution by a failure to execute the law: "the President is not the protector of the country against the Congress. The Constitution did not give him that prerogative."[19]

Before the 1974 reform was passed, the House majority compromised between these positions by acknowledging that there are certain circumstances in which the president should have impoundment powers but not exercise them unilaterally. A small-scale budget reform bill containing new impoundment-control procedures passed the House in July 1973. In November, that bill was dropped and the impoundment reforms were included in the 1974 Congressional Budget Act already being debated.[20]

In addition to the skirmishes over presidential impoundments, a related political conflict between congressional Democrats and the Nixon administration surrounded the nascent Office of Management and Budget. The Reorganization Act of 1939, which created the Executive Office of the President and moved the Bureau of the Budget (BOB) from the Treasury Department to the Executive Office of the President (EOP), expired just prior to President Nixon's first term. Nixon submitted a plan to Congress to essentially abolish the politically isolated BOB and replace it with a new budget office, which would be more responsive to presidential policy objectives regarding agency management and budgeting. The reorganization plan was contentious, especially in the House, not least because the top officials of the proposed OMB were not going to be subject to Senate confirmation. But the old BOB was too unpopular to survive. The chairman of the Senate Subcommittee on Executive Reorganization, Abraham Ribicoff (D-

CT), charged that BOB was too antiquated and rigid to be responsive to modern presidential administrative needs. This argument, along with a massive lobbying effort by the members of the Ash Council, which drew up the plan, led to Nixon's Reorganization Plan No. 2's passage and OMB's replacement of BOB in 1970.

Under its first three directors, George Schultz, Caspar Weinberger, and Roy Ash, OMB was heavily criticized for its partisan bent, extensive reach into the executive branch, and role in Nixon's impoundments. In 1973, Congress passed a bill requiring that the director and deputy director be confirmed by the Senate (for both present and future officeholders) rather than appointed directly by the president. Nixon vetoed the bill arguing that it violated his constitutional removal power since Congress was in effect creating a new position title by abolishing and recreating the offices to circumvent the president's appointment prerogative. The Senate overrode the veto, but the House did not, and compromise legislation was passed to confirm future directors only.[21]

Nixon's funding-clashes with Congress on both domestic and international programs and appropriations and the related OMB fight were important elements of the Democrat-dominated Congress's desire to curtail presidential power over the budget. But these partisan conflicts also brought out a larger institutional issue: whether Congress would continue to reduce its power over the annual budget process, as had occurred since the beginning of the twentieth century. Congress could rein in Nixon, but should it rein in *the presidency* too? The Senate Committee on Government Operations highlighted this institutional question in a 1973 report, as did Representative William Moorhead (D-PA) before the JSC, economist Charles Schulze, and the House Rules Committee. Even if these arguments have strong partisan components, they still demonstrate the dominant rhetoric of institutional ambition.

The Senate Committee on Government Operations defended Congress's place in the budget process and separation of powers system generally:

Separation of powers could not be sustained if power to make policy and the power to act were joined in the same hands. If executive officials were empowered both to decide what should be spent and to do the actual

spending, there would be no meaningful place for Congress in the governmental structure. Thus, the spending process in the broad and constitutional sense, is a *sine qua non* for legislative purpose and independence. At
stake, therefore, in the attempt to improve the spending process, is the
restoration to Congress of its essential role in American government.[22]

William Moorhead (D-PA) agreed: "I do believe that the people of the
United States recognize that we are in a somewhat of a constitutional
confrontation between the legislative branch of government and the
executive branch and since I have been in the Congress the legislative
branch has declined in power and the executive branch has increased
in power. I express to my friends that I don't consider this to be a partisan
political matter of Republican versus Democrat. I think it is a
constitutional question of the executive versus the legislative."[23] And
the House Rules Committee also defended Congress's role:

Budget reform and impoundment control have a joint purpose: to restore
responsibility for the spending policy of the United States to the legislative
branch. One without the other would leave Congress in a weak and ineffective position. No matter how prudently Congress discharges its appropriations responsibility, legislative decisions have no meaning if they can be
unilaterally abrogated by executive impoundments. On the other hand, if
Congress appropriates funds without full awareness of the country's fiscal
condition, its actions may be used by the President to justify the improper
withholding of funds. By joining budget and impoundment control in a
complete overhaul of the budget process, H.R. 7130 seeks to ensure that
the power of appropriation assigned to Congress by the Constitution is
responsibly and effectively exercised.[24]

Institutional Issues

So why did congressional control of the budget appear elusive to so many
institutional actors? The following criticism Nixon offered in 1972 was
repeatedly echoed by economists and members of both parties: "The
Congress suffers from institutional faults when it comes to federal
spending. . . . Congress not only does not consider the total financial
picture when it votes on a particular spending bill, it does not even contain
a mechanism to do so if it wished. . . . The Congress, thus, has no sure

way of knowing whether or when its many separate decisions are contributions to higher prices, or possibly to higher taxes."[25]

One important aspect of Nixon's criticism was the fact that tax-writing and spending were completely separate in Congress: the House Ways and Means Committee and the Senate Finance Committee dealt with revenues, debt legislation, and entitlements, while the House and Senate Appropriations Committees dealt with some, but not all, expenditures. Even within the appropriations and tax committees, subcommittees were responsible for investigating the details of the bills in their jurisdiction only and, according to the Senate Finance Committee, "adequate attention has not been devoted to budget totals."[26]

Reduced congressional budgetary control over annual appropriations was also related to fragmented institutional arrangements. For fiscal 1974, only 44 percent of all federal expenditures were authorized by appropriations committees and subcommittees, since large entitlements were handled by tax-writing committees. At the same time, authorizing committees would grant agencies the ability to contract for obligations that did not necessarily translate into outlays for that budget cycle. Overall, only 60 percent of the estimated fiscal 1975 budget required action by Congress that year, but technically only 34 percent was "controllable."[27] Table 3.2 makes this dramatic decline quite apparent.

In light of the controllability problem, the JSC argued annual spending ceilings might be necessary, but to be "effective and meaningful" they should be placed on both new budget authority and outlays (i.e., expenditures and net lending). But the JSC also acknowledged that a coordination problem would be inevitable for enforcing such a ceiling. *In fiscal 1973, for example, approximately one hundred sixty legislative actions had a direct or indirect relationship to budget authority and spending.*[28] The House Rules Committee made a similar comment on the dispersed budgetary power of the Congress: "The excessive fragmentation of the budget process in Congress makes it difficult for Congress to effectively assess program priorities or to establish overall budget policy. At the very least, priority setting means that competing claims on the budget are decided in some comprehensive manner rather than in isolation from one another. This is not now the case. . . . The total is the sum of many individual actions, most of which are taken without any real cognizance of their impact on the economy."[29]

**Table 3.2: Controllability of Budget Outlays: A
Comparison of Fiscal Years 1967, 1971, and 1975**

Percent of Total Outlays	1967	1971	1975
Relatively uncontrollable under present law			
Open-ended programs and fixed costs:			
Payments for Individuals..................	25.5%	35.0%	42.0%
Other..	7.8	8.5	8.9
Outlays from prior-year contracts and			
obligations.............................	23.6	19.5	16.0
Subtotal, relatively			
uncontrollable outlays..........	56.9	63.0	66.9
Relatively controllable outlays....................	47.3	41.3	34.1
Other Outlays/Adjustments......................	-4.2	-4.3	-1.0
Total Budget Outlays......................	100.0	100.0	100.0

Source: Adapted from Historical Tables, *The Budget of the United States
Government, Fiscal Year 1986* (Washington: Government Printing Office, 1985),
Table 8.1.

Additional challenges to coordination surrounded the new openness of the budget process. Beginning in the early 1970s, broader participation by interested organizations, wider access to budgetary
information, more relaxed procedures for adding budget bill amendments and discussing alternatives, and an enlargement in the number
of budget participants in Congress meant increases in competing claims
on federal dollars. As Allen Schick describes, before the 1970s, the
Appropriations and Ways and Means committees were essentially run
behind closed-doors, and affected interests outside, and even within,
government had a difficult time gathering budget data. To compensate, states, local governments, and institutions like Brookings began
to publish analyses of the federal budget and interest groups began to
monitor budget activity more closely. The Ways and Means Committee expanded its membership, established subcommittees, and began
to allow amendments to budget bills. This new openness affected budget outcomes in that "with the expansion of budgetary participation, it
is harder to deprive an affected interest without a fight."[30]

Related to the pressures of coordination and increases on spending demands was the problematic use of continuing resolutions to fund government programs and agencies. Continuing resolutions are extensions of current spending levels in the absence of new fiscal year budgets. They exist so that programs and agencies can remain funded even if Congress has not passed the necessary appropriation bills by the beginning of the fiscal year. In an average year prior to the 1974 act's passage, half or more of the required appropriations bills were still awaiting passage on July 1. Although these resolutions are one way of preempting budget crises, they have two major shortcomings, according to the House Rules Committee in 1973. First, continuing resolutions prolong the period of uncertainty about spending outcomes, which can be particularly burdensome to state and local governments awaiting new funding information. Second, continuing resolutions can create inefficient spending strategies in agencies, as they give agencies incentives to spend funds rapidly because apportionment controls do not apply to these resolutions.[31]

Due to these various institutional issues, congressional spending and budget process problems were addressed five times between 1967 and 1972, but no sustained coordination between revenues and expenditures was attempted. Congress enacted various spending ceilings, but they were not successful, according to the Senate Finance Committee, because of conflicts between the tax-writing and spending committees, as well as "uncontrollable" increases in exempted programs ranging from Vietnam War funding to entitlements and farm subsidies. A Senate report found that "experience with exceptions has demonstrated that there is no general agreement as to the number of programs which should be given the favored status of exemption. As a result, once exemptions are started, this seems to represent an invitation to amend the bill by adding additional programs to the list of exemptions. This, of course, seriously erodes the effectiveness of any overall limitation."[32] As the following summary of these ceilings shows in Table 3.3, the use of spending ceilings did not fulfill fiscal expectations.

In light of these failed experiments, the JSC's final report argued that spending ceilings were useful but should not be the sole means of controlling expenditures. From the JSC's perspective, it was the inability of Congress to evaluate revenues and outlays from a broader perspective that undermined its ability to prioritize spending and coordinate

Table 3.3: Summary of Congressional Spending Limit
Legislation and Results, 1967–1972

Year	Spending-Reduction Legislation	Result
1967	across-the-board reductions in controllable programs without expenditure ceiling	some reductions, but failed to meet amount specified
1968	ceilings on outlays and obligational authority combined with tax legislation, exempting six categories of expenditure; president authorized to withhold amounts from obligation to meet limits	more reductions achieved by action on individual bills than through ceiling
1969/ 1970	ceilings written into supplemental appropriations bills, exempting uncontrollable expenditure; ceilings adjustable according to congressional action	no significant impact
1972	limits added to debt ceiling bill	ceiling nullified in conference due to disagreements over presidential power to enforce them

Source: Adapted from Schick, *Congress and Money*, 32-42.

fiscal policy.[33] In addressing these problems, the JSC's report presented arguments regarding why these problems exist and how the new institutional structures the committee recommended would attempt to avoid the usual pitfalls of spending caps. The JSC noted that for a spending ceiling to be effective, it must be placed on both new authority and new outlays, but this would involve an unwieldy number of participants, as mentioned above. A second major problem regarding meaningful spending ceilings was the unpredictability of relatively uncontrollable appropriations. A third problem was that ceilings were usually enacted early in the budget cycle when information on budgetary needs was not clear, and therefore the ceilings were unrealistic.

Related to all these issues was the persistent problem of "backdoor" spending, which gets around the spirit, if not the letter, of spending caps.[34] To better coordinate both backdoor and reviewed appropriations, the JSC unanimously recommended new standing budget committees in each chamber to coordinate the work of the revenue and appropriations committees as well as lay down and enforce new expenditure caps. These proposed committees would enforce any new ceilings on budget outlays, new budget authority, and net lending and would draw up annual concurrent resolutions to coordinate all congressional budget activity. Congress could then impose tax surcharges or other forms of taxation on individuals and corporations to ensure that the concurrent resolutions are adhered to.

Agreements on spending caps would be proposed at the beginning of the budget creation cycle and reported by the budget committees and then revised and enforced after the authorizing committees have done their work and the budget committees have gathered more relevant information. Finally, the proposed budget committees would regularly submit to both chambers tabulations on the effects of existing and proposed legislation on overall expenditure goals as well as future impact for the next three to five years.[35]

The spending ceilings outlined by the JSC would not be legislated firmly in advance but left to the budget committees to decide each budget cycle. All new budget authority and outlays had to be within the set ceilings of that year. The JSC also proposed a "rule of consistency" to ensure that any increase in allocation be offset by an accompanied provision for specific revenue to pay for the expenditure(s). The funds to cover this allocation could come from new revenue or from a decrease in funds to any one or more budget categories (similar to "pay-as-you-go" provisions in the 1990 Budget Enforcement Act).

In a working paper for the Select Committee on Committees, Alice Rivlin (with the Brookings Institution at the time, and later the first Congressional Budget Office director) outlined a slightly different diagnosis of the institutional problems plaguing Congress and why the JSC recommendations were inherently flawed. She argued that the main problems with congressional budgeting are a lack of deliberations on large spending issues and priorities, agencies' spending too much time and focus on annual budgeting issues, and a lack of analysis and commitment to future impacts of any one year's budget. In effect, she proposed triennial budgeting to cope with Congress's fiscal burdens.[36]

In light of all these criticisms of congressional budgeting and presidential impoundments, as well as the JSC reports, members of the House and Senate proposed more than two hundred and fifty reform bills and resolutions. Although the overall theme of these bills was to rein in the executive and increase control of the budget in Congress, various rules and spending ceilings to control majority power were heavily supported by the JSC. Ultimately, however, Congress rejected such self-imposed limitations on its legislative prerogatives.

Passage of the Bill

Implementing the JSC's recommendations meant major changes for important congressional power centers, committees, and interests, and these controversies were given significant attention in congressional deliberation. The Appropriations, Ways and Means, and Finance Committees would be most affected by the reforms, and their competing interests were discussed by the JSC in both reports. Although the Appropriations Committee made up almost half the participants in the JSC, the revenue committees' preferences were largely heeded for two reasons, according to Schick. First, the congressional and public consensus was that overspending, not undertaxation, was the cause of the budgetary crisis, and, second, the Ways and Means Committee was extremely powerful at this time, whereas the Appropriations Committee's jurisdiction had been gradually eroded by the growth of backdoor spending and other uncontrollable expenditures.[37]

From the perspectives of the House leadership, the JSC's proposal was generally supportable but controversial in parts. The House Rules Committee reviewed the legislation in 1973, and, as it was an arm of the Democratic leadership, it had to reconcile numerous majority party interests. As Schick explains, Representative Richard Bolling (D-MO) led the negotiations and reached a compromise between the two main factions opposed to the JSC recommendations: liberals concerned with tightening spending requirements and the likely conservative composition of the proposed Budget Committee and the Appropriations Committee, whose leaders thought the proposed reforms eroded too much of its power.[38] The bill the Rules Committee reported had diluted the influence of the Appropriations and Ways and Means Committees in the new House Budget Committee, leaving more seats available to the general House membership, whose Democrats at the time leaned more to the left than the members of these committees.[39] To satisfy the Appropriations leaders, the first budget resolution in each annual cycle under the new requirements would have soft targets instead of firm ceilings. The Rules report also argued that early spending limits deprive Congress of the flexibility needed to respond to changing circumstances, and they reduce the utility of the appropriations process. This need for congressional control over the process was an argument in favor of eliminating the "consistency" amendment discussed above and other restrictive rules on floor action: "Points of order could have been raised at many stages of the process and legitimate legislative initiatives would have been blocked. The constant objective of budget reform should be to make Congress informed about and responsible for its budget actions, not to take away its power to act."[40]

The minority view of the Rules Committee was in support of the budget-process reforms but against the added impoundment provisions, arguing that excessive federal spending aggravates inflation and that the anti-impoundment provisions will eliminate "one of the few remaining defenses" against it. At the same time, the minority view pointed out that if the new congressional procedures were successful, there might not be a need for impoundments at all. But if the new budget process did not succeed in reducing spending, then the president's impoundment powers were very necessary. In light of these points on both sides, Representative John Anderson (R-IL) argued that in recent decades, "while the Executive function grew stronger and more centralized, the congressional budget function grew weaker and more fragmented. . . . Partly because of our conditioned dependence on the Executive over the years, and partly because of the great proliferation of spending responsibilities and decisionmaking powers in the Congress, the sad fact is that we do not have a rational budget process we can call our own."[41]

H.R. 7130 ultimately passed with only twenty-three votes opposed, while S. 1541 endured similar tensions and success. Senator Lee Metcalf (D-MT) headed the new Subcommittee on Budgeting, Management, and Expenditures of the Government Operations Committee, which had primary jurisdiction over the budget reform bill. Like the House Rules Committee, the Senate subcommittee also strayed from the JSC's recommendations regarding the proposed Budget Committee. According to Allen Schick, Metcalf's committee voted to remove all membership quotas from the proposed Senate Budget Committee (SBC), allowing members who did not serve on either Appropriations or Finance. Although this new recommendation had bipartisan support, the subcommittee was also split on the use, flexibility, and implementation of targets and ceilings, which were generally supported by conservatives and viewed suspiciously by liberals who voiced concerns regarding who would enforce the limits.[42]

Representative John Conyers (D-MI) conveyed this concern when he appeared before the Subcommittee. The following exchange demonstrates intra-institutional concerns in light of power transitions within Congress.

SENATOR ROTH (R-DE): Would you agree that basically, whatever the [budget] committee is, or however you set up the ceiling and you set up the priorities under the ceiling, the final decision should be made by the House and Senate as a whole so that every Member does have a voice? . . .

MR. CONYERS: Yes. . . . I would be willing to agree to that because otherwise, we would be vesting in the hands of a small number of Members in the Senate and the House the most important decision of every session of Congress. We would be saying that we are not going to let the executive branch tell us how to legislate and how to project the financial considerations of this Nation, but we would also not be doing it ourselves. We are going to let a small number of men in each body make these decisions, which I don't think would settle pleasantly in the contemplation of most of the Members of the Senate and the House, and for a very good reason.[43]

Economist Charles Schulze of the Brookings Institution (and former director of the Bureau of the Budget) highlighted other issues surrounding the target/ceiling proposal:

If the Congress having set such a ceiling continues by its individual actions to provide funds in appropriations, in back door authority, and so forth, in excess of the ceiling it sets, what that ceiling really does is give the President a directive to impound. Second, and perhaps more important, if all the Congress does is set a ceiling, then over the long run I can guarantee that the Congress' basic authority over priorities and its power over the purse will deteriorate. . . . You could vote for a high authorization, a high appropriation, and at the same time vote for a nice tight overall ceiling.[44]

And Senator Brock (R-TN) agreed: "Unless we do [more than a ceiling] the Congress simply cannot establish national priorities. That is the nub of the question: Do we or do we not have the will and having the will do we establish the structure for the Congress to speak for the American people, in determining the national needs and national allocations of resources."[45]

The issue of ceilings was partially resolved by the Operations Committee chairman, Sam Ervin (D-NC), who worked with Senators Edmund Muskie (D-ME) and Charles Percy (R-IL) to forge a compromise. The compromise was based on the subcommittee's recommendations for a complicated process of enforcing spending limits as well as procedures for limiting backdoor spending and pet project amendments, increasing timely authorization legislation, and increasing budgetary information flow.[46]

The resulting bill had four phases for congressional budgeting: informational and analytic (the proposed Congressional Budget Office and budget committees organizing the requests and estimates), consideration and adoption of the budget resolution (containing ceilings on total and recommended budget outlays and authority), the appropriations process (enacting budget authority with consideration given to the resolution through scorekeeping provisions), and the reconciliation process (determining spending totals and reducing appropriations or enacting a second resolution if ceilings are exceeded).[47] The new reform bill was then referred to the Senate Rules and Administration Committee at the request of one of the Rules Committee's members, Majority Whip Robert Byrd (D-WV). Senator Byrd organized a forty-five-member working group, which wrote a compromise bill.[48] The new bill included the Senate in the appointment of CBO's director and detailed membership requirements of the Senate Budget Committee,[49] among dozens of smaller compromises between the House and Senate plans. After four days of debating the working group's report, the Senate passed it 80 to 0.[50]

The most contentious issue in the conference committee was impoundments, but other issues also needed to be resolved. A year earlier, in light of Nixon's withholdings, both chambers passed legislation on impoundment control that allowed this action but differed on congressional oversight. As is detailed in the next section, the 1974 compromise differentiated between presidential spending rescissions and deferrals.[51] The other compromises allowed a more flexible target for the first budget resolution and softened the authorization deadline requirements. The conference bill also provided that the new process begin with fiscal 1977, with an option to begin in fiscal 1976, but mandating that the impoundment control provisions begin immediately.

Support for the conference report in the House and Senate was overwhelming, and the reform was described frequently as "landmark" and "historic." On the floors of both chambers, supporters cited spending and inflation control as top issues that the Budget Act would address, as well as the institutional power the act gave to Congress. But there were consistent worries as well. Some of the act's supporters, especially in the House, wondered whether members would have the "will" to make the budgetary controls work and whether the new budget timetable was truly workable within already crowded congressional calendars. Related to this last point were reservations concerning the complexity of the new budget resolution and reconciliation processes and how the budget committees may not be responsive enough to the concerns of a wide range of members in light of the time pressures put upon them. Other members argued that the new backdoor spending control procedures were an improvement over the old processes but still not strong enough.[52] As the following chapters show, all of these concerns became the centerpiece of subsequent reform efforts in the 1980s and 1990s.

The final bill passed the House on June 18, 1974, by a 401 to 6 margin, and the bill passed the Senate 75 to 0 on June 21.[53] The budget reform bill was signed by President Nixon on July 12, 1974, less than a month before his resignation.

Provisions of the 1974 Act

The main principles of the 1974 reform set it apart from its successors because the new procedures were not designed to restrict the powers of congressional majority preferences nor mandate deficit reduction. In response to fiscal, political, and institutional pressures, the Congressional Budget Act was meant to create a more disciplined budget process controlled by Congress. The act was designed to increase congressional budgetary power in relation to the president in three ways: new legislative measures that would not be subject to presidential approval, increased information independence from the president's budget office, and reductions in unilateral presidential impoundment powers. In response to intra-institutional pressures, the act also largely maintained existing budget-related committee jurisdiction and flexibility by not requiring set spending ceilings and created new entities and processes that would give rank-and-file members power.[54]

Although the 1974 act was partly inspired by spending and deficit concerns, the new procedures could be used theoretically to increase spending and deficits if a majority of Congress wished. A major step in this "deficit neutrality"[55] was the shift from using firm annual spending ceilings in the late 1960s to more flexible targets created in the first budget resolution during each annual legislative cycle. Related to this point, the act ignored many of the JSC's proposals for mandating restrictive rules if spending increases were proposed without compensatory revenues or spending reductions in other areas. These rejected provisions would have mandated points of order if they were violated and could only be waived with a two-thirds vote.[56] As the House Rules Committee argued in its report, these and other rejected JSC recommendations would have stifled congressional ability to pursue its spending prerogatives through normal majority-driven legislative procedures.

However, other key JSC recommendations were retained because without them the new process would not have the kind of control that was needed to increase Congress's understanding of the macro-level ramifications of its myriad budget-related actions. According to the 1974 act, the first budget resolution must be in place before specific spending, revenue, entitlement, or debt legislation could be considered. Without this requirement, the coordination of spending and revenue, which the first resolution mandates, would be far less likely. Congress did lose some powers to act on certain spending preferences, but the important difference between the 1974 act and subsequent acts was that these restrictions were largely self-imposed and could be waived with a smaller majority than later, more restrictive rules changes. By contrast, the impoundment provisions provided a clearer mechanism for congressional control over executive spending powers while still maintaining the mechanism for executive withholdings.

The Budget Committees

The 1974 act created two budget committees that would theoretically represent a broad spectrum of interests in each chamber. The House Budget Committee (HBC) was given a strict formula for membership distribution: five members from Appropriations, five from Ways and Means, eleven from other standing committees, and one from each of the two parties' leadership.[57] Neither the Senate Budget Committee's number of members nor the selection process for choosing the members was included in the act (but the new Committee was born with the JSC-recommended fifteen seats). The members of both the HBC and SBC were to be fully determined by the party caucuses, but SBC members could serve indefinitely.[58] With the help of mostly permanent and separate staffs, the three basic duties given to the budget committees in the 1974 act were: to report two concurrent resolutions on the budget each year; to make several macro-impact reports of proposed and existing programs; and to oversee the operations of the Congressional Budget Office.[59] The budget committees were not designed to have any subcommittees to help in these tasks, but they immediately instituted a practice of *ad hoc* task forces whose primary functions were to "study" rather than "legislate" programs and budgets. Unlike the division of the Appropriations Committee's work into subcommittees for each of the thirteen annual spending bills, the Budget Committee's task forces were predominantly cross-categorical in their budget areas.[60]

The Congressional Budget Office

One of the 1974 act's purposes was to provide Congress with information independence from OMB, which had been considered a secretive and partisan arm of the executive since it replaced the Bureau of the Budget in 1970. The Speaker of the House and the President *Pro Tempore* of the Senate appoint the CBO director after considering the recommendations of both chambers' budget committees "without regard to political affiliation and solely on the basis of his fitness to perform his duties."[61] The director has a four-year term that is not concurrent with the president's and is removable through a resolution by either chamber. The Congressional Budget Office "was to provide a bastion of neutral analysis, loyal to the institution of Congress, rather than to committees or parties."[62]

The three main analytic responsibilities of the CBO in the act were: to monitor the economy and estimate its impact on the budget; to improve the flow and amount of budgetary information within Congress; and to provide costs and effects analyses of alternative budgetary choices. The CBO was mandated to provide information related to all kinds of budgeting bills and issues to the budget committees, as well as by request to the Appropriations, Ways and Means, Finance, and, as a last priority, other standing committees and individual members. In addition, CBO was mandated to provide temporary personnel upon request to the Budget, Appropriations, and tax committees. In all of these functions, according to the list of duties in the act, assisting the budget committees was to be the first priority of CBO.[63] On or before April 1, the director was mandated to submit to the budget committees a report on fiscal policy for the year beginning that October, as well as provide information updates "from time to time." This main report should include alternative levels of total revenues, total new budget authority, and total outlays (including surpluses and deficits), level of tax expenditures under existing law (taking projected economic factors into account), as well as budget authority and outlays for major programs and functional categories. In analyzing alternatives to current or proposed policies, CBO should take into account how these proposals "will meet major national needs and affect balanced growth and development of the United States." The 1974 act also provided support for the goal that CBO would have the resources and information necessary to become an effective budgeting arm of the Congress.[64]

The New Budget Timetable

A theoretically self-disciplining timetable was included in the 1974 act as a response to accusations that Congress's old procedures did not look at budget totals, and it also arguably allowed time for the CBO and budget committees to perform their new duties. The most important dates provided under the timetable were the presentation of the president's budget, action on the first and second concurrent congressional resolutions, action on a reconciliation bill (if one was

Table 3.4: 1974 Congressional Budget Act Timetable

On or before:	Action to be completed:
November 10	President submits current services budget.
15 days after Congress convenes*	President submits his budget.
March 15	Committees and joint committees submit reports to budget committees.
April 1	CBO submits report to budget committees.
April 15	Budget committees report first concurrent resolution on the budget to their houses.
May 15	Committees report bills and resolutions authorizing new budget authority.
May 15*	Congress completes action on first concurrent resolution on the budget.
7 days after Labor Day	Congress completes action on bills and resolutions providing new budget authority and spending authority.
September 15*	Congress completes action on second required concurrent resolution on the budget.
September 25*	Congress completes action on reconciliation bill or resolution, or both, implementing second concurrent resolution.
October 1*	Fiscal year begins.

          * major annual events

Source: P.L. 93-344, Section 300.

deemed to be necessary), and a new official start of the fiscal year, as seen in Table 3.4.[65]

The information-gathering stages for the new congressional budget process were to end by mid-April, and then the major focus of the new procedures would begin—the two concurrent budget resolutions. The first concurrent resolution was a formal reply to the president's budget proposal and occurred after committees with jurisdiction over budget authorization, expenditures, appropriations or revenues formulated their recommendations and transmitted them to the budget committees.

While changes could occur later, the first resolution ideally would establish the ground rules for the year by setting targets for the committees and Congress as a whole to meet, including recommended and estimated levels for total budget outlays and new budget authority, budget outlays and new authority for each of the nineteen functional budget categories, surplus or deficit ("whichever is appropriate in light of economic conditions and all other relevant factors") revenues, and appropriate level of debt and debt ceiling changes. This first concurrent budget resolution is not a bill submitted for presidential approval. Rather, it is a framework within which the entire Congress makes budget decisions, determines priorities, and makes allocations. As an agreement between both houses and between each house and their committees regarding future action, an important step toward the first resolution is each chamber's Budget Committee hearings. During these hearings after the transmission of budget estimates from the various standing committees, the budget committees receive testimony from members, representatives of federal departments and agencies, the general public, and national organizations "as the Committees deem desirable."[66]

By April 15, assuming all committee and CBO reports are submitted and hearings have ended, the budget committees would report the first concurrent resolution to their chambers. An accompanying report must include a comparison of Budget Committee recommendations and the president's; an estimation of total, new, and categorical outlays deemed "controllable" or not; revenue sources and totals; underlying economic assumptions, objectives, and data, as well as alternatives considered, total and categorical five-year budget impact projections; and statements of significant changes to state and local government funding.[67]

The first resolution adopted by the two chambers provides funding levels for the upcoming fiscal year plus the next two years.[68] A joint explanatory report would accompany the first resolution to spell out the appropriate levels of total outlays and new authority among each of the committees that has jurisdiction over budget bills and resolutions. Based on this first resolution, scorekeeping by CBO would advise committees as they worked on authorizations and appropriations.[69] After passage of the appropriations bills, Congress would "reaffirm or revise" the first concurrent resolution through a second binding resolution just fifteen days before the new fiscal year was to begin. This second resolution restates or revises spending and revenue totals as well as directs the authorizations committees to determine and recommend changes of specific dollar amounts to accomplish the new spending totals. The committees are generally given only dollar amounts to reduce their authorizations, leaving the specific changes to programs and functions to the discretion of the committees.[70] If only one committee is directed to make changes, it should report a reconciliation resolution or bill directly to the chamber, but if more than one committee makes changes, then the Budget Committee would report the new changes together. An additional provision in the second resolution is for the revenue committees to determine and recommend changes to the federal debt if necessary.[71]

Regarding the dramatic changes to the budget process with the new budget resolution and reconciliation processes, Howard Shuman summarizes the political issues at stake: "by giving members of the House and Senate the opportunity to vote on the total amounts instead of the mere details of cuts, in the consideration of both the budget resolutions and the reconciliation bills, the act provides a method of cutting the 'sacred cows' not available under previous procedures."[72]

The Impoundment Provisions

The 1974 act begins the Impoundment Control title with an unusual description that illustrates the interbranch conflict surrounding the reform: "Nothing contained in this Act, or in any amendments made by this Act, shall be construed as—(1) asserting or conceding the constitutional powers or limitations of either the Congress or the President; (2) ratifying or approving any impoundment heretofore or hereafter executed or approved by the President or any other Federal Officer or employee."[73] Distinguishing between the use and approval methods of deferrals and rescissions forms the heart of impoundment control and increased congressional input. In the case of temporary withholding in deferrals, congressional nonaction means the president's proposal goes forward, but in the case of permanent rescission, congressional nonaction means the rescission will not take place.

A "deferral of budget authority" occurs when the president, the director of OMB, the head of an agency or department, or any official or employee of the U.S. government proposes withholding or delaying approved appropriations. This deferral, which could be done through establishing "reserves" for that agency in times of changed requirements or savings gained through greater operating efficiency, must be explained in a special message transmitted by the president to the Congress. If either house passes an "impoundment resolution" of disapproval, the funds must be released according to their original obligations. While there is no deadline for the House or the Senate to act, no approved deferral can go beyond the fiscal year.[74]

By contrast, a rescission is defined as the permanent withholding of funds, which can be a part of a project or its entire budget authority. In cases of rescission the president must still transmit a special message to Congress that includes the amount he is rescinding; which other account or department could potentially receive the funds; the reasons why the budget authority is rescinded; the estimated fiscal, economic, and budgetary effects of the proposed rescission; and "all facts, circumstances, and considerations relating to or bearing upon the proposed rescission or the reservation and that decision to effect [the change], and, to the maximum extent practicable, the estimated effect of the proposed rescission or the reservation upon the objects, purposes, and programs for which the budget authority is provided."[75] If Congress wants to approve the rescission, it must pass a rescission bill approving all or part of the president's reduction proposal within forty-five days of receiving the president's special message. Ultimately, then, the Congress had the last word, even with its silence, as lack of positive action on a presidential rescission request killed it.

Conclusions on the 1974 Act

The 1974 Congressional Budget and Impoundment Control Act was a landmark reform, purposefully designed to regain lost institutional budgeting power through new structures, internal processes, and interbranch checks. Unlike the failed experiments with congressional budgeting in the mid-1940s, the 1974 act is also unique in twentieth-century budget history because many of these provisions are still standing, despite attacks on them in the 1980s and 1990s. And while the harsh institutional self-criticism seen in its legislative history links the 1974 reform with those that followed years later, this diagnosis did not deter the majority party from keeping power close at hand.

Strategy and Reform

The 1974 Congressional Budget and Impoundment Control Act demonstrates Kiewiet and McCubbins's theories on the strategic advantages of majority party delegation of power to internal agents and the regulation of external agents gone astray. As is evidenced by the legislative action and rhetoric surrounding the bill's background and passage, and how these actions and arguments relate to the structures of the reform, three kinds of majority party spending power were increased in 1974.

First, the new budget committees were created as internal agents of the majority party, and the use of this kind of principal-agent strategy has been demonstrated by several scholars of the congressional budget process. There has usually been a close relationship of the party leaders' and caucuses' preferences to the ideology, geography, and seniority levels of the budget committees. Since 1977, House Democratic members are nominated by the party's Steering and Policy Committee and approved by the entire caucus in separate votes for the Appropriations, Ways and Means, and at-large members.

Prior to 1977, the chairmen of Appropriations and Ways and Means each nominated three members from their committees, so the shift to the Steering Committee bolstered the party leadership's power. Democrats in the Senate vote in their Conference on nominees put forward by a steering committee. In both the House and the Senate, Republican leaders select the Budget Committee members through their Committee on Committees. The term limits imposed on the HBC members give party leaders more opportunities to change the committee, whereas the permanence of the SBC has created a more independent power source.[76]

Reflecting on the first five years of the new budget processes, Schick argues that "from the start of markup in HBC through the completion of floor action, House Republicans have been outsiders, rarely courted or consulted by the [majority] Democratic Party."[77] Kiewiet and McCubbins's analysis of ideological relationships between committee members and party caucuses further shows that, especially in the House, both parties' members on the Budget Committee have been slightly more ideologically extreme than their congressional parties overall.

These facts further lead Kiewiet and McCubbins[78] to conclude that such strategic internal delegation can serve party interests loyally.

Second, the 1974 act's other internal budgeting processes and structures were designed to avoid the external delegation and strict internal mechanisms that would mitigate congressional majority power. Despite the Joint Study Committee's recommendations, Congress rejected annual spending ceilings, which are meant to reduce majority spending prerogatives, in favor of softer targets drafted annually and enforced internally by the budget committees. In addition, the Congressional Budget Office was meant to provide a less-partisan source of budget information than the president's Office of Management and Budget but still reflect the majority's preferences through the choice of the director.

Third, the 1974 act rejected executive-enforced spending limits and reduced the president's impoundment powers by creating new oversight controls on their use. The increased powers that President Nixon demanded and often unilaterally exercised were not considered viable solutions to spending problems by the Joint Study Commission or to the other legislative committees investigating budget reforms. In addition, the new impoundment regulations regarding presidential deferrals and rescissions are easily related to the desire of the majority party to mitigate powers previously delegated to an external agent who had arguably abused the delegation.

Although Aaron Wildavsky's evaluation of the 1974 act is meant to be a criticism of its results, his argument underscores the theory that internally focused agents and processes could be extremely useful for majority party spending goals: "The new budget process was a form of government of congressmen, by congressmen, for congressmen. It created rules for Congress, but any majority can change such procedures. Legislation in the House and Senate often is considered under rules tailored for the occasion; amendment of those rules on the floor is common enough. Congressmen would follow the budget act's rules only if they wanted to do so; they would want to do so only if they valued the process itself more than they valued what they would lose if they obeyed the act."[79]

Without even analyzing the appropriations outcomes of the Congressional Budget and Impoundment Control Act, we can conclude that there are many aspects of the 1974 act's legislative history that demonstrate what a principal-agent strategy might look like in the design and rhetoric of budget reform. At the same time, the act's background and extraordinary bipartisan support show that larger political and institutional issues also determined its form.

Institutional Self-Diagnosis and Reform

The protracted battles with President Nixon over impoundment, the larger issues of presidential usurpation and abuse of power, and the internal power shifts away from congressional centralization and hierarchy all shaped the goals and processes of the 1974 act. The external politics behind the reform led to calls for increased congressional power, but the internal politics meant that in the creation of the new budget process, centralized authority would be largely eschewed in favor of the continuation of broad power distribution but with greater coordination of the disparate parts.

And looming behind these important background factors was Congress's institutional capacity problems with budgeting. The fiscal and partisan issues that helped trigger Nixon's impoundments, and the reform movement generally, were very much tied to two major congressional problems of budgeting. Although government spending is the result of both executive and legislative actions, the spending pressures within Congress as a representative body were well accommodated by its fragmented budget processes consisting of over a hundred actions that did not reconcile spending with revenue. In addition, dramatic increases in spending pressures since the midcentury led to various kinds of backdoor spending processes that circumvented annual appropriations reviews. As was said repeatedly throughout the reform process, Congress lacked control over its budgets.

The next three chapters demonstrate that, even after these particular contexts faded and the main actors changed, similar institutional problems continued. These institutional problems contributed to vocal anti-Congress sentiment that advocated a reduction in congressional majority power over annual budget outcomes. In other words, a lot of "strategic behavior" related to the 1974 act and afterward can be better understood in relation to these institutional issues. The 1974 reforms were initially considered a fiscal success and may have satisfied the various needs of institutional leaders and rank-and-file members, but they did not fix the representational problems that were widely considered to be the heart of the issue.

After the first use of the new congressional budget process in 1976, the chairmen of the two budget committees, Representative Brock Adams (D-WA) and Senator Edmund Muskie (D-ME), announced that actual outlays were billions of dollars below the amounts allocated in the budget resolution: "Fiscal year 1976 ended at midnight yesterday and for that year Congress lived within its spending ceiling and is below its deficit target. . . . The successful operation of this new budget process is historic. . . . It shows that Congress has recaptured from the Executive its constitutional role in controlling the power of the purse."[80] These sentiments faded within a few years as deficits began to rise dramatically, and congressional budgeting processes were again blamed and targeted for change.

In this sense, the goals of better budget control and coordination arguably lived on, but the principle of increasing congressional majority power did not. As the subsequent reform movements demonstrate, many institutional budgeting problems highlighted in the 1974 reform period were diagnosed again and again throughout the next two decades. Ultimately, the Congressional Budget and Impoundment Control Act itself came under fire for exacerbating the very difficulties it was meant to mitigate.

4

CONGRESS ATTACKS DEFICITS (AND ITSELF) WITH GRAMM-RUDMAN-HOLLINGS

*Why should Congress embark on a dangerous and perhaps unconstitu-
tional course? Congress already has the ability to make the cuts
necessary to achieve the deficit reduction targets in Gramm-Rudman-
Hollings. What it lacks is the will to make the difficult choices
necessary to meet those goals.*

　　　　　　　—Senator Dennis DeConcini (D-AZ), 1985[1]

. . . bad idea whose time had come.

　　　　　　　—Senator Warren Rudman (R-NH), 1985[2]

The 1974 Congressional Budget and Impoundment Control Act and
its Gramm-Rudman-Hollings amendments a decade later were very
different responses to similar institutional self-diagnoses. As Chapter
3 emphasized, the framers of the 1974 budget reforms acknowledged
that institutional deficiencies in congressional budgeting contributed
to federal spending problems, but they also argued that restructuring
and enhancing congressional power over the annual budget process
would lead to more responsible fiscal outcomes. Gramm-Rudman-
Hollings I and II marked an important shift, in both congressional
action and rhetoric, from such defense and enhancement of legislative
budgeting prerogatives observed in 1974. The fiscal and political
pressures resulting from burgeoning deficits and debt in the 1980s
brought a new wave of internal and external criticism of Congress. But
this time, the reformers, largely from the Republican side, argued

congressional budgeting power exacerbated, rather than solved, long-standing legislative budgeting problems.

Although the 1974 act was also born from political and fiscal pressures related to deficit spending, the processes created by the Congressional Budget Act did not specifically advocate or tilt toward balanced budgets since they would accommodate a high-deficit budget if the majority wished. The 1985 and 1987 acts, by contrast, were not meant to be compliant to majority votes. As Allen Schick says, Gramm-Rudman-Hollings was "premised on the notion that if left to its own will, a congressional majority would not be able to control the deficit."[3] Putting this assumption into law, the new reforms created firm ceilings on total annual deficits, mandated that legislation exceeding these ceilings be subject to points of order on the floor, and mandated external "sequestration" if the ceiling was violated in the passed budget. Why would Congress do this to itself? Once again, the driving force of reform was the growing deficit, which brought out partisan differences on past and future fiscal policies and inspired a more general exploration of Congress's deeply rooted budgetary challenges related to representation.

So despite some early institutional protectiveness among House Democrats, congressional ambivalence surfaces during the deficit wars of the mid-1980s. When Gramm-Rudman-Hollings (GRH) was first proposed in 1985, House leaders, especially Majority Whip Thomas Foley (D-WA), were somewhat warm to the idea of spending ceilings but quickly dismissed the first proposal offered by the three senators (two Republicans and a Southern Democrat), which gave extraordinary power to the president (also a Republican) to execute measures to keep the annual budget within the target. Foley also insisted on exempting major programs from possible cuts and tried to get the Congressional Budget Office more involved in the new process. Later that year, the House and Senate compromised on a different agent to execute any necessary across-the-board cuts—the Comptroller General of the General Accounting Office. Even House Democrats agreed to relegate a more institutionally defensive alternative to an ultimately ignored fallback plan in which the budget committees together exercised a similar power. And two years later, after the first GRH was declared unconstitutional, Democratic majorities in both chambers did little to stop the new delegation of power to the president's OMB to perform the sequestration. Although GRH theoretically constrained both branches' policy proposals, the reform did not protect the Congress as much as it could have.

The other legislative action that seems to defy principal-agent expectations is the creation of deficit ceilings themselves. As was discussed in Chapter 3, the framers of the 1974 budget reforms explicitly rejected proposed spending ceilings and related rules changes because they were thought to be antimajority. By contrast, the framers of the 1985 and 1987 acts emphasized deficit ceilings and strict rules to enforce them on the floor precisely because, they argued, *Congress could not be trusted to deliver deficit reduction under normal legislative procedures.* Perhaps the outcomes of these ceilings could deliver the substantive goals of the majority party, but this kind of partisan strategy became blurred in 1985 and 1987 when both parties supported them in different majority circumstances. The transaction cost politics approach to delegation also does not explain the GRH reforms. As stated before, Epstein and O'Halloran argue that members will not support delegation of distributive powers, especially during divided government. Neither is true in these cases. But Epstein and O'Halloran are correct that collective action problems are often behind delegation movements, and these challenges stem from balancing responsiveness and legislative effectiveness.

Although intra- and inter-party politics constitute a large part of the GRH story, both principal-agent and transaction-cost politics approaches to delegation are ultimately unsatisfying because they do not sufficiently emphasize deeper institutional problems that transcend these issues. If principal-agent strategies are being pursued by the majority party, we can expect to observe certain legislative actions related to this behavior in the reform period. We would see the majority party's pursuit of internal and external delegation through the creation or utilization of processes, committees, institutions, and rules that the party could control. Yet the legislative backgrounds of both GRH reforms included rejected alternatives that were internally protective and still attempted to address structural difficulties related to budgeting. So the cost-benefit calculations emphasized by formal theories are much more complicated than the simple binary choice to make or buy.

The winning argument in the deficit battles emphasized how Congress was not up to the task of deficit reduction. While I emphasize such rhetoric in the case studies, I do not deny that much congressional self-criticism behind these changes had partisan subtexts nor that many congressional Democrats overtly blamed the Republicans for the deficit, and vice versa. Nevertheless, the dominant rationale in the legislative history of these acts is more explicitly anti-Congress than partisan in nature. In addition, many opponents of the GRH reforms, from both parties, also took a largely institutional angle in their defense of congressional prerogatives. In the end, the actual partisan differences on the reforms are clear in the legislative history but somewhat clouded in the final vote tallies: both the 1985 and 1987 reform votes were along party lines, but they were attached as riders to urgent debt-ceiling increases, so it is hard to differentiate who supported one or both parts of the bills.

More important, such fiscal and political contexts of the reforms reflected a decade of institutional soul-searching over long-standing and new constraints on Congress's capacity to make low- or no-deficit budgets. As in 1974, two major and related institutional problems continued to plague congressional budgeting. First, pressures for spending and against taxation are very difficult for members to resist in a representative and fragmented institution. The often-repeated phrase that members do not have the "will" to make tough budget decisions stems from these fundamental legislative issues. The spending and fragmentation problems contributed to the rising deficit despite the 1974 procedures instituted to reconcile outlays and revenues. Second, the percentage of discretionary funds in the annual budget was shrinking to a point that Congress really only controlled about 25 percent of federal appropriations. Therefore, even deliberate reductions in controllable spending would not necessarily translate into deficit reduction due to the nature of backdoor spending and related precommitted funding that had been utilized especially since the middle of the century.

But unlike 1974, institutional ambition within Congress did not dominate the debates over how to address these issues, and vocal anti-Congress sentiment became the norm in budget battles, even among the majority party. The main argument of this book is that, despite varying political contexts of the five major changes to the budget process since the early 1970s, the institutional problems with congressional budgeting tie them together as a pattern. But at the same time, cross partisanship—meaning that a stable group of mostly southern conservative Democrats joined forces with the Republicans—characterizes each reform's history more than strict bipartisanship.[4]

In light of these and other factors informing the legislative history of the mid-1980s reforms, GRH is characterized more by institutional ambivalence than abdication. External delegation was not the only solution to these issues, and Congress also took less-publicized, internally focused steps to correct problems that the 1974 reforms failed to address or did not fully reform. Although the dramatic concept of an outside agent cutting the federal budget across-the-board received a lot of attention, other aspects of the Gramm-Rudman-Hollings Acts of 1985 and 1987 are interesting for how they shed light on Congress's less-visible institutional development. Between the 1974 act and GRH I, Congress made several informal changes to the new congressional budget process to improve complicated or faulty procedures that were straining its committees and calendars. Some of these alterations were codified in the 1985 and 1987 acts.

Yet in spite of all these changes, the 1985 and 1987 acts did not, in effect, dramatically reduce congressional budgeting power because many important aspects of the reforms were ignored or abandoned and the deficit continued to increase rather than decline. Despite several sequestrations and infamous last-minute budgeting maneuvers to meet the letter of these laws over the years, the ceilings and rules adopted in 1985 and 1987 were widely considered to have failed when measured by each reform's stated deficit-reduction schedule, which mandated zero deficits by the early 1990s. This fact can either be heartening to champions of congressional power or evidence that many of the institutional self-diagnoses made during the reform period were actually correct.

Background of Gramm-Rudman-Hollings I

The fiscal, partisan, and institutional history of GRH I was dominated by rhetoric and action that emphasized Congress's responsibility for the burgeoning federal deficit. While the dramatic tax cuts and increases in military spending proposed by President Ronald Reagan in his first term, and supported in Congress, arguably contributed to higher deficits during the decade, the focus of public debate outside and within Congress was largely on the institution's irresponsible spending structures and proclivities rather than the president's fiscal policy agenda.

Fiscal Issues

Fiscal problems related to the deficit drove partisan tensions and institutional self-diagnosis in the 1980s that ultimately placed blame for budgetary imbalance squarely on the shoulders of the Congress. While the fiscal policies created through the 1974 budget process were largely successful for the first five years, they appeared to fail dramatically in the early 1980s. Despite oil price shocks and stagflation, the first five years of the process were marked by relatively low levels of deficit and debt.[5] But during the early years of the Reagan administration, levels of deficit spending and debt rose dramatically due to Reagan's first economic program coinciding with a recession.

In his budget message to Congress in March of 1981, President Reagan explained how his supply-side economic philosophy would translate into budgetary improvement. He argued that reductions in government spending, tax rates for individuals and corporations, and federal regulatory requirements, combined with a "rational" control of the money supply by the Federal Reserve, targeted spending increases in the military, and maintenance of "safety net" programs for the most needy, would together promote economic prosperity and a balanced budget. The economic predictions made by the administration for this program over a three-year period were that by 1984, eight million new jobs would be created, the unemployment rate would fall to 6.4 percent, inflation would be 5.7 percent, and the interest rate on three-month Treasury bills would average 7.0 percent. In addition to these economic and fiscal policy achievements, Reagan predicted the fiscal year 1984 budget would be in surplus.[6] But deficits shot up immediately following the passage of Reagan's program, the Federal Reserve tight-money policy, and other related issues and stayed in the twelve digits consistently through the 1980s, as seen in Table 4.1.[7]

The fact that the Reagan budget plan and the Fed's policies led to an immediate increase in the deficit was not a surprise to some. In 1982, Rudolph G. Penner (a former Nixon and Ford administration

Table 4.1: Federal Budget Deficit and Debt, Fiscal Years 1975–1988

Fiscal Year	Deficit (in billions)	Deficit as % of GDP	Total Public Debt (in billions)	Debt as of GDP
1975	$53	3.4%	$395	25.4%
1976	74	4.3	477	27.6
1977	54	2.7	549	27.9
1978	59	2.7	607	27.4
1979	41	1.6	640	25.6
1980	74	2.7	710	26.1
1981	79	2.6	785	25.8
1982	128	4.0	920	28.6
1983	207	6.1	1,132	33.1
1984	185	4.9	1,300	34.0
1985	212	5.2	1,500	36.5
1986	221	5.1	1,737	39.8
1987	150	3.2	1,889	41.0
1988	155	3.1	2,051	41.4

Source: Congressional Budget Office Historical Tables; www.cbo.gov.

official and a future CBO director, but at this time he was with the American Enterprise Institute) argued why the 1981 budget and tax actions had failed: "While I agree with the goals of those actions, and while the goals—higher defense spending, higher private capital formation, lower inflation, lower marginal tax rates, lower non-defense spending and lower deficits—were not logically inconsistent, the administration and the Congress got their numbers wrong. The enacted reductions in long-run revenues were far in excess of the prospects for lower long-run spending, and massive long-run deficits became ingrained in any reasonable budget projections."[8]

By mid-1984, the economy's growth slowed abruptly and continued to be sluggish for the first three quarters of 1985, and GRH I was proposed that October. According to Penner, by then CBO director, the causes of the 1984 slowdown were widely considered to be related to a reduction in inventory investing and continued decline in net exports. Consumer demand remained strong, but foreign competition continued to dominate certain goods markets. The subsequent trade

**Table 4.2: Controllability of Annual Budget Outlays:
Fiscal 1974, 1980, 1986**

Percent of Total Outlays	1974	1980	1986 (est.)
Relatively uncontrollable under present law Open-ended programs and fixed costs:			
Payments for Individuals..............	40.3%	41.7%	41.4%
Other...	11.0	10.8	16.0
Outlays from prior-year contracts and obligations	17.1	17.5	19.2
Subtotal, relatively uncontrollable outlays	68.4	70.0	76.6
Relatively controllable outlays	34.8	30.2	26.2
Other Outlays/Adjustments....................	-3.2	-.2	-2.8
Total Budget Outlays...................	100.0	100.0	100.0

Source: Adapted from Historical Tables, *The Budget of the United States Government, Fiscal Year 1986,* Table 8.1.

deficit was partially a result of the growing budget deficits because high interest rates attract international capital, which raises the value of the dollar and causes American exports to become more expensive abroad.[9]

The rising deficit also resulted from a larger problem of mandatory spending. Increasing levels of prior-year government commitments had been an important constraint on the budget process beginning in the 1970s.[10] The growth of entitlements and indexing benefits, multiyear spending commitments, and interest payments on the national debt all decreased annual budget flexibility for the Congress and president. Even though the 1974 act addressed some of these problems by creating procedural hurdles for the establishment of new mandatory funds, discretionary spending declined as a percentage of both the federal budget and GNP as GRH was debated.[11] Although new entitlement legislation was rare after the 1974 act, such spending increased during the same period because of increased program participation and benefit indexation, among other factors, thus further constraining Congress's fiscal maneuvering room, as shown in Table 4.2.

Partisan Issues

These fiscal pressures were heavily intertwined with inter- and intra-party conflicts, the politics of divided government, and criticism of congressional budgeting practices. Ronald Reagan's victory in 1980 brought Republican control of the Senate and thirty-three Republican seats in the House. Although House Democrats retained more seats on paper, a disciplined Republican minority and bloc of conservative Southern Democrat "boll weevils" produced a working majority for Reagan's first two economic and budgetary plans. But despite the bipartisan effort to pass Reagan's first budget and tax legislation, Reagan's budgets soon after became "dead on arrival" as House Democrats consistently fought with the Senate and president on taxes and spending.[12] Ultimately, as Senator Daniel Patrick Moynihan (D-NY) said, GRH was hammered out through political bargaining and compromise: "A majority of Democrats agreed to dismantle the domestic policies of Franklin D. Roosevelt in return for a majority of Republicans agreeing to dismantle the defense policies of Ronald Reagan."[13]

Party-line votes and conflicts on budget resolutions noticeably increased during Reagan's first term. Since the mid-1970s, the House traditionally had far more party votes on budget resolutions than the Senate, but during the Republican majority in the Senate from the 1980 to 1986 elections the Senate too became increasingly polarized.[14] But Senate Republicans did not necessarily agree with Reagan's budget priorities in light of the increased deficit problem. In 1985, with deficits looming in the $200 billion range, a three-pronged budget conflict emerged between Senate Republicans, House Democrats, and President Reagan. A deficit-reduction approach offered by Senate Majority Leader Robert Dole (R-KS) and Budget Committee Chairman Pete Domenici (R-NM) included holding defense spending to the current year's levels while allowing an inflation-rate increase, a one-year freeze on cost-of-living-adjustments (COLAs) for all federal pensions (including Social Security), small domestic program reductions, and $59 billion in tax revenue increases over a three-year period.[15]

President Reagan rejected the defense and tax proposals, and the House Democrats rejected the cuts in domestic programs and COLAs. Further efforts to enact cuts in the deficit through reconciliation in-

**Table 4.3: Sample of Public Opinion
on Reagan's "Responsibility" for Deficits**

Do you feel President (Ronald) Reagan's economic policies are directly
responsible for the recent increases in the federal budget deficit, or not?

	1/86	1/87	1/88
Yes	38%	52%	53%
No	46	35	31
Not sure	16	13	16

Source: Modified from Cambridge Reports National Omnibus Survey, Roper
Center Public Opinion Online (Question IDs: USCAMREP.86JAN, R007,
USCAMREP.87JAN, R009, USCAMREP.88JAN, R008, accessed through Lexis-
Nexis).

structions attached to the budget resolution fell apart too. With twenty-
two Senate Republicans up for reelection in 1986, Gramm- Rudman-
Hollings was a novel proposal to deal with these fiscal and political
problems: "Thus, the spring offensive of 1985 collapsed, but the basic
thinking remained. The Senate Republican leadership was still con-
vinced that the deficit had to be cut and that this could be accomplished only through a balanced approach. . . . An added conclusion
was that the Senate Republicans could not count on White House
leadership in overcoming the political problems of reducing the deficit. . . .
The Senate decided it would have to come to terms with the House,
regardless of the president's wishes."[16]

Despite this background of conflict between Senate Republicans
and President Reagan, the original GRH proposal gave substantial
amounts of power to the president to make effectively unilateral spending cuts. After negotiations with the House Democrats, however, this
delegation to the president was transferred to the Comptroller General in the 1985 act. But why delegate at all? In public opinion, some
indicators showed President Reagan was blamed when asked directly
about his relationship to fiscal policy, as Table 4.3 shows. While these
data do not completely fit with other slices of public opinion on the
causes of deficits summarized in Table 4.4, which largely put the responsibility on Congress's shoulders, altogether they show a public

ambivalence about the nation's fiscal policy, which was absorbed by Congress throughout the budget reform process.

Institutional Issues

Beginning several years before Gramm-Rudman-Hollings, the 1974 act's new institutions and processes were periodically reviewed by Congress through committee hearings and reports on how the congressional budget process was faring. Before the deficit dramatically increased in the mid-1980s, defenders argued the new process had minor problems but was evolving to suit the needs of Congress by keeping discretionary spending more coordinated with revenue and other related policies than before the act. Nevertheless, some critics of the process argued that too much of the budget remained immune from review as mandatory spending increased as a percentage of the budget and that greater enforcement measures were needed to truly coordinate revenue and outlays. But by the mid-1980s, the 1974 act's processes were so heavily blamed for high deficits, that mere incremental corrections were argued to be insufficient by many inside and outside Congress.

Beginning in the late 1970s, the problem of missed deadlines in the appropriations process was a focal point for both defenders and critics of the existing process. Defenders of the process pointed to the flexibility of the budget act regarding Congress's preferences and schedules, and critics argued that the act's processes were too complicated and fragmented to be done on time. Authorization bills (especially in the areas of foreign aid, defense, and health and human services) were often not passed prior to their related appropriations bills, as the rules required. Furthermore, not once since 1977 had all thirteen regular appropriations bills been signed into law by the start of the fiscal year, and, notably in fiscal years 1986 (as GRH was debated) and 1987, not one of the appropriations bills was passed on time.

The government was often functioning on a catch-all continuing resolution, which allowed the government to keep its commitments by maintaining current spending levels until budget resolutions were passed. This problem of missed deadlines was often related to the complicated calendar established by the 1974 act, in which authorization bills, appropriation bills, and the second budget resolution had to compete for floor time between May 15 and September 15. These deadline and timing issues relating to the successes and failures of the Congressional Budget Act, among other problems, were discussed in a comprehensive review of the budget process in 1979. Testifying before the Task Force on the Budget Process of the House Budget Committee, Allen Schick argued that the institutional success of the budget process stemmed from Congress's adherence to its major provisions while maintaining legislative prerogatives related to majority budget power: "Under the aegis of the Budget Act, Congress has adopted almost a dozen budget resolutions, hundreds of authorizations, more than 50 appropriation acts, and a handful of major tax laws. These separate actions have been effectively linked together by committee reports, scorekeeping data, cost estimates, and crosswalk procedures. Congress thus has been able to preserve its diversity as a legislative institution while establishing an integrative framework for making program and financial decisions."[17]

According to Schick, the successes of the 1974 act were observable also through the alteration of the legislative calendars to focus on budget procedures and even in the increase in budgetary conflict. Schick argued that the sometimes-dramatic clashes over the annual budget resolution were the healthy result of better-informed members having an increased appreciation for the ramifications of the Congress's budget actions on other legislative interests. Alice Rivlin, then director of CBO, similarly testified that the 1974 processes empowered Congress to set, adjust, and abide by aggregate targets and ceilings for expenditures and receipts as well as have greater capacity to set fiscal policy.[18] But supporters of the 1974 act also acknowledged numerous difficulties with the new budgeting procedures. Schick and Rivlin, among others who appeared before the Task Force, made many suggestions for making the process more timely and comprehensive as well as for further enhancing congressional power over budget outcomes.

Echoing these themes, Representative Jamie L. Whitten (D-MS), an important legislative figure in the 1974 reform, suggested ways to improve the process:

If we can solve the problem of failing to enact authorizing legislation in a timely fashion, can bring entitlement programs into the annual appropriations process, improve the macroeconomic focus of the budget, put greater emphasis on the revenue side of the process, review more carefully Federal credit programs, avoid the delay of enactment of appropriation bills and include off-budget agencies in the unified budget, we will have a more effective and more workable budget process. This does not require a massive overhaul of the existing system—indeed I feel that would be a big mistake. What we need now is just some fine tuning to eliminate some of the problems we've discovered.[19]

An additional question surrounding the 1979 review of the congressional budget act was the untapped procedure of reconciliation created in 1974. Although it had not yet been utilized,[20] reconciliation was a potentially powerful centralizing tool for Congress to bring expenditures and revenues into agreement by commanding authorizing committees to comply with the second budget resolution.[21] Reconciliation debuted in 1979, just prior to the HBC hearings, but became so contentious in the conference committee between the House and Senate Budget Committees that the reconciliation instructions were removed after two months of stalemate.

One of the main problems with reconciliation was the timing of the procedure in the original act. Schick testified that the ten days allotted between adoption of the second resolution and the reconciliation bill were not sufficient for the process to work. The lateness of the reconciliation procedure calls into question whether anticipated savings can be realized. Because reconciliation compels controversial revisions in existing law, it can be expected to stir up a great deal of legislative conflict at a stage in the congressional budget calendar when conflict can least be afforded.[22]

Schick recommended that the reconciliation process be used at the beginning of the budget cycle during the first budget resolution instead of at the end of the process.[23] This advice was taken without much fanfare by Congress as it debated President Carter's last budget proposal for fiscal year 1981. The first budget resolution contained instructions to each chamber's authorizing committees to cut spending by $6.4 billion in the Senate and $5.3 billion in the House. The resolutions also called for amendments to increase revenues by $4.2 billion in the Senate and $3.9 billion in the House. The final result of the fiscal year 1981 reconciliation bill was a combined spending cut and tax increase of $8.2 billion.

Days before President Reagan's inauguration, CBO Director Rivlin cited the new reconciliation process to defend congressional budgeting: "In the face of a changing economic situation, and in an election year, the fact that they completed the required budget and did reconciliation for the first time is evidence of the strength of the process."[24] But only months later, the Reagan administration's novel use of the budget resolution and reconciliation procedures made the congressional budget process much more dramatic. Six weeks prior to the May 15 deadline of the first resolution, SBC's ranking Republican and Democrat, Senators Pete Domenici (R-NM) and Ernest Hollings (D-SC), introduced a concurrent resolution, which proposed revising the *current* fiscal year's budget approved in Carter's last year. This unusual strategy for altering the budget was legal under a little-known provision of the 1974 act, Section 304, which said that the last second concurrent resolution could be revised, even during the fiscal year in which it took effect. The new resolution proposed new total numbers for spending reductions for fiscal 1981, as well as the following two fiscal years. Despite controversy over the economic assumptions, statistical methods, and sudden changes in fiscal policy, the Reagan administration and its congressional allies succeeded in getting overwhelming support for what was ultimately called the "Gramm-Latta" substitute budget bill. Reconciliation instructions attached to this first resolution began the informal withdrawal of the second resolution, which was later dismissed by law.[25]

In 1982, criticism of the flexibility of the congressional budget process in light of this prior-year use led to three different congressional committee hearings on amending the 1974 act. Although many of the 1979 Task Force's suggestions were informally instituted—including deferred enrollment of some spending bills and nonbinding multiyear planning budgets—other problems emerged from the 1981 budget and tax actions. The new round of proposals to strengthen the budget act focused on the almost annual *ad hoc* procedural changes to the resolution and reconciliation provisions, problems related to conflicting economic analyses and assumptions, how more off-budget spending items should be included in the budget, and, of course, the burgeoning deficit.

Hundreds of bills were proposed in 1982 to limit the growth of federal spending and/or prohibit federal budget deficits. Some of the more popular bills called for a balanced budget amendment to the Constitution.[26] Despite the extensive discussions on revamping the process that fall, no major changes passed both chambers. The overall consensus was that the 1974 processes were sound but, like the conclusions that emerged from the 1979 hearings, the process should include still more off-budget items and stricter enforcement procedures.

In light of the pressures of the balanced budget proposals, the 1974 process was consistently defended for its flexibility in two ways: the process can be used in various ways to coordinate budget choices (there had been as few as one and as many as four budget resolutions in various years), and the 1974 procedures maintained institutional power for congressional majorities. In hearings before the HBC in September 1982, Rudoph G. Penner spoke of the strength of the 1974 processes. Despite an especially tough budget resolution fight that year because the dramatic 1981 tax cut had to be partly repealed, Penner did not agree with critics who argued that the intense fights over that year's budget resolution reflected poorly on the process: "the process is not perfect but I believe that the problems of this year and the time-consuming nature of the deliberations are more a reflection of the fundamental difficulties of the decisions that had to be made than they are a reflection of important flaws in the decisionmaking process. . . . Obviously, if difficult choices are not made explicit, decisionmaking is easier, but considerably less rational."[27]

In hearings before SBC, the vast majority of those testifying also argued that the process was fundamentally sound, although it could use some improvement. Those opposed to the balanced budget amendment testified that more flexible, statutory-based commitments to rein in deficits were preferable. Former Representative Robert Giaimo (D-CT) and former Senator Henry Bellmon (R-OK) argued that if such a balanced budget amendment were to be added to the Constitution, inevitable attempts to get around its provisions would seriously undermine Congress's credibility.[28] Again, discussions on tinkering with, not replacing, the 1974 reforms centered around the merits of two-year budget cycles, stronger enforcement mechanisms for the now-binding first budget resolution, permanent membership for the HBC, and earlier deadlines for authorization and appropriation work to be finished.

Senator Hollings did not agree that this kind of tinkering would be enough: "I am feeling like I am in Alice in Wonderland. We are praising each other about the wonderful result and how we have got the one budget resolution rather than the two, and we have refined the process and we have constrained ourselves and we have avoided the turf fights and everything else, as we give each other the good government award. . . . Where are these tools for discipline . . . and what should we do now, facing these high deficits?"[29]

Chairman Domenici responded indirectly to Senator Hollings by arguing that congressional majorities, not the budget process, drive deficit spending: "I think we are supposed to be a priority-setting Committee, but when you look at whether we can really do that or not, the answer is probably, no, we cannot. There is valid criticism for the deficits that exist, but I look back on the last two years and we are only a committee of the Congress. We cannot be bigger than its desire, and we cannot force beyond its desire. . . . I am not so sure that in looking at amending this process that we are not asking the process to do too much"[30]

Beginning the same month as the HBC and SBC hearings was a new Task Force on the Budget Process that was reappointed by Claude Pepper (D-FL), chairman of the Rules Committee. In addition to the September 1982 sessions, the Task Force also held hearings in 1983 and 1984.[31] In 1984, the Task Force submitted a report on its proposed amendments to the 1974 act. In its report, the Task Force pronounced the 1974 processes fundamentally sound but proposed several amendments to the act to strengthen the process. The committee recommended: a single annual budget resolution with total entitlement authority and functional category breakdown included and mandatory reconciliation instructions attached (with additional resolutions optional); earlier deadlines for the president's budget submission, congressional budget resolution,[32] authorization and appropriations legislation; strengthened controls through new points of order for committee and aggregate totals which violate program or total spending limits; and expanded coverage of off-budget agencies, credit obligations and guarantees, and tax expenditures.[33]

No major changes to the budget process passed in 1984, but many of these proposed changes would ultimately be included in the 1985 Balanced Budget and Emergency Deficit Control Act the following year, along with the more famous dramatic deficit control procedures. Even some original supporters of the 1974 act finally conceded that

Table 4.4: Sample of Public Opinion on
Others' Responsibility for Budget Deficits

In thinking about the federal budget deficit, I'd like to know how responsible you feel various people have been in helping to cause the large federal budget deficit.

	American Public	Congress
Very responsible	17%	44.5%
Somewhat responsible	53.5	50
Not at all responsible	29.5	5

Source: Modified from *Time,* Yankelovich, Skelly and White, Roper Center Public Opinion Online (average from 1/84 and 8/84; Question IDs: USYANK.845661, Q34AD and Q34AB, USYANK.845673, Q35D and Q35B, accessed through Lexis-Nexis).

Who do you think is primarily responsible for the federal deficit? Do you think it is:

	9/84	12/84	4/85	7/85	11/85	9/86
President Reagan and his administration	19%	24%	27%	20%	25%	24%
The Congress	26	27	24	28	27	29
Democrats in office before Reagan	30	28	33	31	31	30
Not sure	27	21	20	22	18	20

Source: Modified from *Time,* Yankelovich, Skelly and White, Roper Center Public Opinion Online (Question IDs: USYANK.845693, Q30, USYANK.845701, Q 18, USYANK.855714, Q7, USYANK.855731, Q18, USYANK.855733, Q16, and USYANK.865772, Q56, accessed through Lexis-Nexis).

the processes were too complicated and/or flexible to handle the large-scale deficit reduction that became a major political issue, one that landed in Congress's lap first and foremost.

Still, it is unclear why Congress explicitly (among most Republicans) or implicitly (among most Democrats) accepted so much blame for deficits rather than deflecting it to the president, as both branches are technically responsible for budget policy. One reason may be that public opinion at the time generally blamed Democrats more than Republicans in Congress for deficits, and the Congress more than the president. But, as Table 4.4 shows, the public did not *completely* fault the Congress for deficits and, as was said above, when asked directly, increasingly put the blame on President Reagan after GRH I and II were put into effect. At the same time, of course, the public did not blame themselves first for the country's fiscal problems. While congressional finger-pointing at the voters would be a risky strategy to be sure, members and leaders could have used this time to educate the public instead of bashing themselves. As Table 4.4 shows, there was enough blame to go around. While these data may not overwhelmingly fault the Congress as an institution, they certainly reveal public skepticism about the federal government's handling of its fiscal responsibilities, which Congress internalized during the Reagan years.

Passage of the Act

On September 25, 1985, Senators Phil Gramm (R-TX), Warren Rudman (R-NH), and Ernest Hollings (D-SC), with twenty-one other cosponsors, introduced an amendment to a national debt ceiling extension bill.[34] The general outline of the original proposal called for a five-year deficit-reduction schedule. If CBO and OMB estimated that the deficit of a given year would exceed that year's ceiling, the proposal would trigger across-the-board spending cuts on eligible discretionary programs.

Democratic leaders in the House balked at some of the cutting provisions. Although Majority Whip Thomas Foley (D-WA) had previously said the GRH proposal was "an excellent opening to deal with the terrible deficits and mounting debt that had continued to haunt our country's economic future," he advocated for more program exemptions while also speeding up the deficit-reduction timetable.[35] Since interest payments on the debt, Social Security, and prior-year contracts would be exempt from the cuts, about half of the federal budget would qualify for reductions. Under the original proposal, the president would compile a list of cuts and submit them to Congress. These "sequestrations" would go into effect unless Congress submitted a reconciliation bill or resolution adhering to the ceiling within thirty days, which would be subject to the normal presidential veto and congressional override procedures.

By attaching this novel reform to the debt-ceiling legislation, which was needed to prevent a government default by mid-October, the sponsors ensured relatively quick responses in both chambers.[36] With no

committee hearings, economic or other analyses, and limited floor debate,[37] the Senate added the GRH amendment to the debt-ceiling legislation on October 9, by a vote of 75 to 24, and passed the combined
bill on October 10, by a 51 to 37 vote.[38] Criticizing the Senate's quick
action, Representative David Obey (D-WI) said, "you have the right
to ask whether it is true that the Senate is the greatest deliberative
body in the world."[39]

Although there were no conventional hearings and markup sessions in the House either, three committees heard testimony from outside authorities on the Senate plan. House Budget Committee hearings
began on October 9 but on October 11 the House decided to go directly to conference with the Senate. Although generally supportive of
the goal of balancing the budget as soon as possible, scholars and economists appearing before the committee, as well as some of the Democrats on the panel, expressed concerns with the transfer of congressional
budgetary power to the president entailed in the Senate's bill as well as
the general idea of a formula-driven fiscal policy when the president is
making controversial tax and spending moves. But the members of
Congress who supported GRH, largely Republicans, were adamant that
the proposal properly showed primary concern for the end of deficit
reduction while still maintaining a balance of power, as shown by the
House sponsor of the bill, Representative Connie Mack (R-FL): "I think
most of us would want to come up with a solution that maintains a
balance of power and not transfer power, and in my humble opinion,
that is what we have come up with in this particular proposal. . . . And
it is an indication, I think, of Congress'—I think the word to use is
really inability to deal with the problem."[40] Concerns on the other side
were voiced by Representatives Pat Williams (D-MT) and Barbara
Boxer (D-CA), respectively:

I don't agree that Congress cannot act, and it seems to me that history, with
the exception of the most recent history, indicates the reverse is true. . . .
But if one accepts that the Congress can't respond, it would seem to me
that the way to cure that would be to give the Congress additional tools,
not take away from us the tools that we have.[41]

I don't like Gramm-Rudman because I think it's giving away our powers.
It's as simple as that. I came here to do something and I'm going to stand

up and be counted, rightly or wrongly, thrown out of office or reelected, on what I do.[42]

Other notable exchanges surrounded the testimony of Charles L. Schulze, former head of the Council of Economic Advisers and the Bureau of the Budget, who was particularly prescient in his remarks about the bill's problems. In addition, Schulze questioned whether Congress could really adhere to the deadlines and ceilings as well as the fiscal ramifications of exempting most government programs from the sequester sword. To him, Rep. Bobbi Fielder (R-CA) made this remark, which is telling on partisan and institutional grounds: "You aren't in a position where you're required to make the decisions and therefore you can accept waiting for that crisis so that a better, more perfect decision can come along. That's not going to happen.... It is a measured step, it begins to force us into a direction that will result in a lower level of Federal spending, which is one of my personal goals, and as a result of that, we will at least be less in debt than we are today."[43] To which Schulze responded: "My point is that you will follow Gramm-Rudman for about 3 years, 2 years, maybe. It will make some modest contribution. But precisely because this is based on the proposition you can solve the budget deficit problem without touching taxes and Social Security, it is going to leave you fundamentally where you were, because you are not going to cut that much ultimately out of civilian and defense spending."[44]

On October 11 and 21, the Joint Economic Committee held hearings and similar arguments were waged on both sides. Chairman David Obey opened the meeting with harsh words for the proposal and its supporters. Obey argued that the reason conservative Senators voted for the proposal was to get social spending under control, and the reason liberal Senators voted for the proposal was to get military spending under control. This is the heart of what Obey called the political impasse.

I don't think that we really have those deficits because of any economic impasse. I think we have those deficits because we have been faced with a political impasse. Now, after 5 years of searching for something called the political will to deal with them, instead, Members of the Senate seemed to have desperately grasped at straws looking for some kind of institutional magic wand that can do what the politicians apparently don't have the guts to do, which is deal with the problem at hand rather than structure formulas to require it to be dealt with in the future in a massive way.[45]

Senator Alfonse D'Amato (R-NY) responded that, although the proposal has some faults, it at least addresses the very problem Representative Obey pointed out. This kind of negative self-diagnosis became the dominant argument: "We lack the political will in Congress to make the necessary deficit reductions, to make the necessary cuts that are going to reduce the deficits. We just simply don't do it, and I believe that we have to have the kind of discipline which the Gramm-Rudman proposal mandates. . . . If the Congress can't do it, then the Congress will give that opportunity to the President."[46]

Economists testifying before the committee did not question the pros and cons of the power transfer to the president but rather the fact that the proposal would be unlikely to reduce the deficit substantially. Herbert Stein, of the Enterprise Institute and former chairman of the Council of Economic Advisers (CEA) under President Nixon, argued that the fear of across-the-board cuts would give appropriations committees and subcommittees incentives to overestimate their needs as a protection against sequestration—action which would not lead to a net reduction in the deficit. He suggested that instead of an across-the-board cut the president be given greater discretion to make targeted spending reductions and to impose income tax surcharges if necessary. After all, Stein concluded, "we have to visualize the possibility that if this thing is enacted it will extend beyond the term of the existing President."[47]

Economist Walter W. Heller, former chairman of the CEA under Presidents Kennedy and Johnson, agreed with Stein's concerns and also raised other issues about the methods and assumptions of the proposal. Both testified that the Gramm-Rudman method of reducing spending by across-the-board cuts could be very harmful for national defense since the reduction formula could reduce combat readiness while sparing less-necessary pork-barrel weapons projects.[48] Heller added that such a formula would also mean cuts without regard for a government program's merit and quality-of-service. Heller also took issue with two aspects of the economic side of GRH. First, the politicization of economic forecasting would be continued through the proposed process of splitting the difference if CBO and OMB forecasts clash. Second, large-scale cuts in a recessionary period could have an extremely negative effect on an economy that could benefit from government-based demand stimulation. In addition, a recession would inherently test the limits of the Gramm-Rudman ceilings because automatic spending goes up as more people seek benefits: "In failing to distinguish between deficits caused by economic recession and slow growth from those that are caused by tax and spending policy—that is the basic difference between cyclical and structural components of the deficit—the Gramm-Rudman plan takes us back to the dark ages of budget thinking and practice."[49]

In testimony before the committee, both deficit doves and hawks agreed the plan was flawed. Alan S. Blinder of Brookings questioned the economic need for zero deficits in 1991, a year seemingly drawn at random by the co-sponsors of the bill, or in any other year regardless of the economic condition of the country. Blinder further questioned why taxation was not a part of the balanced budget proposal since the tax reductions stemming from the 1981 Economic Recovery Tax Act (ERTA) legislation arguably contributed to the current problem.[50] And deficit-hawk economist Franco Modigliani, winner of the 1985 Nobel Prize in Economics, emphasized in his testimony that the proposal was worthy only for its laudable end of reducing deficits and spending. However, postponing pain through later-year cutting, and the lack of emphasis on tax increases, made the goals less realizable.[51]

On October 17, constitutional and balance-of-power issues dominated hearings held by the Legislation and National Security Subcommittee of the House Committee on Government Operations. Although the subcommittee was ostensibly concerned with the proposal's impact on defense spending and military readiness, Chairman Jack Brooks (D-TX), a conferee for the House, first called attention to a letter Judiciary Chairman Peter Rodino (D-NJ) sent to him regarding Rodino's constitutional objections to Gramm-Rudman. Rodino argued that giving near-unilateral power to the president to make budget cuts seemed highly offensive to constitutional structures and Supreme Court precedent. Rodino charged that GRH violated the legislative and appropriation prerogatives of the Congress, bicameralism, and the presentment clause and would therefore be considered an unconstitutional deviation from the legislative process according to the Supreme

Court's ruling in *I.N.S. v. Chadha*:[52] "The Gramm-Rudman proposal seeks to circumvent these constitutional requirements, as did the legislative veto, except that Gramm-Rudman attempts to do so by delegating unconstitutional powers to the president, rather than to one or both Houses of Congress. . . . While under the Constitution Congress *can* delegate the authority to implement laws, it *cannot* delegate the authority to repeal laws."[53]

In the bill's defense, James C. Miller III, the newly appointed director of OMB, responded using President Reagan's argument that the congressional budget process should not be held sacred if it is obviously broken.

Over the years, sincere efforts have been made by men and women of good will in both parties to solve the chronic problem of overspending by the Federal Government, but the problem has not been solved. We cannot escape the simple truth that the budget process has failed. . . . This legislation will impose the discipline we now lack by locking us into a deficit spending reduction plan. . . . If Congress cooperates and passes this legislation, we can send a clear and compelling message to the world that the U.S. Government is not only going to pay its bills, but we are also going to take away the credit cards.[54]

Specifically countering the charge that the proposal dramatically enhances presidential power, Miller argued that the president's budget proposal would be as constrained as Congress's in order to live within the specified targets. Furthermore, the president would be merely executing the cuts mandated by a formula-driven sequester. In other words, Miller said, the presidential power to make the cuts is really "ministerial," so this bill was no line-item veto. Miller also echoed Senator Gramm's original defense of the bill by saying that the threat of the sequester would be a powerful incentive for the Congress and president to work together to adhere to the targets and avoid sequestration.[55]

Representative Mike Synar (D-OK), also a conferee, sat in on the hearing and questioned Miller on the constitutional ramifications of the Gramm-Rudman proposal. Miller described four general constitutional issues that had come up in conversation with various members and Administrative officials. Synar replied:

You tell me you have talked about it. We are in a potential constitutional crisis here, and the Senate staff yesterday, in briefing the conferees, made it very clear as I go down this list [of Constitutional clauses potentially affected by Gramm-Rudman] that no legal analysis has been done. Now what is going to be really interesting is if we go through this whole exercise in the next 15 days and pass a law, which we all want to do, that will not stand the most minimal constitutional challenge. Since the administration has endorsed this proposal, I think at a minimum some type of constitutional analysis must have been done, or must have been considered, or is being considered.[56]

Although Charles A. Bowsher, the Comptroller General, agreed with Synar that the proposed transfer of power to the president would be immense, he was more concerned with how both branches could use their other powers to undercut the principles of the act. Bowsher emphasized that the president would be given a lot of discretion in deciding which programs would be considered "controllable" (in other words, capable of being cut) or not. The seemingly mechanical across-the-board reductions would actually resemble political choices more than the sponsors would admit. Likewise, Bowsher anticipated that Congress members would try to "game" the procedure by altering the status of their pet programs to the "uncontrollable" category by indexing the benefits or funding the program through advance-contract authorizations, among other tricks considered to be backdoor spending. Overall, Bowsher expressed the General Accounting Office's (GAO) stance on the issue to be deficit reduction through annual substantive, not procedural, legislation,[57] which is ironic as Bowsher was later in a position to defend the reform in the subsequent Supreme Court case.

Rudolph G. Penner, director of CBO, expressed somewhat similar discomfort with the kind of powers the Gramm-Rudman proposal would give to his office as well as OMB. GRH would direct both budget offices to prepare economic forecasts and assess the impact of the proposed budget on the deficit. In the likely event that these offices do not agree on their forecasts, and the subsequent deficit the budget would cause, the deficit estimates of CBO and OMB would be averaged. If the averaged amounts were higher than the year's ceiling, the sequester mechanism would be triggered.

This resolution would significantly change CBO's role by endowing it with powers far beyond anything envisioned when the institution was created. . . . Given the record of economists, it will not be difficult to convince anyone that economic forecasting is a very uncertain art. Reasonable men and women can differ widely about what the future holds, and even if there is agreement on an economic forecast, there is an added layer of uncertainty involved in translating that forecast into an estimate of budget totals. . . . It is hard to think of other instances where unelected officials have such power to do good and evil.[58]

Penner suggested OMB and CBO present their forecasts and estimates to Congress and allow members to decide which set to use as a basis for budgetary debate or whether the two estimates should be averaged. Despite the possibility of further politicizing the process of forecasting, and perhaps weakening the intent of the legislation, Penner argued such a congressional debate and vote would give more accountability to the process.

As the hearings came to a close, even supporters of the measure seemed to be holding their noses. In addition to the famous quotation by Senator Rudman cited at the beginning of this chapter, "Senator Dole is reported to have said to Senator Rudman, 'Don't get up and explain it again. Some of us are for it.' And Senator John H. Chafee (R-RI) called it 'the worse thing except for anything else.'"[59] On November 1, the House passed a measure designed by its conferees by a 249 to 180 party-line vote. Only one Republican and two Democrats voted against the rest of their caucuses. On November 6, the Senate passed its latest version of GRH by 74 to 24, and the House rejected it by 177 to 248. The Senate's version was largely the same as the original. The House version mandated a stricter schedule for deficit reduction, allowing a smaller deficit in fiscal 1986 than the Senate plan would allow,[60] and targeted fiscal 1990 for the elimination of the deficit. Additional disagreements between the House and Senate plans surrounded who would mandate the reductions and which programs would be excluded from any sequester.

At the same time, agreement on larger principles was clear: mandatory deficit reduction and new congressional budget procedures would pass that year. In December, the final conference report narrowed the differences. Representative Leon Panetta (D-CA) concluded

Table 4.5: Final Conference Report for Gramm-Rudman-Hollings I— Comparison of House and Senate Positions on Major Issues

Issue	House	Senate	2nd Conference
Sequestration order triggered by report of	CBO Director	CBO and OMB Directors	Comptroller General
Fixed or flexible outlay ceilings	Flexible (based on economic growth)	Fixed	Fixed
Fiscal year target for zero deficit	1990	1991	1991
Severability / Fallback plan	Not severable; No fallback	Severability possible; fall-back included	No severability; fallback included

Source: Modified from House Conference Report 99-433, 1985, Parts I, II, and VII.

that "even liberal Democrats who were appalled by the plan still voted for it because support in the House for the basic concept was so strong that the Republican Senate version could have won."[61] The differences between the chambers and the final conference report are shown in Table 4.5.

Again, although GRH I would, on paper, constrain the president's policy choices through the deficit ceiling and possible across-the-board cuts in defense and nondefense, remarks on the floor defending the proposal still focused upon Congress's general inability to come to budgetary agreements with its various parts. For example, Senator Robert Packwood (R-OR) explicitly faulted Congress for deficits, even as he defended the GRH bill for giving the president less power than detractors assumed.

Those of us who support the Gramm-Rudman-Hollings procedure are saying we would rather reduce the deficits with the concomitant good for the economy and the lowering of interest rates. We would rather do that, even if it means delegating to the President the power to put into effect ministerially these spending cuts, than do nothing and have the deficits.

If Congress, in two tries, is unable, for whatever reasons, to get its act together, if we cannot do it because a Democratic House and a Republican Senate cannot agree, or conservatives cannot agree with liberals, that is our fault. It is not the public's fault and certainly not the President's fault.[62]

Others, such as Senator J. Bennett Johnston (D-LA), who opposed the measure, spread blame for current deficits all around and focused on representation-related conflicts in the federal government.

First, how did we get here? We got here because of the failure of the process—because of the failure of the President of the United States, in my judgment, to do his duty; because of the failure of the Congress, in my judgment, to do its duty; because of the failure of the people of this country to understand what it is all about; and I might say finally to our friends in the fourth estate, the failure of the press to tell the people what the facts are. In a word, Mr. President, we got here because the people, the Congress, the President, and the press all want that which never was and never can be. That is, they want a balanced budget without cuts, without pain, without taxes, without taking the blame, without taking the responsibility, without measuring up to those duties of statesmanship which require occasionally that we say "no" to our most profligate desires to spend and to avoid pain. None of us as institutions—not the President, not the press, not the people, and certainly not Congress—have been equal to the task. . . . What we ought to do in Congress, in my judgment, is live up to our constitutional duty. The duty of this Congress is to raise money and to appropriate money, among other things—that is, to set priorities, to micromanage the budget, to decide what things are more important and how important and when, and how revenues should be raised and when.[63]

The bill based on the second conference report passed the Senate by 61 to 31, and the House by 271 to 154 on December 11, 1985, and President Reagan signed it on December 12.[64] Although President Reagan was an early supporter of the bill, he raised the possibility of a presidential veto after the Defense Department openly criticized the sequestration process as a threat to military readiness—a point Senator Moynihan (D-NY) also argued on the Senate floor. In his statement on the bill, Reagan reiterated these concerns, as well as the looming possibility that the law would be declared unconstitutional, specifically wondering whether congressional officers (the director of CBO and the Comptroller General) can perform executive functions relating to the sequestration procedures, as well as the provision authorizing the president to terminate or modify defense contracts if approved by the Comptroller General (CG).[65]

Hours after Reagan signed GRH into law, Representative Synar filed suit in federal district court in the District of Columbia challenging the sequestration procedure. Although Representative Synar and his allies opposed the legislation on constitutional grounds to protect Congress's legislative prerogatives, other members of Congress voted against the bill because it excluded some politically sensitive entitlements from cuts. Senator William Roth (R-DE) said the passed bill contained a "political bias in the deficit reduction mechanism" because of the exempted programs.[66]

Ironically, the time and attention Congress gave to the GRH bill derailed that year's budget reconciliation legislation that should have been passed by the start of the fiscal year on October 1. The fiscal 1986 budget resolution called for a $75.5 billion reduction in appropriations over a three-year period and was not passed as of the December adjournment. A continuing resolution was passed to keep the government funded for fiscal 1986 until the new GRH procedures could be instituted.[67]

Major Provisions of the 1985 Act

On the surface, the Gramm-Rudman-Hollings proposal had one main point: reduce congressional majority power over the annual budget process. By setting annual spending ceilings that were very difficult for Congress to change, as well as be enforceable by an outside agent, majorities would have a difficult time spending beyond the limits, although the first years of the ceiling were relatively generous regarding anticipated deficits. But in light of the years of criticism of the 1974 processes, GRH also strengthened the congressional budgeting processes in more subtle and long-lasting ways. While neither aspects of the reform brought the deficit under control as planned, the determination to both give away and consolidate institutional power

Table 4.6: Maximum Deficit Amounts in Gramm-Rudman-Hollings I

Fiscal Year	Maximum Deficit (In Billions)
1986	$171.9
1987	144.0
1988	108.0
1989	72.0
1990	36.0
1991	zero

Source: P.L. 99-177, Sec. 201.

demonstrates a continued ambivalence about strengths of congressional budgeting.

Deficit-Reduction Schedule, New Timetable, and Sequestration Provisions

Deficits are defined as the amount by which outlays are greater than receipts in a given fiscal year. In calculating the deficit under the procedures for mandatory reduction, receipts and outlays relating to the Social Security trust fund and Federal Disability Insurance trust fund are included. Budget authority, receipts, revenues, disbursements and outlays of other "off-budget" federal entities are also included in the calculation of the federal deficit.[68] For sequestration to be triggered, the budget bill passed by both chambers must exceed the ceiling by $10 billion, except in fiscal 1986 and 1991, where no cushion was allowed. Table 4.6 summarizes the maximum deficits allowed in each year and the target goal of zero deficits by fiscal year 1991. The new deficit schedule's enforcement was woven into the new timetable for presidential and congressional action on the budget, as shown in Table 4.7.

Gramm-Rudman-Hollings I mandated that the president's budget proposal "be prepared on the basis of the best estimates then available" and adhere to that year's spending ceiling but also detail what would happen if Congress did not adhere to the president's estimates and outlay proposals.[69] Assuming that the appropriation bills have been passed over the summer, the CBO and OMB would take "snapshots" of the

Table 4.7: Budget Action Timetable for Routine and Sequestration Processes

On or before:	Action to be completed:
1st Monday after Jan. 3*	President submits his budget.
February 15	CBO submits report to HBC and SBC.
February 25	Committees submit views and estimates to HBC and SBC.
April 1	SBC reports concurrent budget resolution.
April 15*	Congress completes action on resolution.
May 15	Annual Appropriation bills may be considered in the House.
June 10	House Appropriations Committee reports last annual appropriations bill.
June 15*	Congress completes action on reconciliation legislation.
June 30*	House completes action on annual appropriation bills.
August 15**	(OMB and CBO take "snapshots" of the deficit.)
August 20**	(OMB and CBO report to the GAO.)
August 25**	(GAO issues report to the president.)
September 1**	(Presidential order is issued.)
October 1*, **	Fiscal year begins. (Sequestration order takes effect.)
October 5**	(OMB and CBO issue a revised report reflecting final congressional action.)
October 10**	(GAO issues a revised report to the president.)
October 15**	(Final order is effective.)
November 15**	(GAO compliance report issued.)

Source: P.L. 99-177, Title III, *major annual events, **sequestration-related events (if triggered).

deficit as of August 15. Each director would submit a report to the Comptroller General five days later estimating total levels of revenue and outlays Congress has authorized and assess the impact of these numbers on the annual deficit, taking into account economic growth indicators. The directors would also determine how much the deficit would exceed the $10 billion cushion added to the ceiling in all but fiscal 1986 and 1991, and any difference between the budget offices would be averaged.[70]

Taking into account the directors' reports, the Comptroller General's report to the president on August 25 would detail which funds would be sequestered, and the funds would be divided equally between defense and nondefense discretionary programs, which totaled about one-third of the annual budget.[71] The president would then issue a "sequestration order" on September 1, which may not modify the estimates or reductions of the CG's report, and an accompanying message detailing the amounts sequestered.[72] Upon receipt of the president's message, the House and Senate would refer it to the legislative committees responsible for those programs. On October 5, the directors would issue a revised report taking into consideration any additional congressional action to reduce the deficit, which was not mandated by the act, and on October 10, the CG would revise his estimates in a report to the president. On October 15, the president issues his final order to eliminate the deficit excess identified by the final CG report, and the CG must submit a compliance report by November 15.[73] The points of order related to proposals in excess of the deficit ceilings could be suspended if a declaration of war was in effect, and if economic growth is estimated to be less than 1 percent according to either of the directors. In the case of recession, the majority leader of each chamber could introduce a Joint Resolution suspending the act's sequestration procedure, unless the Joint Resolution followed the order's report by the president.[74]

Strengthening the 1974 Budget Processes

The 1985 reform increased congressional budgetary information by mandating a comparison with the president's figures in the concurrent resolution report and specifying the economic assumptions and alternate assumptions considered by the budget and conference committees.[75] Whenever a committee reports a bill, resolution, or amendment proposing any of these changes, it must now submit a report prepared in consultation with the CBO director on the immediate and long-term impact of the proposed legislation on various budget totals. To assist in information gathering and making the calendar more efficient, the presidential budget and first concurrent resolution were mandated a month earlier than the 1974 requirements. Furthermore, backdoor spending would be limited through restricting procedures for proposing new future obligations. No new spending, budget, credit authority, new entitlements, nor changes in revenues and total debt limits may be proposed until the concurrent resolution is adopted.[76] This provision includes all "off-budget" programs, credit, and other obligations (except Social Security, which was removed from the unified budget, but its revenues and outlays were still counted toward the deficit number). The resolution may be revised at any time after its adoption, even while the fiscal year is under way. The revisions still must adhere to the maximum deficit amounts.[77]

Enforcement of the reconciliation instructions was also strengthened by requiring them with the first budget resolution, dropping the inefficient second resolution, and designating several kinds of stricter budgeting rules. Congress must act on the reconciliation instructions within thirty days. Budget and spending legislation proposals in excess of the ceilings would be out of order, with a three-fifths override vote necessary in the Senate to waive rules and a majority in the House, with a few exceptions.[78] Committees were given ten days to publish their internal distribution of outlays, budget authority, entitlements, and credit, and, if not, the committee's legislation could be subject to a point of order.[79]

Expedited Judicial Review and Fallback Procedures

The framers of GRH anticipated that members of Congress would challenge the law's constitutionality and, therefore, added provisions for expedited judicial review and a fallback process in case the sequestration was declared unconstitutional. Any member or any other person adversely affected under action related to the sequestration procedure could bring his or her case before the U.S. District Court for the District of Columbia "for declaratory judgment and injunctive relief on the ground that any order that might be issued pursuant to section 252 violates the Constitution." In addition, the District Court's order could be reviewed by appeal to the Supreme Court directly, and "it shall be the duty" of both Courts to expedite the cases as much as possible.[80]

The 1985 act also created an alternative and internally driven procedure for issuing a sequestration order if the enforcement clause of the act was declared unconstitutional. Specifically, the Comptroller General's role in preparing the sequestration report was anticipated to

be constitutionally suspect. If the Comptroller General's role was declared unconstitutional, the directors of CBO and OMB would submit
their reports to a Temporary Joint Committee on Deficit Reduction,
which would be composed of all members of HBC and SBC. The chairmen of these committees would preside as co-chairmen of the Joint
Committee, and the actions taken by the Joint Committee would be
determined by majority vote. No later than five days after receiving
the directors' reports, the Joint Committee would report a joint resolution to their chambers. The resolution's time on the floor would be
expedited by strict rules precluding filibusters, substitutes, and mo-
tions to table, and only two hours of debate would be allowed before
an up or down vote. If enacted, the resolution would be submitted to
the president in lieu of the Comptroller General's report.[81]

Fiscal and Legal Outcomes of GRH I and Background to GRH II

Since the 1985 act did not pass until fiscal 1986 was underway, the
ceilings and timetables were altered for GRH's first year. According to
the act, the maximum deficit reduction for fiscal 1986 could be only
$11.7 billion (in effect a $37.2 billion cushion). The directors' snapshots
were taken on January 10, 1986, and on January 15 Charles Bowsher,
the Comptroller General, received their reports. On January 21,
Bowsher issued his revised report to the president, making only minor
adjustments to the snapshots. On February 5, the House rejected a
Republican resolution to force Congress to make the cuts through a
revised budget resolution, so the sequestration order took effect on
March 1.

Reductions in retirement cost-of-living-adjustments and other automatic spending increases eligible for sequester, among other programs, were reduced almost equally in defense and nondefense outlays
for the combined $11.7 billion reduction. In the final calculation, only
20 percent of the budget was eligible that year for cutting. Due to the
pending litigation discussed below, Congress immediately convened
the temporary joint committee established in the fallback procedures
and voted to preserve the cuts by packaging them into a bill that was
approved and signed.[82]

The potential cuts for fiscal 1987 were estimated to be more severe than those of fiscal 1986, and the budget process was complicated by the District Court's decision in February and the Supreme Court's decision in early July that, as predicted, nullified the CG's role in the sequestration procedure. The congressional fallback procedure's attractiveness was arguably quite limited that year with the off-year election just months away. As Shuman[83] argues, both the Congress and the president were in no-win situations before the 1986 election since they could be portrayed as weak-willed if they did not make the required cuts themselves or draconian if they did. However, both situations were somewhat alleviated by the directors' snapshots in August, which, when averaged, brought the estimated deficit to $163.4 billion, $19.4 billion above the year's target.[84] Although conflict between the House and Senate on the budget resolution was not resolved until the end of June, over two months late, deficit reduction was not as painful as anticipated since the actual cutting needed to be only the $9.4 billion above the $10 billion cushion allowed by the act for fiscal 1987.

Through various outlay postponements, tax windfalls, and other piecemeal savings, no sequestration report was necessary that year since the predicted deficit fell exactly into the spending ceiling before October 1. These "golden gimmicks" and "smoke and mirrors" alterations, as some legislators called them, were made at the last minute, and deficit spending was set at $151 billion, well within the $10 billion cushion. Soon after the fiscal year began, however, CBO estimated that the actual deficit had grown by $30 billion.[85]

Bowsher v. Synar

On February 7, 1986, the United States District Court for the District of Columbia handed down its opinion in *Synar v. US.* The three-judge panel unanimously declared the sequestration portion of GRH to be unconstitutional. The plaintiffs, Representative Synar and the National Treasury Employees Union, challenged the constitutionality of the act's broad delegation of legislative power and, in addition, the constitutionality of Congress's delegating sequestration powers to the Comptroller General. The panel held that since the delegation to the Comptroller General was an unconstitutional violation of the separation of powers structure, the larger question of whether the act generally violated the "delegation doctrine" did not need to be settled. However, the panel did delve into three aspects of the delegation question in response to the plaintiffs' contentions. The panel argued the act did not delegate a "core function" of legislative power; nor was the breadth of power delegated so broad that it violated general legislative prerogatives; nor did the delegation potentially "undo" previous legislation in a manner dissimilar from other kinds of previously upheld administrative delegation.[86] "Through specification of maximum deficit amounts, establishment of a detailed administrative mechanism, and determination of the standards governing administrative decisionmaking, Congress has made the policy decisions which constitute the essence of the legislative function."[87]

The constitutionally offensive part of the delegation for the three-judge panel was the Comptroller General's executive function in the act in light of Congress's removal powers over him. Although the president appoints the Comptroller General with the advice and consent of the Senate, the Comptroller General could be removed by a congressional joint resolution.[88] Thus, the panel argued, the Comptroller General can be construed as a legislative agent. Since a legislative officer is arguably precluded from actions of "an executive nature," the Comptroller General lacks the degree of independence from Congress to perform executive functions. The panel concluded by defending its focus on the Comptroller General issue rather than delegation doctrine: "the more technical separation-of-powers requirements we have relied upon may serve to further the policy of that doctrine more effectively than the doctrine itself."[89]

In July 1986 the Supreme Court affirmed the District Court panel's decision in *Bowsher v. Synar*.[90] The majority opinion, written by Chief Justice Burger, held that the "separation of powers doctrine" articulated most recently in *INS v. Chadha* (1983) supported the lower court's decision. The question of constitutionality again surrounded the role of the Comptroller General and Congress's removal powers. Two of the three other opinions filed in this case disputed the majority's argument on the removal issue. In his dissent, Justice White did not agree with the majority's characterization of congressional removal power, which he argued had a minimal impact on the independence of the Comptroller General. Justice Blackmun's dissent argued that the constitutional flaw brought to light by this case was not the sequestration provisions of Gramm-Rudman but the removal power itself. Furthermore, Justice Blackmun noted that the majority's opinion put too much weight in a removal power that had never been used. In addition to the removal question, the broader issue of delegation was noted in Justice Stevens's concurring opinion, joined by Justice Marshall. Stevens agreed with the majority's conclusion that the primary sequestration procedure is unconstitutional, but on different grounds. He argued that Congress could not delegate powers to an individual agent of the Congress that would allow him to make nationally binding public policy. In both GRH cases, the original fallback provision was determined to be fully constitutional. However, in subsequent congressional hearings and debates on how to repair the 1985 act, the fallback procedure was ignored in favor of delegation to OMB.

The Balanced Budget and Emergency Deficit Reduction Reaffirmation Act of 1987

In the wake of the *Bowsher* decision, Congress had several options for saving GRH: take enforcement power away from the Comptroller General and give it to a legitimately "executive" office; change the removal laws concerning the Comptroller General; or permanently utilize the original fallback provisions, which meant Congress would itself make the cuts. Within a month of the Supreme Court's decision, the first choice was proposed as an amendment to the 1985 act by its original authors: OMB and CBO would make a joint report to the Comptroller General, who could make some modifications if necessary, but then report it back to OMB, which would replace the Comptroller General as executor of the sequestration. Other proposals called for a new executive position to be created called the "Director of Deficit Reduction," which could even be held by the existing Comptroller General, but this suggestion did not go very far.

Despite the fact that the Democrats retook the Senate in the 1986 elections, giving it a ten-seat majority, and the House Democrats gained five seats, giving it an eighty-one-seat majority, the Congress passed the 1987 amendment to GRH with additional power for the Office of Management and Budget. Although the 1987 act did not restore the kind of presidential discretion desired by the original act's authors, the fact that a Democratic Congress agreed to the power shift makes the

GRH II reforms substantially different from the 1974 act's attempt to *regain* congressional power from an opposition president.

In late July 1986 three weeks after the Supreme Court's decision, the Senate's Committee on Governmental Affairs met to hear testimony on the various new options to keep the deficit-reduction mechanism created by the act. Discussion focused somewhat on problems with GRH I[91] but mostly entailed the pros and cons of the OMB's extended role in the so-called Gramm-Rudman-Hollings II proposal. Senator Gramm defended the proposed change to OMB's role by arguing that OMB's discretion would be more limited than critics feared.

Let me begin by making it clear that we are not talking about the setting of public policy in trying to estimate the deficit. We are talking about a green eyeshade function. That does not mean that there is not discretion in green eyeshade functions, but it is more important to understand that the discretion is not related to public policy. It is related to technical judgment [regarding inflation, deficit, and growth projections]. . . . The Director of OMB already has discretion in terms of his input with CBO in the initial process. From that point of view, other than having two bites rather than one, there is no really relevant change in the process here.[92]

Perhaps anticipating criticism of this defense of OMB, Senator Hollings added that the president's budget office, and Director James Miller III, were more respectable at the present than in the early Reagan years: "Two years ago, with Stockman, no chance. I wouldn't trust him to do anything. . . . He was the worst charlatan I have ever seen in Government in my 35 years of service. Now, we have . . . a new Director of the Office of Management and Budget. We have seen how they have treated Gramm-Rudman-Hollings and their responsibilities thereunder."[93] And defending the general need for congressional delegation to other institutions, Senator Hollings added, somewhat countering the public opinion data presented at the opening of the chapter, "we are all operating within the arena of an attentive public. . . . This bill was got together not by politicians around the conference table, but by the American families around the kitchen table. . . . You take a poll . . . and ask, 'Who is responsible for the deficit,' and they will say, 'The Congress.' They don't say President Reagan."[94]

Before both the Senate Committee and the House Government Operations Committee, which began hearings the next day, Comptroller General Charles A. Bowsher argued that although GAO would support Congress's giving additional powers to OMB, his first recommendation would be for Congress to adhere to the original fallback procedure. In the House hearings, William H. Gray III (D-PA), the chairman of the House Budget Committee, also defended the original fallback procedure.

I tend to favor, as the trigger, not OMB's finger pulling it, not someone else pulling it, but collectively the finger of the House and Senate making those tough decisions. That is what we were sent here for. And I think basically the Gramm-Rudman II approach is a faulty one that raises serious constitutional questions, in terms of the role of the OMB Director, as well as the Congress giving away its legislative authority to set priorities, particularly when we know the Congress [for the last two budget cycles] bipartisanly rejected the policies of the administration.[95]

Further discussions in the House hearings concerned the role of OMB in allegedly "cooking the books" over the years, as Congressman John Conyers (D-MI) put it as he asked President Reagan's second Budget Director James Miller III whether OMB could be trusted in the proposed new position of sequestration reporter. Miller strongly defended the agency's record as well as the technical nature of the powers delegated to it, largely echoing Gramm's defense in the Senate.[96]

In testimony in the fall of 1986, after the Democrats regained their majority in the Senate, legislators did not seem to be as concerned with the sequestration enforcement issue. In March and April of 1987, the House Subcommittee on Legislation and National Security of the Committee on Government Operations met again to discuss larger issues and problems facing the federal budget process. The chairman of the subcommittee opened with what he hoped would be the focus of the hearings: "The primary purpose of the hearings is to determine whether our current budget problems are the results of a flawed budget process or simply the product of inaccurate or unrealistic budget numbers. If the problem turns out to be bad numbers, the solution is clear—get better numbers. If the problem turns out to be one of bad process, however, we will have to consider the possibility that the President and the Congress may not be playing proper roles in the budget process."[97]

The usual budget policy experts appeared before the committee, including Allen Schick, Alice Rivlin, and Charles Schulze. Their conclusions were similar to those they expressed beginning in the late 1970s: simplify the congressional calendar through multiyear appropriations, streamline the interaction of the major budget-process committees in each chamber, bring credit budgets into the fold of the federal budget, avoid omnibus spending packages and catch-all continuing resolutions, and stem the increases in mandatory spending (especially entitlements). While criticizing the deficit problem and agreeing that additional tinkering may be necessary, all of these scholars were vehemently opposed to transferring additional budgetary power from Congress through the line-item veto, which was then gaining some consideration, as well as against the then-perennial balanced budget amendment proposals.[98]

By late June, the new GRH II proposal was the only amendment to the 1985 law to have received major floor attention. In addition to technically resolving the separation of powers question through the use of OMB, this amendment also addressed some of the institutional concerns listed above. Ensuring relatively quick deliberation, once again the amendment was attached to a new statute to raise the debt ceiling. Despite conflicts between the chambers, the debt issue forced resolution of the differences quickly: the conference report was issued on September 21 and a federal government default would take place on September 24.[99] The House did not offer any process-related amendments to the debt-ceiling legislation, so the Senate's plan for altering the deficit-reduction yearly timetable and proposed alteration of the sequestration executor dominated the conference report (summarized in Table 4.8).

Again, it is notable that the House lacked a counterproposal to the Senate on all these important issues, especially who or what should perform the sequestration. Although GRH I was clearly driven by partisan politics, the Democrats seem to have given up the institutional protectiveness shown by their leadership two years before. Along these lines, on the House floor, Ways and Means Chairman Dan Rostenkowski (D-IL) defended the conference report:

In order to make the process constitutional, authority for administering the automatic cuts is vested with [OMB]. I want to emphasize that OMB will have no discretion to determine where the cuts will be made. The automatic cuts will continue to be equally divided between defense and non-

**Table 4.8: Conference Report for Gramm-Rudman-Hollings II—
Comparison of House and Senate Positions on Major Issues**

Issue	House	Senate	Conference
Sequestration order triggered by report of	No proposal	OMB Director, giving "due regard" to CG report based on joint Budget Directors' report	OMB Dir. giving "due regard" to CBO Director's report
Fixed or flexible outlay ceilings	"	Fixed	Fixed
Fiscal year target for zero deficit	"	1992	1993
Severability / Fallback plan	"	None	None

Source: House Conference Report 100-313 (1987), Part III.

Table 4.9: Maximum Deficit Amounts—A Comparison between GRH I and II

Fiscal Year	GRH I Maximum Deficit	GRH II (In Billions)
1986	$171.9	N/A
1987	144.0	N/A
1988	108.0	$144.0
1989	72.0	136.0
1990	36.0	100.0
1991	zero	64.0
1992	N/A	28.0
1993	N/A	zero

Source: P.L. 99-177, Sec. 201 (GRH I) and P.L. 100-119, Sec. 106 (GRH II).

defense programs . . . OMB cannot change this. . . . The reinstatement of the automatic trigger provides needed discipline to the deficit reduction process. . . . No one wants the automatic cuts to go into effect. But no real deficit reduction is going to take place unless the Gramm-Rudman-Hollings trigger is cocked.[100]

Representative David Obey disagreed:

In Wisconsin if you hire a carpenter and they screw up the job the first time, you do not bring them back twice more. But that is not the way we are doing it here. In 1981, we were told in the Gramm-Latta bill that if we just follow their prescription on budgeting and taxes we would get to a zero deficit. . . . Two years ago the same carpenters came and said, "We have a new idea." So we passed Gramm-Rudman. . . . The same carpenters are back here for the third time.[101]

Similar pros and cons were debated on the Senate floor. Carl Levin (D-MI) also defended the conference report:

Gramm-Rudman has been a favorite pincushion of editorial writers and academics. Indeed, many of them and some of our colleagues see it as the ultimate copout. . . . But the real copout would be to see budgetary gridlock and to do nothing about it. Gramm-Rudman is a way—even if it is an awkward way—to break that gridlock. It is a way to force decisionmaking from elected officials who do not like to inflict some pain now, even to avoid greater pain later. This pain is as evenly applied as we know how in this Gramm-Rudman fix.[102]

And Senator Pete Domenici disagreed:

[GRH II] may appear to be the only game in town, but it is a pretty rotten game . . . do not forget. . . . There is a reconciliation bill languishing in the committees. It is the only instruction around. It was voted in by the Congress of the United States. . . . Turn to that as the instrument. Put that together. Negotiate with the President. There is nothing in the world wrong with that.[103]

The conference agreement passed the House on September 22 by a 230 to 176 vote, and the following day the Senate passed it 64 to 34.[104] Once again, there was a possibility of a presidential veto due to President Reagan's fear of defense cuts through the sequestration process, which was echoed by Secretary of Defense Caspar W. Weinberger and Secretary of State George P. Shultz. Nevertheless, Reagan signed the bill on September 29, in part at the urging of Treasury Secretary James A. Baker, who feared a government default if the debt-ceiling legislation was delayed.[105]

Table 4.10: Budget Action Timetable for GRH II Sequestration Process

On or before:	Action to be completed:
August 15	OMB and CBO takes "snapshots" of the deficit.
August 20	CBO reports snapshot information to OMB and Congress.
August 25	OMB reports sequestration calculations to president and Congress; president issues order executing OMB report.
September 1	Presidential order is issued.
October 1	Fiscal year begins. Sequestration order takes effect.
October 10	CBO issues revised report to Congress and OMB on additional congressional action.
October 15	OMB submits final report to President and Congress
October 20	Majority leaders introduce (by request) joint resolution affirming president's order.

Source: P.L. 100-119, Sec. 251 (as amended).

The 1987 act made several adjustments to the Gramm-Rudman procedures. In response to the problems of adhering to the initial deficit limit, GRH II softened the deficit-reduction ceilings to an extent that the new requirements essentially allowed Congress and the president to avoid real deficit reductions for two years, as shown in Table 4.9. The $10 billion cushion remained in all years except for fiscal 1993.[106]

The 1987 act also made adjustments to the calendar for the sequestration process to take the new role of OMB into account and give Congress more time to make the necessary reductions to avoid sequestration if desired, summarized in Table 4.10.

Some other aspects of the 1985 act were retained as others were altered. Important provisions of GRH I that were retained included the composition of the overall cuts, half from defense and half from nondefense categories, and various exemptions and limitations that ultimately eliminated two-thirds of the budget from sequestration. The president was again given discretion in shifting cuts within defense budgets that would deviate from across-the-board rules but still allow the total requisite reductions. Rules changes in GRH II included out-lawing the application of government asset sales to deficit-reduction targets, early "prepayments" of loans, and other accounting actions that had been used the year before to offset spending. In addition, re-visions were made in the methods of calculating the baseline totals of spending, which had the effect of broadening the base spending eli-gible for cutting. Rules changes in the Senate restricted extraneous provisions in reconciliation bills and future spending increases that did not affect the current year's totals. In addition, a three-fifths majority in the Senate would be needed to overturn rulings on points of order related to these and earlier GRH regulations that could themselves be waived by a three-fifths majority. Previous practice allowed the rulings to be overturned by a simple majority.[107]

Preliminary budget process reforms included in Title II of the 1987 act included nods to the budget experts and legislators who argued that the budget process should include a credit budget and multiyear spend-ing bills. The 1987 act specifically says that the CBO and GAO should begin measuring the costs and allocations associated with federal credit and loan programs for fiscal years 1987 and 1988 and report their find-ings to Congress. In addition, an "experiment" in multiyear budgeting was specifically authorized.[108] Again, power was both given away and internally strengthened—at least on paper. Although the focus of the reform, deficit control, was a failure, more subtle changes in the budget process addressed persistent problems in the 1974 procedures.

Conclusions on Gramm-Rudman-Hollings

The heart of Congress's harsh self-diagnosis beginning in the mid-1980s is the tension between particularistic and fragmented legislative structures necessary to represent local interests with its responsibility to be a nationally focused and responsive legislative body. Even as deficit ceilings and an across-the-board sequestration process were predicted by outside analysts to be doomed to failure, Congress maintained that it was a realistic and necessary way of restraining itself. While fiscal pressures related to the deficit and serious party differences on spending drove the GRH plan, the lack of "will" on the part of Congress to balance the budget on its own was repeated again and again. Although the new deficit-reduction procedure would technically rein in presidential power to propose deficits in annual spending, both the overall rhetoric and new oversight powers given to OMB in 1987 made the nature of the reform more anti-Congress than anti-president.

Strategy and Reform

Kiewiet and McCubbins say strategic delegation is "logical" to the extent that a majority party in Congress, the principal, has reward and sanction powers over the agent, and the agent is better at performing the task than the principal would be. The evidence that Kiewiet and McCubbins present to support the logic of various congressional budgetary delegations is the proximity of budget resolutions and bills drawn up by the agents to the overall caucus preferences. In the 1970s and 1980s, they argue, internal agents such as the budget-related committees produced spending blueprints that were in line with the Democratic majority's spending goals in specific policy areas. Enacted budgets were also in line with these preferences, despite various delegations to the executive branch.[109] Although Kiewiet and McCubbins do not discuss whether the Comptroller General and OMB were direct agents of Congress, it is possible to assume that they would conclude that the GRH delegations were strategic, successful, and thereby rational because of their spending outcomes.

The roll calls of the acts can also be used as evidence that Republicans and conservative Democrats initiated these reforms to ensure overall reductions in federal spending. In addition to these groups' presumed interest in protecting various specific spending preferences, they had been very critical of congressional spending overall and had reasons to believe that taking power away from congressional majorities would help ensure lower deficits. Although there are mixed results from the ceilings enacted in 1985 and 1987, since they were set high initially and largely circumvented, it is still possible to conclude that GRH I and II were strategic delegations because spending powers were taken away from the main source of the problem.

Even granting that the above arguments are true, I do not believe they tell the main story behind these acts. First, even if the budget outcomes were ultimately amenable to majority preferences, there is little indication that the external recipients of power were chosen because of their principal-agent potential. In fact, legislative action and rhetoric behind the act indicate that the Comptroller General and OMB were chosen precisely because they were not directly related to majority power—especially as OMB was chosen in GRH II after the Democrats had regained control of the Senate in the 1986 off-year elections. Second, and related to this point, Congress created a seemingly reasonable fallback plan in the original GRH to enact the across-the-board cuts itself through a temporary joint committee but abandoned this procedure after the first year and did not include it in the next round of reform.

Since Kiewiet and McCubbins acknowledge that agency losses are greater with external delegation, especially to opposition party-controlled agents, it would seem more potentially strategic, successful, and rational, from the majority party's perspective, to delegate power to this internally controlled temporary committee. Furthermore, the deficit ceilings and restrictive rules of both laws further mitigated majority party power, even if the ultimate spending distribution outcomes were acceptable to the party. All this is not to deny that real individual and party-level incentives to support these reforms existed in the mid-1980s. There is no question that deficits were unpopular in the electorate, at least theoretically, and both parties had incentives to show their support for deficit reduction. The fundamental question is why the passed deficit-reduction solutions went automatically with reduction of congressional power. A decade before, despite similar criticisms of congressional budgeting processes (albeit with much smaller deficits) congressional power and majority prerogatives were protected.

Institutional Self-Diagnosis and Reform

Three kinds of institution-wide challenges to congressional budgeting largely shaped the criticism of controlling procedures as well as the solutions in 1985 and 1987. First, in the background and debates over both Gramm-Rudman laws, the problem of "political will" to make the necessary cuts or to raise taxes was raised by members of both parties. Political will problems stem partly from the inability of individual representatives to resist constituent pressures related to spending and taxation. The amalgamation of these individual pressures obviously leads to deficits if revenue is insufficient. I argue that this "will" problem is inherent in a representative institution such as Congress, which wields real budgeting powers, and is a challenge to low- or no-deficit budgeting. Related to these challenges are the inherently fragmented structures of Congress, which are necessary for division-of-labor and to further ensure representation of specific constituency interests. Despite the 1974 reforms, which were meant to reconcile the actions of various authorization, appropriation, and tax committees, deficits rose dramatically. And despite early successes, the 1974 act often seemed to contribute to coordination problems with unrealistic calendars for budget action and the additional layer of activity in the budget committees.

Second, the shrinking percentage of "controllable" funds is an institutional challenge to congressional budgeting. This percentage hovered above one-third of the budget in 1974 and one-quarter in the mid-1980s. There are several methods for ensuring that certain spending commitments are shielded from annual budget review and control, and, while this legislative spending protection may help in constituent representation, it also contributes to budgetary fragmentation and loss of institutional control over annual spending numbers. Although some of these "backdoor" spending items are truly uncontrollable, such as the level of mandatory interest payments on the debt, others are technically controllable but politically dangerous, such as various entitlements, and some are simply government projects with multiyear spending authorizations that must be honored by subsequent Congresses. Without making real inroads into the controllability problem, budget reform may not work.

Third, these institutional budgeting problems have contributed to, and are reflected in, Republican-led anti-Congress sentiment inside and outside the institution. Unlike 1974, the pervasive criticism of congressional budgeting practices in the mid-1980s did not translate into reforms that would enhance congressional power over budget outcomes. Although internal budgeting procedures were incrementally improved to address several persistent problems with fragmentation, enforcement, and off-budget items, the real focus in the GRH laws was reducing congressional majority power. Although deliberations over the acts brought many institutional power questions to the surface, most members appeared to favor ceding power, even to opposition or otherwise difficult-to-control agents. While these votes may have been cast with a "true interest" in deficit reduction and/or an eye to the next election, there was a real disconnection between the individual and institutional ambition.

At the same time, this delegation-based reform is notable for reducing presidential budgeting power as well. Presidential power to propose a budget was theoretically reduced by the preset deficit limits entailed in the 1985 and 1987 legislations, as well as the provision of the law that disallows presidential alteration of the Comptroller General's sequestration order. Louis Fisher laments that presidents operating under these laws did not challenge the constitutionality of these constraints *on their powers*:

I do not see how Congress can interfere with the President's constitutional duty to present legislative proposals that *he* "shall judge necessary and expedient." . . . The White House evidently finds it in its interest to relieve the President of the personal responsibility for submitting a national budget, given the magnitude of current deficits. GRH is a convenient way for the President to duck responsibility . . . [and] under the terms of the original GRH, the President had to issue an order under his own name but without the slightest ability to control the content. I thought that procedure was repugnant both to separation of powers and to the principle of presidential responsibility.[110]

As deficits climbed even higher in the wake of GRH II, a new wave of reform again highlighted institutional challenges to balanced budgets. The fact that delegation to automatic mechanisms and external enforcement did not seem well-suited to the deficit-reduction task in the mid-1980s did not preclude another experiment with these kinds of processes in the 1990 Budget Enforcement Act. Although the new solutions were arguably better suited to the old problems when measured by deficit reduction through the 1990s, the same institutional question arose regarding why Congress (more than the president) could not deliver deficit reduction through normal legislative processes. And again, the answer emphasized the institution's controversial fiscal outcomes related to its duties and structures of representation.

5

OLD PROBLEMS AND NEW TOOLS OF SELF-RESTRAINT

The Budget Enforcement Act of 1990

Despite the fact that all of us in Congress say we want a balanced budget—we have failed to gain control over the budget. In the eyes of many Americans, we are the problem and not the key to the solution.
— Senator Orrin Hatch (R-UT), 1990[1]

We need budget reform that will require us to make our deadlines and that will impose discipline on Congress—the negligent keeper of the country's purse.
— Senator John McCain (R-AZ), 1990[2]

The enforcement provisions in this package go further than just enforcement of the package. They change the body and soul of the congressional budget process.
— Senator Herb Kohl (D-WI), 1990[3]

Congress revisited the federal budget process, and the related issue of how to discipline itself better, just three years after Gramm-Rudman-Hollings II was passed in 1987. In their discussion of the 1990 Budget Enforcement Act (BEA), James A. Thurber and Samantha L. Durst summarize the pressing bundle of issues the government faced: "the budget reforms of the 1970s and 1980s, in spite of their goals, did not curb federal spending, reduce the deficit, force Congress to complete budgeting on time, reorder national spending priorities, allow Congress to control fiscal policy, or eliminate the need for continuing resolutions. Clearly, something needed to be done to counteract these loopholes."[4]

But why was Congress responding to these problems once again with reforms that weakened its ability to increase and shift spending items while enhancing executive power to shape and monitor the budget process? As the 1990 budget agreement's taxation, spending, and procedural elements helped lay the foundation for dramatic economic improvement through the decade, it is an important piece to the puzzle of why deficit reduction was correlated with congressional power reduction.

Of course, similar to GRH, the president's hands would be tied under the new rules too, but again Congress was more explicitly under attack, and this legislative history is evident in the reform's process changes. Rejecting the failed GRH I and II approach of strict deficit ceilings, the BEA curtailed both branches' fiscal powers through discretionary spending caps and pay-as-you-go entitlement rules. These rigid new processes were meant to regulate certain kinds of congressional spending legislation and tradeoffs that authorization and appropriations committees had allowed traditionally. In addition, the BEA expanded the president's Office of Management and Budget powers to "score," "umpire," and "sequester" various kinds of congressional spending and tax provisions. This aspect of the reform is notable because OMB was explicitly chosen to perform these functions over the nonpartisan Congressional Budget Office, which was relegated to a fallback position if OMB abused its BEA powers. Although a small group of Democrats fought this delegation to President Bush's OMB before and after the BEA was passed, they were defeated.

Due to these and other actions, I argue in this chapter that strategic theories of delegation only partially explain the Budget Enforcement Act. As in chapter 4, I base this conclusion in part on the unmet expectations of principal-agent strategy in the legislative actions and rhetoric behind the act. If the new agents and structures created by the 1990 act could better assist the realization of majority party preferences and the majority leaders had important controls over the agents, the delegation-based reform could be seen as a long-term partisan strategy. But in legislative action during the 1990 reform period, the Budget Enforcement Act continued the legacy of GRH I and II by not only severely restricting current and future congressional spending decisions through self-imposed barriers, but also by delegating enforcement provisions to outside and opposition-party agents arguably beyond the easy control of majority party leaders.

In addition, the BEA delegations to OMB at the expense of CBO do not fit with Epstein and O'Halloran's transaction cost politics approach, which says Congress will delegate to reduce the cost of its information-gathering and collective action problems. Through the 1980s, CBO was widely considered to have more accurate deficit projection numbers and was a less partisan office than OMB, yet OMB was again chosen as the arbiter of the new rules, despite the fact that the Democrats were the majority in Congress and the final conference report suggested reservations about OMB's ability to perform the sequestration function fairly. Although Congress allowed this delegation as part of a famous tax bargain with President George Bush, the public legislative history shows most members who opposed the 1990 act were far more concerned about the numbers in the budget package than the new enforcement procedures.

The institutionally focused rhetoric dominating the speeches and testimony of the 1990 act's proponents show Congress still bore the brunt of blame for the country's fiscal situation. This rhetoric may not have been "sincere" in all cases, but the close connection between the institutional rhetoric and structural changes give it weight as a source of explanation for these developments. As in 1974, 1985, and 1987, the background of the 1990 budget-process reform includes years of congressional self-diagnosis of its institutional capacity to budget responsibly. Related to the fiscal and political pressures clearly evident behind all of these reform movements is persistent internal and external criticism of Congress's institutional budgeting structures. Similar to the background of the 1974 Congressional Budget Act and the two GRH acts, the BEA's legislative history brings to the surface often-repeated challenges to congressional budgeting: high constituent demands in a fragmented policy process under severe fiscal constraint and shrinking discretionary maneuvering room. The events of 1990 should be seen in this larger institutional context, even as the policy problem of the deficit and the partisan tensions surrounding how to deal with this issue under conditions of divided government are the foundations of this history.

In the end, Congress may have properly diagnosed its budgeting problems and acted responsibly to correct them in making the 1990 reforms. While both GRH reforms were failed experiments in painless solutions to the deficit problem, the 1990 agreement and those that followed (especially in 1993 and 1997) showed how Congress and the president could make tough political decisions through representation, deliberation, compromise, *and* restrictions made in advance.[5] However, even assuming that the Budget Enforcement Act was a success, the trend of delegation to rein in deficits prompts important questions about what Congress's legislative role should and can be as it balances local and national exigencies.

Background of the 1990 Act

There are many potential suspects to blame for high and persistent deficits, including fiscal policy choices by elected officials, monetary policy, other economic cycles and international pressures, and a demanding electorate. Yet, once again, the Congress ultimately shouldered the bulk of responsibility for the failures of the GRH reforms to control unbalanced budgets.

Fiscal Issues

When President George Bush took office in January 1989 he inherited a variety of economic and budgetary challenges. The national debt had tripled under President Reagan to almost $3 trillion, signs of economic recession had started after more than six years of steady growth, inflation was around 4.5 percent, interest rates were high, and the cost of the savings and loan bailout was estimated at roughly $500 billion. President Reagan's final budget included new taxes and user fees of almost $13 billion and estimated that the deficit would match the GRH II target of $100 billion. OMB's optimistic economic assumptions regarding real GNP growth, the consumer price index, and Treasury bill and bond rates were integral to the administration's meeting this deficit ceiling, at least on paper.[6]

President Bush sent a moderately revised fiscal 1990 budget to Congress after taking office, without a tax increase and retaining most of the OMB's economic estimates. In this revision, Bush estimated the deficit to be even lower than Reagan's projections—roughly $95 bil-

Table 5.1: Federal Budget Deficit and Debt, Fiscal Years 1988–1991

Fiscal Year	GRH II Ceilings (in billions)	Actual Deficit	Deficit as % of GDP	Total Public Debt (in billions)	Debt as % of GDP
1988	144	155	3.1	2,051	41.4
1989	136	152	2.8	2,190	40.9
1990	100	221	3.9	2,411	42.4
1991	64	269	4.6	2,668	45.9

Source: Congressional Budget Office Historical Tables; www.cbo.gov.

lion. But this budget proved to be politically contentious and ultimately exceeded the mandated deficit ceiling by more than 100 percent. In addition to his "no new taxes" pledge while campaigning, Bush also proposed targeted tax breaks and a "flexible freeze" on spending to keep domestic discretionary spending increases at or below the inflation rate. Many of these spending proposals were rejected by congressional Democrats, among other disagreements, and the sequestration provisions of GRH II were triggered after the fiscal year officially began on October 1, 1989.[7] Despite a last-minute deficit-reduction bill and small round of sequestration-ordered cuts in late November, OMB estimated the following July that the deficit for fiscal 1990 was over $160 billion (counting the Social Security surplus[8] but not the savings and loan bailout). Ultimately, the official fiscal 1990 deficit was over $220 billion (shown in Table 5.1).

Fiscal pressures related to the deficit continued in the following budget cycle. GRH II mandated a $64 billion deficit ceiling for fiscal 1991, but the actual deficit was projected to exceed the limit by tens of billions. Even with the GRH rule allowing an additional $10 billion deficit cushion before a sequestration is triggered, OMB admitted in mid-1990 that the predicted deficit in President Bush's fiscal 1991 budget would not come close to the target. President Bush abandoned his infamous tax pledge soon after in the summer-long budget summit negotiations.[9]

Former CBO Director Rudolph G. Penner made a tongue-in-cheek remark when he said if only OMB had continued its process of presenting unrealistic economic forecasts, the 1990 budget agreement that produced the Budget Enforcement Act might not have been necessary. The sudden deviation from OMB-generated rosy scenarios, Penner argues, was largely due to a sharp increase in real interest rates that spring, which "frightened administration economists, and it became clear that they were anxious to attempt a grand budget compromise."[10] But the current budget process under GRH had other flaws in its assumptions and processes that reflected misunderstandings about fiscal policy.

The problem is that the deficit in any one year is far more influenced by the economy and other factors outside the direct control of Congress than it is by the spending and tax policies. . . . Moreover, the targets were extremely ambitious, and therefore unrealistic, given the powerful political constraints that inhibit policy changes. . . . Gramm-Rudman's most important feature was that it did not require the achievement of its deficit goals. It required only that Congress and the administration promise to achieve them when the following year's budget was formulated. This created a powerful incentive to make optimistic assumptions regarding the path of the economy and the deficit.[11]

So the deficit and debt climbed steadily upward.

In addition to the overall increase in annual deficits, the perennial problem was also how to cut them in light of Congress's shrinking control of the budget. As discussed in chapters 3 and 4, most mandatory spending is technically controllable only by altering the original authorizing statute, but the kinds of programs entailed in these outlays are politically risky to reduce. Other kinds of mandatory spending are holdovers from previous commitments relating to federal projects that are not completed in one budget cycle. And some outlays are truly uncontrollable, such as net interest payments on the national debt that are fixed through prior-year deficits and current interest rates. In fiscal 1991, for example, interest payments on the debt were roughly 14.5 percent of total outlays (included in Table 5.2 in the "other" category). By the mid-1980s, the percentage of effectively uncontrollable outlays began to hover around more than 70 percent of the budget, up from roughly 65 percent ten years earlier.

Despite the various restrictions on entitlement spending entailed in the Gramm-Rudman agreements, between 1985 and 1990 the an-

**Table 5.2: Controllability of Annual Budget Outlays,
Fiscal 1986, 1988, 1990**

Percent of Total Outlays	1986	1988	1990 (est.)
Relatively uncontrollable under present law Open-ended programs and fixed costs:			
Payments for Individuals...................	40.7%	42.1%	44.8%
Other...	16.4	16.2	15.1
Outlays from prior-year contracts and obligations	18.3	17.6	18.4
Subtotal, relatively uncontrollable outlays	75.3	75.9	78.4
Relatively controllable outlays	27.5	27.3	24.5
Other Outlays/Adjustments......................	-2.9	-3.1	-2.9
Total Budget Outlays.............................	100.0	100.0	100.0

Source: Adapted from Historical Tables, *The Budget of the United States Government,* Fiscal Year 1989, Table 8.1.

nual growth rate of spending on mandatory programs grew at twice the rate of spending growth on discretionary programs (7.2 percent and 3.75 percent respectively). In addition, inflation-adjusted spending on discretionary programs, including defense, fell at an annual rate of 3.4 percent during these years, while spending on mandatory programs rose at an annual inflation-adjusted rate of about 1.8 percent. As noted before, decreased controllability, as seen in the Table 5.2, makes fiscal maneuvering much harder for both the president and Congress as they struggle with decreasing spending for deficit control.

In light of these trends of increasing deficits and decreasing annual discretion, Congress convened several sets of hearings in 1989 and 1990 featuring current and former members of the executive and legislative branches and state and local officials. Despite varying opinions on the economic causes and effects of high deficits, as well as debates on the merits of the Bush budget proposals, one theme from all these hearings was that GRH II's ceilings would not be met honestly.[12] A GAO report on the deficit, included in the record at a Senate Committee on

Governmental Affairs hearing entitled "Critical Issues and Problems
Facing the New Administration and Congress," summarized many key
points made in later hearings.

There are no quick or painless solutions to the federal government's budget
problems. The apparently simple or painless answers will not work. We
cannot "grow" our way out the problem. Public demand for government
services . . . grows as fast as revenues. . . . We cannot "freeze" our way out
of the problem. Much of the budget is concentrated in politically sensitive
entitlement programs . . . or in interest costs. . . . We cannot "sequester"
our way out of the problem through mechanistic, formula-based program
cuts of the sort prescribed by Gramm-Rudman-Hollings legislation. With
between 70 and 80 percent of the budget exempted for a variety of reasons,
the rest of the government would be gutted if the machinery were allowed
to operate without restraint. . . . The GRH approach has accomplished
little more than constraining the growth of the deficit.[13]

As was discussed in chapter 4, several assumed economic ramifications of high deficits prompt these kinds of concerns. High deficits
lead to high interest rates to entice domestic and foreign lenders. Among
other concerns related to the value of the U.S. dollar and balance of
trade issues, high interest rates theoretically depress domestic capital
investments and flexibility in monetary policy while giving some powers over the U.S. economy to foreign lenders, who take their profits
and interest payments abroad.[14] As deficit projections remained high
in 1990, fiscal 1991's budget policy negotiations ultimately included
major reforms for the congressional budget process. With the off-year
election approaching and divided government in place, party politics
also played an important role in this legislative history.

Partisan Issues

Allen Schick reminds us that by 1990, the politics of divided government
informed budget conflicts and policy for all but four years of the budget
process created in 1974. Schick also partly attributes divided government's existence to Americans' paradoxical calls for "smaller government
and bigger programs": "Inasmuch as the budget divides the parties—
note the frequent party-line votes on budget resolutions—it is hardly
surprising that Democrats and Republicans, entrenched in their own

branches, cannot take sufficient steps to put the deficit problem behind them. . . . Each party has been able to escape full responsibility for the deficit, and therefore the impulse to take vigorous action as well, by blaming the other side."[15] While not responding to Schick directly, Senator William V. Roth (R-DE) had a slightly different take on one of the results of divided government on the budget process: "In many ways, I think that [the deficit] is a product of divided government. There are different philosophies and different priorities and the easy way to work out these controversies is to add more to everything, without blaming either the Congress or the White House or the House or the Senate because there are differences here among us."[16]

In either case, although inter-party conflicts mattered in annual budget summits and outcomes under the Bush administration, one can argue that *intra-party* conflicts mattered even more in the case of the 1990 budget skirmishes. Similar to budget conflicts under Reagan, northern Democrats in Congress were generally hostile to Bush's insistence on capital gains tax reductions, allegedly "regressive" targeted tax increases, and protective spending proposals regarding military funding.[17] At the same time, in the fiscal 1991 budget negotiations, notable differences emerged between House and Senate Democrats over entitlement cost-of-living freezes. But the more widely cited conflict was between Bush and his party regarding his abandoning the "no new taxes" pledge. This struggle was aggravated when Ed Rollins, Co-Chairman of the National Republican Congressional Campaign Committee, advised Republican congressional candidates to oppose the president's revised budget plan, which was conceived with congressional leaders and announced September 30, a day before the fiscal year began and a little over a month before the off-year election.[18]

After the defeat of this first budget summit package, largely due to multilateral disagreements in the House on October 5,[19] and the self-imposed withdrawal of House Republicans from the budget negotiations, congressional leaders regrouped with administration officials and produced the compromise Omnibus Budget Reconciliation Act at the end of October. The new budget package was a five-year agreement entailing targeted revenue increases and spending cuts. Related to this specific budget battle and the demise of GRH II, as well as the previous decade of rising deficits, persistent institutional problems with congressional budgeting were raised by both sides. This self-criticism transcended party affiliation and touched upon challenges to congressional budgeting articulated since the early 1970s.

Institutional Issues

After GRH I and II failed to control the deficit, presidential candidate Bush vowed to push for better budgetary "discipline" in 1988. In budget-process-reform language, "discipline" usually means reducing congressional majority powers over annual spending decisions. In his partisan and institutional criticism of congressional budgeting under Democratic control, Bush reflected public opinion on the deficit. As in the 1980s, Congress generally felt the brunt of fiscal criticism in the polls more than the president, and such trends are reflected in the years surrounding the 1990 budget deal, as Table 5.3 indicates.

In light of the continued unpopularity of the deficit, the president and numerous members and leaders of Congress variously argued for a balanced-budget amendment, enhanced presidential rescission powers including a line-item veto, a two-year budget cycle, and a new joint budget resolution (which would require the president's signature) to replace the concurrent budget resolution (which did not).[20] Many of the same issues had been debated for two decades and were given serious consideration once again in several sets of hearings from 1988 through 1990 on improving the congressional budget process. The Senate Governmental Affairs Committee met to discuss the multiyear budgeting issue, among other budget-related topics, in June 1988. The committee had before it nineteen different proposals to reform the budget, and most dealt with biennial budgeting in some way. In his opening statement, Chairman John Glenn (D-OH) acknowledged that the budget process frustrates most members, consumes a lot of congressional time, and yet important deadlines and deficit goals were often missed: "The important question, however, is not whether the process is frustrating, but whether it has broken down completely and if so, how can we fix it. By itself, budget reform will not create the political courage to make tough choices. Nevertheless, budget reform can create a greater presumption in favor of lower deficits, whether by making the presentation of budget information more meaningful, the

Table 5.3: Sample of Public Opinion on Responsibility for Budget Deficits

Which [important institution], if any, is most responsible for the deficit in the U.S. federal budget?

	1/88	12/88	8/90
Congress/Leaders	45%	47%	59%
The President	27	15	12
Other	15	—	—
Both equally (vol.)	—	30	24
None/Don't Know	13	7	5

Source: Modified from Gallup Organization, Roper Organization, and CBS/NY Times, Roper Center Public Opinion Online (Question IDs: USGALLUP.TM0188, R19A, USROPER.88CSEF, R01, and USCBSNYT.082190, R26A, accessed through Lexis-Nexis).

Is it mainly the Republicans in Congress, or is it mainly the Democrats in Congress, or both who are responsible for not making a serious effort to reduce the federal budget deficit?

	8/90
Republicans	9%
Democrats	11%
Both	74%
Don't know/no answer	6%

Source: Modified from CBS and NY Times, Roper Center Public Opinion Online (Question ID: USCBSNYT.082190, R26B, accessed through Lexis-Nexis).

process of budget choice more useful, or the monitoring of budget performance more effective."[21]

As was mentioned in chapters 2 and 4, biennial budgeting had been discussed in budget-process-reform hearings since the late 1970s and was specifically stated to be a worthwhile "experiment" in the GRH II legislation.[22] According to supporters, the merits of a biennial budget include a reduction in cumbersome and complicated budget deadlines and conflicts and an increase in time for congressional oversight of agency performance. The problems with a biennial budget include the need for appropriations flexibility as agency needs change, as well as the complicated and controversial art of economic and budget forecasting for multiple years into the future. An additional intra-institutional question with biennial budgeting concerns the decreased powers of the appropriations committees under any kind of multiyear budgeting cycle.

Senator Wendell Ford (D-KY) testified before the Senate committee that his two-year budget proposal was not "an anti-Gramm-Rudman-Hollings bill" in that the structures of GRH II would remain in place. One budget resolution and one set of appropriations legislation would pass in the first session of Congress, and the second session would be devoted to authorization, oversight, and compliance-related legislative activities. In this proposed cycle, if the budget were not in place by the start of the fiscal year, permanent continuing appropriations provisions would supplant the usual need for continuing resolutions.[23]

Senator William V. Roth (R-DE), a co-sponsor of the Ford bill, emphasized biennial budgeting as something that 85 percent of the Congress said they supported, according to a study by the Center for Responsive Politics.[24] In addition to the legislative and oversight advantages in such a process, biennial budgeting would reduce repetitive budget-related actions and provide greater understanding and accountability than the often-used continuing resolutions passed after the fiscal year has begun, which are quickly debated and subject to an up-or-down vote. In addition, Roth argued, the extensive fragmentation of the current congressional budget process and the problems of missed deadlines needed to be redressed.

There is no question that the Budget Act of 1974 was a major improvement over what had been a virtually uncontrollable and haphazardous [sic] process. The 1974 Act provided the Congress with a mechanism to formulate and evaluate an overall fiscal strategy. It helped put individual appropriation bills into perspective regarding the entire budget. Yet, while it strengthened the Congress's hand in making budget decisions, it weakened the ability of Congress to get its work done efficiently and effectively. . . . A biennial budget could help to moderate Government spending by forcing the Congress to abide by its budget decisions. To the American people, Congress appears hamstrung by its own procedures and unable to cope with the most urgent fiscal problems of the Nation. We owe it to the American people to reform the process. A two-year budget cannot substitute for political will to reduce the deficit, but it does provide an effective means to help get our fiscal house in order.[25]

The ranking member of the Senate Budget Committee, Pete V. Domenici (R-NM) argued that the biennial budget was one of a few important reforms he recommended for the congressional budget process. Arguing, like Senator Roth, that the 1974 processes were flawed but fundamentally sound, Domenici testified that incremental reforms such as a new budget cycle, broader binding allocations in the budget resolution, a joint budget committee, and earlier deficit-reduction triggers, among others, would reduce intra-institutional budgeting conflicts.[26] Domenici also agreed with Roth that the budget process was too fragmented. The 1974 structures and deadlines were simply put atop the existing ones, which largely entailed separate revenue, appropriations, and authorization processes, and then the GRH processes were added to those. As Comptroller General Charles Bowsher argued in his testimony, through these many layers, coordination had declined:[27] "So, you are trying to push through four or five or six different systems here and call it a budget process and I think what you have got to do is you have got to simplify that back down to one or two processes. I think the leadership, rather than the budget committees, is key."[28]

The question of who or what would impose internal discipline on the process was also raised in joint Senate hearings of the Budget and Governmental Affairs committees in October 1989. These hearings began a week after sequestration had been triggered on the fiscal 1990 budget. Budget Committee Chairman Jim Sasser (D-TN) opened the hearings with the question of whether this latest sequestration trigger was evidence that GRH was working, or whether it indicated persistent problems with congressional budgeting. Citing still-rising deficits, the multiple methods used to "game" the GRH procedures,[29] OMB underestimations of annual deficits due to optimistic economic assumptions, and the sequestration procedure's unwieldy enforcement mechanism, Sasser argued that new reforms were necessary. But while he thought the goal of procedural reform is generally laudable, as were the goals of GRH, Sasser argued that such action does not get to the heart of the issue.

In the final analysis, I think it is obvious that I do not believe, for one, that process is really the problem. In fact, Gramm-Rudman was itself a process solution to a fundamental problem of political will. The problem with this budget is not process. The problem of this budget is we simply do not have enough funds to operate this Government and meet the needs that all of our constituents wish us to meet, or we simply don't have the political will to make the cuts and make the savings that need to be made.[30]

Despite this acknowledged challenge of "political will," Senator Robert W. Kasten Jr. (R-WI) argued that GRH had actually helped reduce the deficit relative to GNP, the annual level of government spending growth, and total government spending relative to GNP. According to Kasten, GRH's "deficit-neutral" rules for new spending, in which new spending had to be offset with new revenues or other shifts, were important factors in these developments. But stronger discipline was still necessary, and Kasten offered his opinion that enhanced presidential rescission power and a constitutional balanced-budget amendment would be useful to supplement the existing budget process: "The repeal of Gramm-Rudman . . . would be tantamount to an admission on the part of Congress that we are unwilling to live within our means. I can think of no worse signal we could possibly send to the American people and the financial markets. . . . To throw in the towel this soon would be a shocking abdication of fiscal responsibility on Congress's part."[31]

In addition to these kinds of pronouncements, the bulk of the hearings again surrounded various proposals for two-year budget cycles, as well as other bills related to committee restructuring to combine authorizations and appropriations, create a new joint leadership budget committee, incorporate debt-limit legislation into the budget process, place Social Security off-budget, and enhance executive rescission powers (cited more extensively in the next chapter). Senator Rudy Boschwitz (R-MN) argued that the long-held assumption of annual automatic spending growth is a very important problem behind the deficit and debt issues, and he implied that this issue must be addressed first—regardless of the form that any new budget processes take: "Congress has always handled the budget process in a manner that defies common sense. One of the biggest gimmicks that Congress has used is the current services budget baseline that assumes automatic spending growth in all programs. This means that Congress may assume that the services offered by a $100 million program in 1989 will cost 120 or 130 million dollars in 1990, a significant increase before the budget process even begins. That way, if Congress ends up spending $110 million we can pat ourselves on the back."[32]

The final notable hearing touching upon these and other institutional issues took place in March 1990 before the Task Force on Budget Process, Reconciliation, and Enforcement of the House Budget Committee. Task Force Chairman Marty Russo (D-IL) opened with the argument that recent deficit trends and various budgeting gimmicks undermine the credibility of the budget process: "Nobody who has viewed the process close up in recent years takes assertions about the budget seriously anymore. . . . Reconciliation and appropriation bills are filled with timing shifts and other gimmicks, which help reach some arbitrary deficit reduction target in the budget year, but do not contribute to long-run deficit reduction. The president submits a budget that relies on very optimistic economic and technical assumptions and questionable savings proposals to meet the Gramm-Rudman deficit target. Congress attacks the assumptions and proposals as phony, but uses them in the budget resolution anyway."[33] Later in the hearing, Russo added:

The bottom line is, that if the only way out is to say you are for a constitutional amendment to balance the budget, or for a line-item veto rather than having the political will to do the job, you are never going to be able to face the problems that need to be solved. . . . And nobody here has the political will to want to do that. We are all politicians and unfortunately, the problem we face is, How do you fix the budget? . . . We have to either increase taxes, which the last time we said that, the Democratic nominee for President got one state in the Union, or we have to do it with spending cuts . . . and just a little small section called non-defense discretionary programs are the ones that are going to face cuts.[34]

Russo also explained why he and House Budget Chairman Leon E. Panetta (D-CA) place some of the blame for these problems and for the budget deficit predicament on the sequestration processes of the GRH reforms. Russo argued the sequestration process is flawed in the allocation of spending cuts, as well as the deficit targets themselves. By contrast, Russo and Panetta's proposal for reform included pay-as-you-go spending procedures, multiyear budgets and enforcement processes, and incentives for the president to propose revenue increases, among other proposals.[35]

Representative Richard K. Armey's (R-TX) opening statement agreed that the budget process was a concern, and he specifically pointed to the fragmented nature of spending decisions and methods for gaming the process, such as authorizing committees' classifying certain spending as entitlements to ensure insulation from Budget, Ways, and Means and Appropriation Committee controls. These problems with entitlement growth and the "cutting the President out of the process" were directly related to the 1974 reforms, Armey argued.[36] Armey therefore defended the budget reform goal of constraining Congress and the government generally to reduce deficits and spending through better process discipline: "We have three legs of the fiscal triad—taxing, spending, and borrowing—and we put a constraint on one of the three legs. . . . I guess what I would be looking for in process reform is something that more definitively defines constraints, and I suppose I would prefer for the definition to be on spending, not on borrowing . . . could we come up with a super Gramm-Rudman that really got to the jugular of the matter, as opposed to the heart of the matter as I think Gramm-Rudman did."[37]

By contrast, former CBO Director Alice M. Rivlin testified that although the deficit was not caused by the budget process, bad processes such as GRH can aggravate the high deficit trend. Although the pre-GRH process in the early 1980s led to high deficits, Rivlin argued that the numbers were brought down soon after through revenue increases and multiyear budget agreements that restrained spending growth. In light of even higher deficits since GRH, process reform may be generally laudable, but

it is not a substitute for political leadership or the will to act. . . . Process changes cannot solve the budget problem but can impede its solution, especially if they focus attention on the short run. . . . Gramm-Rudman-Hollings was a well-intentioned effort, but is now doing more harm than good. . . . If I were queen for a day I would say to the Congress, scrap Gramm-Rudman-Hollings and return to the process that preceded it. You do not need specific dollar targets. You do not need the bizarre threat of sequestration. You do not even need to take Social Security out of the budget calculations. Just keep passing serious, "ungimmicked" 3-year budget resolutions, 3 or 4 or 5 years, until you are running a surplus in the unified budget [translating into a balanced operations budget].[38]

Henry Aaron, an economist at Brookings, also argued GRH was a procedural mess that hid the real need for major policy changes to eliminate deficits. Although the kinds of "sticks" used in GRH seemed to encourage evasion of budget reality, the elimination of such devices would not necessarily be the best answer. Aaron recommended that the sequestration provisions be replaced with more restrictive chamber rules mandating a point of order if targets were ignored. This reform would also entail a five-year deficit-reduction plan and would specifically exclude popular gimmicks such as asset sales, as well as the operating budget of Social Security, from the spending base. The fundamental advantage of the bill making these changes "is that it places responsibility for reducing the deficit where it belongs—on officials elected to make decisions, not on a formula to which those same officials can abdicate their duty."[39]

The final witness in this set of hearings, former CBO Director Rudolph G. Penner, another perennial voice in congressional budget reform history, agreed with Rivlin and Aaron that GRH resulted in declining confidence in the budget process and had to be replaced but not with rigid mechanistic solutions. Penner argued the process itself needed to be less fragmented by having a joint budget committee, which Senator Domenici supported, in order to reduce the lengthy annual budget resolution conference committees. Penner also emphasized (as did President Bush) that an enhanced presidential voice early in the debating process through the signing of a joint budget resolution would result in presidents having a greater stake in the resolution of the process and therefore more incentive to cooperate with Congress. In the same vein, he also said increasing presidential rescission power was important.

Russo was skeptical of some of Penner's suggestions: "Now if we give [the president] enhanced rescission authority and give him a bigger stake, how does that help us make him much more honest in the beginning? I mean, the bottom line is, he has to tell us exactly where he thinks the economy is going to go. It is in no President's political

interest to say things are not good. Jerry Ford tried that and Jimmy
Carter tried that and they were not reelected." And Penner responded:

> With regard to the power of the Presidency and the budget process, we
> have a very peculiar system in this country. In every other democracy that I
> know, budgeting is an Executive function. That is certainly true in any
> parliamentary system. In our system, the legislature does it. I think we are
> generally served well by the division of power created by our Constitution,
> but at this moment, the power of the President in the budget process is
> even less than the drafters of the 1974 process wanted it to be. . . . So I do
> think that we now have to find a way to increase the President's power not
> to spend money, and the enhanced rescission proposal would force the
> Congress to go on the record and say that spending that the President says
> is not worthwhile is indeed worthwhile. That would be valuable discipline.[40]

As Russo and Panetta's discretionary spending cap plan became
the dominant force in reform, many of these institutional questions
were raised by the participants in the reform negotiations. In the end,
as Penner feared, mechanistic solutions ultimately won out. But in their
relative flexibility and lack of firm deficit-reduction targets, the worst
aspects of GRH were argued to have been eliminated, while the necessary discipline was still imposed on Congress by strict internal rules
and external enforcers.

In all of these congressional hearings some partisan debates and
accusations were present, but the institutional problems and solutions
had definite and repeated themes. The ultimate shape of the 1990 reform movement eschewed the strongest attempts to reduce annual congressional majority power through permanent multiyear budgets,
mandatory balanced budgets, or the line-item veto, but it still addressed
new methods of imposing "discipline" on Congress. Some thought that
the problem with GRH was not that its process overly constrained
congressional prerogatives, but that it did not constrain them enough.
Even those who advocated the abolition of the sequestration threat
advocated replacing it with other procedural obstacles to increasing
annual spending. But others continued to argue that the problem was
simply political will.

An additional institutional issue in the 1990 budget act's background,
not overtly discussed in these hearings, was the internal struggle be-

tween the appropriations and budget committees in the House and Senate. As was detailed in chapter 3, the appropriations committees lost considerable power to the tax-writing and new budget committees in the 1974 Congressional Budget Act. In 1990, however, Senator Robert C. Byrd (D-WV), former Senate majority leader and at the time President *Pro Tempore* and chair of the Appropriations Committee, fought to regain some of his committee's powers. One of the problems with GRH from the appropriations committees' perspective was that they would be pressured to cut programs within their jurisdiction during the budget process and then be vulnerable to a second round of cutting if sequestration orders were necessary because the entire budget still exceeded the deficit targets. From Byrd's perspective, Shuman argues, "the efficient congressional committees and executive branch agencies were penalized, while the spending culprits received probation or were pardoned."[41] In the reforms of 1990, however, punishment would now be narrowly tailored to the perpetrator, at least ideally.

Passage of the Act

As part of the summer budget summit in 1990, a multiyear budget package was tied to new procedural reforms.[42] Although some aspects of the taxation and spending plan were ultimately changed after the House initially rejected it, process reforms remained to help "persuade skeptics, especially financial markets, that the tax and spending goals envisioned by the five-year deal would come to pass."[43] And, according to Shuman,[44] President Bush specifically demanded that process reform be included in any final budget deal in 1990. Proposed reforms of GRH included an extension and revision of overall deficit targets from fiscal 1993 to fiscal 1995 combined with new categorical spending caps for discretionary outlays and budget authority in defense, international, and domestic programs. In addition, the Social Security trust fund would be removed from deficit calculations, as would the activities related to the savings and loan bailout, as had been the case for the current fiscal year. The deficit-reduction ceilings would also be modified under this initial plan to reflect current economic realities and estimates and would be triggered if the budget bill exceeded the ceilings by $15 billion in the later years of the agreement—a $5 billion–greater cushion than existed under both GRH laws.[45] Regarding intra-institutional politics, Appropriations Committee powers were preserved due to "the perseverance, industry, determination, and seething outrage of Senator Byrd."[46]

There was no traditional committee deliberation regarding any of these provisions, which were largely hammered out between the summit members, and most of the provisions survived the conference committee begun October 19.[47] Although there were some differences between the chambers in the proposed alterations in the budget process, the conference committee was dominated by conflicts over the new taxes.[48] As Table 5.4 indicates, at least on the process front, there were few fundamental differences between the House and Senate budget-process-reform proposals to begin with.

As is also shown by Table 5.4, OMB was invested with substantial new powers in the reform. The conference report specifically addressed the reasoning behind OMB's enhanced powers and explained how they might be reduced if necessary.

The conferees recognize that, because of the constraints imposed by the Supreme Court's decision in *Bowsher v. Synar,* the conference agreement vests substantial power to estimate the costs of legislation with the Office of Management and Budget. The conferees are concerned that the [OMB] has not always shown complete objectivity in its estimates. The conferees urge the Congress to scrutinize the scorekeeping of the [OMB] as that Office implements the procedures under this conference agreement. The conferees considered procedures under which Congress would enact into law Congressional Budget Office cost estimates as part of any spending legislation. Should the [OMB] abuse its scorekeeping power, the conferees believe that the Congress should adopt such procedures at that time.[49]

Floor debates on the new Omnibus Budget Reconciliation Act were dominated by issues and concerns surrounding the budget package's tax increases and spending specifics and included heated exchanges regarding which party was responsible for the high deficits and which economic groups were being unfairly burdened in the five-year agreement. The proposed procedural changes received relatively little attention.[50] Nevertheless, some comments on the reforms specifically alluded to the institutional intentions and mixed potential of the new restrictions. Even the package's supporters seemed lukewarm on it.

**Table 5.4: Conference Report for Budget Enforcement Act—
Comparison of House and Senate Positions on Major Issues**

Issue	House	Senate	Conference
Enforcing discretion	mini-seques-trations on spending caps and enforced by presidential order	similar to House	similar to House
Enforcing pay-as-you-go provisions if spending is over caps	president orders cuts from qualify-ing entitlements and discretionary programs	president orders cuts from qualify-ing entitlement programs only	Senate plan
Revising and enforcing deficit targets	new targets and mandated annual revision based on economic changes with modified sequestration processes if targets are exceeded	different new targets than House with revisions possible and continuing GRH sequestration processes	compromised targets with revisions possible
Sequestration orders based on reports by	CBO and OMB with OMB's as final	similar to House	similar to House
Treatment of Social Security	off-budget and not included in deficit estimates or sequestration provisions except for interest receipts	same as House but excluding interest receipts	Senate plan
Enforcement of multiyear spending targets through	annual resolution and reconciliation processes	not specified	5-year budget resolution enforced by points of order
Compliance score-keeping	OMB	OMB	OMB

Source: House Conference Report 101-964, 1990, Title XIII, Sections I-III, V-VI, IX and XII.

Representative John Conyers (D-MI) explained his ambivalence toward the bill and its institutional changes.

For the next 3 years, and perhaps for the next 5 years, our hands will be tied tight. We will have little opportunity to raise new taxes to pay for our mounting social needs, to take advantage of what should be a large peace dividend, and to fund new investments needed to meet our urgent human needs and to make our work force more productive. . . . Such restrictions truly make these budget process revisions a mixed blessing.[51]

And Mike Synar (D-OK) agreed:

Included in the package are certain budget process reforms. Some of these are good in that the Social Security surplus can not be counted as reducing the deficit and a pay-as-you-go system is adopted for future spending. The down side is that the reforms take more responsibility for budget decisions away from Congress and thus further away from the American taxpayer. . . . There is actual deficit reduction in the package, not sham techniques.[52]

Yet Senator Terry Sanford (D-NC) argued the reforms did not put enough constraints on congressional and presidential prerogatives. Senator Sanford argued that the proposed process reforms still allowed budget "loopholes" that weakened the threat of sequestration, favored optimistic OMB estimates, and allowed certain spending programs to be categorized as an "emergency" and thus be exempt from the "meat ax": "Gramm-Rudman opened the door to budgetary games and gimmicks. I do not believe it was designed to do that, but nonetheless it allowed them. This new budget process package is a gimmick in and of itself. It is a gimmick designed to let the White House and Congress off the hook. It is a gimmick that allows the White House and Congress to perpetuate the illusion that we are moving toward a balanced budget while we are actually moving away from a balanced honest budget."[53]

By contrast, although he ultimately voted to pass the conference report, Senator Herb Kohl (D-WI) spoke against parts of the reconciliation bill partially *because* it undercut congressional prerogatives: "Where in years past, we tried—often without result—to match our expenditures with our receipts, now we will focus on preset spending ceilings. These ceilings are written into law. They won't change with the unforeseen needs of the Government or with the changing priorities of this body. . . . Budget policy will no longer be fiscal policy. . . . Budget policy will be appropriations policy: how can we keep within the spending caps we've set—no matter how unrealistic, unresponsive, or irresponsible they are."[54]

These various House and Senate members seem to at least agree that the point of these reforms was to constrain congressional majorities, although they disagree as to whether this discipline was too much or not enough. At the end of the floor debate in the Senate, and without alluding specifically to the budget reforms, Senate Minority Leader Robert Dole (R-KS) summed up the difficulties the entire budget package endured: "Does anyone really think that this Nation should just ignore a $300 billion deficit? Do we just stand around and watch interest rates rise toward double digits as America's national debt spirals out of control? This is the choice that Congress now faces; vote for this agreement, which truly pleases no one, or vote for nothing, which will be a disaster for everyone."[55] To which Majority Leader George Mitchell (D-ME) added: "I hope [the reconciliation bill] does receive the support of a sufficient majority to make a clear statement to the people not only in this country, but abroad, that the American Government can govern, that Congress can act, and that at least on one occasion, we are capable of summoning the courage and will to ask for some part of sacrifice to ensure the Nation's future."[56]

On October 27, the Omnibus Budget Reconciliation Act conference report containing the Budget Enforcement Act passed both chambers in party votes—228 to 200 in the House and 54 to 45 in the Senate.[57] President Bush signed the law on November 5, after four continuing resolutions and two days before the off-year congressional election. An article about the budget summit further asserted that only a few congressional aides had sufficient knowledge to explain the new processes to other aides and legislators: "The confusion is clearly linked to the secrecy surrounding adoption of the new rules. Although the budget process has been the subject of endless public hearings in recent years, this year's changes were drafted in private by a handful of individuals and approved after the barest minimum of debate."[58]

Major Provisions of the 1990 Act

Title XIII of the Omnibus Budget Reconciliation Act was added to the budget package in part to enforce the taxation and spending provisions of the five-year budget agreement. The new structures were also designed to correct some of GRH's worst features, which seemed to encourage paper deficit control during the annual budget process rather than real control when the budget was put into effect. Under the new 1990 rules, the Congress was simultaneously more and less constrained than under GRH. Congress could add new programs and reduce revenues, but these changes would have to be deficit-neutral. Congress could shift funds within the three major discretionary categories, but the category ceilings were set in advance and no funds could be shifted from one category to another. The president and his OMB Director would adjust the spending caps and overall targets to take economic and technical changes into account as well as adjust their "scorekeeping" to restrict Congress.

Although GRH technically remained law, the major provisions of the 1990 Budget Enforcement Act effectively replaced the rigid emphasis on overall deficit targets and across-the-board sequestration threat with a more tailored and flexible spending-control system emphasizing annual appropriations caps. Although the BEA did revise and extend the overall targets and kept the threat of across-the-board sequesters, the BEA more clearly differentiated between the kinds of spending Congress generally could and could not control and between the three main categories of discretionary spending, as well as allowing for new direct spending and revenue decreases under new "pay-as-you-go" rules.

Related to these new provisions were notable potential inter-institutional and intra-institutional power shifts. The inter-institutional power shift was largely from the Congress to the president in the form of increased OMB monitoring, scorekeeping, and revised sequestration-related powers, although the CBO maintained an advisory role in reporting "snapshot" findings regarding how well any one ongoing budget process was likely to meet the spending caps. The potentially important intra-institutional shifts were largely from the budget committees' roles as the powerful annual budget resolution coordinators to the Appropriation and tax-writing committees as the potentially powerful coordinators of the new categorical caps and revenue provisions. Under the rules of the BEA, the congressional budget resolution that formed the heart of the 1974 budget act, and thus the budget committees' power, was less important since the spending caps were already set in advance. Louis Fisher argues that these aspects of the BEA were more political than institutional in nature: "Three basic political goals were embedded in the 1990 statute. The two political branches wanted to avoid fixed targets that had embarrassed them in the past. They agreed to protect the defense budget from legislative raids. And they hoped to finesse the budget crisis at least through the 1992 presidential election year. On those three counts the drafters largely failed."[59] Nevertheless, the structures of the BEA's budget reforms also had many institutional corrections related to years of internal and external criticism of Congress's budget processes.

Deficit-Reduction Schedule, Spending Caps, "PAYGO," and New Sequestration Provisions

As was lamented in congressional committees and on the floors, the GRH targets were never met without some form of gimmickry. One reason for this pattern of congressional and presidential behavior was the inflexibility of the targets in the face of new economic information. Another incentive for rosy economic scenarios and related deceptions was the fact that real deficit reduction after the fiscal year began was not specifically required since GRH sequesters were based on deficit projections during the budget-making process. The new BEA targets, shown in Table 5.5, were not only flexible enough to accommodate changing economic conditions, but the rules *required* the president to adjust them for fiscal years 1992 and 1993 and allowed him to adjust the remaining targets as needed.[60] The huge increases in the targets were meant to reflect a more realistic deficit-reduction schedule as well as a natural ballooning resulting from the exclusion of Social Security receipts from deficit calculations under new BEA rules.

The BEA included several key restrictions on Congress, as well as the president. The new deficit targets were technically enforceable through an overall sequester, after a $15 billion cushion is exceeded, in which the president can mandate across-the-board cuts in eligible discretionary programs, with equal reductions from civilian and defense

**Table 5.5: Comparison of Maximum Deficit Amounts in
Gramm-Rudman-Hollings I, II, and the 1990 Budget Enforcement Act**

Fiscal Year	GRH I (in Billions)	GRH II	BEA
1986	$171.9	—	—
1987	144.0	—	—
1988	108.0	$144.0	—
1989	72.0	136.0	—
1990	36.0	100.0	—
1991	0	64.0	$327.0
1992	—	28.0	317.0
1993	—	0	236.0
1994	—	—	102.0
1995	—	—	83.0

Source: P.L. 99-177, Sec. 201 (GRH I), P.L. 100-119, Sec. 106 (GRH II), and
P.L. 101-508, Part II, Sec. 601(a) (1) (BEA).

accounts. But the extraordinary flexibility that the president now had
to adjust the overall targets, as well as the discretionary spending caps
detailed in Table 5.6, made the actual use of this kind of sequestration
threat very unlikely. The new discretionary spending caps structure
was the heart of the change to the congressional budget process. Discretionary spending refers to the roughly one-quarter to one-third of
the budget that goes through the annual appropriations process and
mostly entails defense spending, agency operations, and grants to state
and local governments, excluding multiyear spending precommitments.
For the first three years of the new rules, budget authority and outlay
caps were specified for the three categories of defense, international,
and domestic spending. For the final two years, these categories were
collapsed for totals in budget authority and outlays. Budget authority
allows agencies to spend money or incur obligations, and the forms of
budget authority are appropriations, borrowing, and contracts. Outlays are the actual disbursements from the Treasury and result from
budget authority granted to agencies in the past as well as the current
year. For this reason, outlays in some categories exceed that year's budget authority in Table 5.6.

Similar to the rules for overall deficit targets, the BEA required the

Table 5.6: BEA's Discretionary Spending Limits for Fiscal Years 1991–1995

Category	1991	1992	1993	1994	1995
Defense (in billions)					
BA	$288,918	291,643	291,785	—	—
Outlays	297,660	295,744	292,686	—	—
International					
BA	20,100	20,500	21,400	—	—
Outlays	18,600	19,100	19,600	—	—
Domestic					
BA	182,700	191,300	198,300	—	—
Outlays	198,100	210,100	221,700	—	—
All categories					
BA	—	—	—	510,800	517,700
Outlays	—	—	—	534,800	540,800

Source: P.L. 101-508, Section 601 (a) (2).

president's budget office to adjust the overall caps for various reasons, including: changes in economic indicators, such as the inflation rate; changes in categorization of programs; and, for the last two fiscal years, changes related to credit reforms. In addition, the president and Congress could exempt "emergency" activities from the overall and discretionary ceilings, such as Persian Gulf War-related funding.[61]

A second kind of sequester was added in 1990 to enforce these discretionary caps if the Congress exceeded them after all executive adjustments were made.[62] In such a case, the sequester would only be put into place for the category in question, after OMB "scores" the appropriation bills for their complicity with the caps, and cuts would be mandated across-the-board in that category's programs only. This kind of sequester could be ordered both during and after the budget-making process for any one fiscal year.[63] Such sequestrations were avoidable in the House and Senate through new point-of-order rule enforcement if proposed legislation threatened the ceilings or by reducing other programs within the category. A notable restriction on efforts to prevent sequestration is that Congress cannot offset spending in one category by reducing another. For example, any "peace dividend" in the military category could not be used to fund new or enlarged domestic discretionary spending.

In addition to these restrictions regarding discretionary funds, pay-as-you-go (PAYGO) rules created a third possible kind of sequester to restrict legislative action regarding direct spending increases and revenue reductions to protect the overall deficit targets.[64] If legislation increased benefits for an entitlement program that exceeded the totals for the authorization committee responsible for that area (as opposed to the appropriations committees' jurisdiction over the discretionary caps), the authorizing committee would have to provide for offsetting program cuts within their jurisdiction or have the program reconciled with new revenue legislation. Similarly, if the revenue committees proposed a tax cut, they would have to propose revenue increases in another area or reconcile the cut with other spending legislation.[65] Although direct spending and revenue targets are adjustable for inflation, recession, and emergencies, similar to the discretionary and overall targets, a "mini sequester" is possible to reconcile these kinds of legislation if a reconciliation bill does not. Such sequesters would reduce all other entitlements not exempted under the GRH rules: "Although each bill need not be deficit neutral, the net result of all bills must be deficit neutral."[66]

These three sequesters could be ordered at the end of the budget cycle, with several discretionary caps sequesters possible earlier. OMB uses "PAYGO scorecards" to demonstrate the effect of enrolled legislation and, if a sequester is necessary, to reduce all discretionary funds or mandate revenue increases.[67] Although GRH II also gave score-keeping and sequestration order powers to the OMB, the addition of two kinds of sequesters in addition to the overall targets was a potentially large expansion of OMB power over the entire budget process, while CBO's role in all three sequesters is largely "advisory."[68] Under the 1987 rules of GRH II, OMB had the power to score the effects of new tax and spending legislation under the economic assumptions that framed any year's budget debates. If OMB determined that the preset deficit limit was threatened by the legislation, sequestration could be ordered, with all three taking place on the same day. How-

Table 5.7: New Budget Action Timetable for BEA Sequestration Process

On or before:	Major action to be completed:
January 21	Notification regarding optional adjustment of maximum deficit amount
5 days before the president's budget submission	CBO sequestration preview report
The president's budget submission	OMB sequestration preview report
August 15	CBO sequestration update
August 20	OMB sequestration update
10 days after end of session	CBO final sequestration report
15 days after end of session	OMB final sequestration report; presidential order
30 days later	GAO compliance report

Source: P.L. 101-508, Section 254 (a).

ever, an overall across-the-board sequester can be avoided if the other two are sufficient to reconcile the budget.[69] "The new process transforms OMB's year-end power into a continuing authority to keep the score on all tax and spending bills as they move through Congress. Armed with this and related powers, the White House would be able to block any legislation it opposes. 'What OMB really had before was the ability to beat Congress over the head with a telephone pole'—a powerful though awkward instrument, a congressional budget aide said, 'Now, it can beat parts of Congress over the head with a baseball bat.'"[70] Along the lines of this argument, Table 5.7 shows OMB's end-of-year power more clearly.

Through preset budget limits and the enhanced power of OMB, the budget committees' powers were reduced. The overall budget totals and discretionary caps were to be set in advance and adjusted by the president, with the details of the programs and internal spending shifts set by the authorizing committees, and the tax committees must act to comply with PAYGO rules. All this seems to imply that the congressional budget resolution and reconciliation process are much less important, according to Shuman: "Except for occasional points of order against proposed violations of the agreement, the function of the budget committees may become ministerial, limited largely to producing a perfunctory annual budget resolution whose essential terms have previously been established."[71]

In addition to the new target and ceilings adjustment powers and the continuation of sequestration-order powers, the executive branch also gained scorekeeping powers that could in effect be used for rescission powers. Shuman argues that under the BEA rules, the president can sign an appropriation, spending, or tax bill and then reduce or impound funds that OMB estimates will exceed PAYGO rules.[72] The Budget Enforcement Act also contained other provisions regarding timetables, enforcement, and the treatment of various programs within the budget. The deadline for the president's budget submission was changed from the first Monday after January 3 in which Congress has convened to the more realistic first Monday in February, although the president was still "urged" to submit the budget as close to January 3 as possible.

As is mentioned above, existing rules in the House and Senate against "budget busting" were expanded to include points-of-order for bills breaching either the budget-year spending limits or future-year spending set in annual budget resolutions through 1995.[73] In addition, the "Byrd rule" in the Senate was a new enforcement provision that, if invoked, prevented extraneous matters from being added to reconciliation bills. A final procedural change led to differences in House and Senate appropriations time lines. Under new rules, House appropriations are allowed to proceed on May 15, even if a budget resolution has not yet been adopted, since the Appropriations Committee can base its bills on the preset spending ceilings. Since the House usually acts on appropriations bills first, this rule could speed the process along in the Senate as well.[74] A final notable new rule mandated that all new revenues be used for deficit reduction.

Social Security trust funds continued to be off-budget, but the BEA also added that its revenues be removed from annual deficit calculations.[75] In addition, a "firewall" provision protected Social Security from Treasury borrowing or the using of Social Security funds for other purposes and established related points of order in the House and Senate to protect against legislation that would reduce the balances in trust funds.[76] Credit reform ensured more specific counting of credit activities and loan guarantees within the annual budget.[77] Stricter regulations concerning the assessment of private government-backed enterprises was another reform meant to make the budget more reflective of federal finances.[78] Finally, as under the GRH rules, many aspects of the BEA would be suspended in the event of war or very low economic growth.[79]

Conclusions on the 1990 Budget Enforcement Act

The most important force behind the BEA was the still-burgeoning federal deficit. Regarding political responses to this policy problem, it is tempting to conclude that the reforms simply reflected the goals of a handful of interested and powerful negotiators in a time of divided government and long-simmering power conflicts between congressional committees. In this view, process reform was added to the extraordinary budget summit agenda of 1990 mostly because it was one of President Bush's prerequisites for abandoning his "no new taxes" pledge, and individual personalities and goals shaped the specifics of the new procedures. The enhanced powers of OMB and the appropriations committees were partly due to the influence of Budget Director Richard Darman and the formidable Chair of the Senate Appropriations Committee and President *Pro Tempore* Robert Byrd among the small group of summiteers. In addition, Democratic leaders involved in the negotiations, such as Leon Panetta and Richard Gephardt (D-MO), may have agreed to the extraordinary new limits on majority party power in order to close the budget deal and reap the political benefits of Bush's rift with House Republicans in the off-year congressional election held just two weeks after the final agreement was hammered out.

While aspects of the timing and details of the reforms undoubtedly reflected these particular events and individuals, long-standing institutional issues were the larger force for reducing congressional budget powers. Despite, or because of, the failure of the GRH experiments, all budget reforms on the table between 1988 and 1990 in one way or another further decreased congressional spending powers. These ideas ranged from biennial budgeting to the line-item veto and balanced-budget amendment to the Constitution, with the latter two coming nearest to success later in the 1990s. The BEA may have been a middle ground between these alternatives and a more realistic method of deficit control than the GRH laws, but it was nevertheless a dramatic new chapter in restraining majorities and delegating congressional budgeting power.

Strategy and Reform

While the 1990 reforms could be interpreted as a mild principal-agent delegation episode, I conclude this kind of substantive outcomes strategy cannot fully explain the Democratic majority party's willingness to cede power to automatic spending caps and external enforcement to an opposition president. As said earlier, the actual numbers contained in the five-year agreement were very contentious and brought out much partisan rancor, but the process reforms themselves curiously received relatively little attention for their potential impact on long-term substantive goals of either party, with a few notable exceptions (highlighted above) during floor debates.

Although the Democrats had to negotiate with an opposition president to get their taxing and spending priorities considered, there is little evidence in public legislative documents or secondary literature that the Democratic summit negotiators reluctantly ceded congressional power, although some members did object to specific OMB powers after the BEA was passed. The better evidence to bolster the strategic approach to delegation is the conferees' explicit defense of giving OMB extraordinary new powers over the annual budget process. If OMB abuses its new powers, the conference report said, Congress should then utilize a fallback procedure using CBO scoring and enact substantive legislation based on those scores. Although the conferees cite *Bowsher* as their explanation for the delegation to OMB, they do not explain how this fallback plan would be squared with the case, nor why the fallback plan should not be the primary way for Congress to hold itself to the terms of the agreement. Evidence of principal-agent strategy is thus the threat of altering the nature of the delegation based on the agent's use of the power. What was not clear in the legislative history of the act is why the Democrats would risk such agency losses in the first place if an internal institution was also considered up to the task.

This CBO/OMB issue also seems to defy important aspects of Epstein and O'Halloran's arguments about the strategic aspects of congressional delegation. They argue Congress can choose to "make or

Table 5.8: Likely Institutional Effects of the 1990 Budget Enforcement Act

Reform	Pres./Exec. Power	Cong. Power	Budget Complexity	Process Openness	Budget Time
Costing/ assumptions	Increase	Decrease	Less complex	More open	More
Firewalls/ sequesters	Increase	Decrease	More complex	More open	More
PAYGO	Increase	Decrease	More complex	More open	More
Five-year budget	Increase	Decrease	More complex	More open	Less

Source: Adapted from Thurber and Durst. "The 1990 Budget Enforcement Act: The Decline of Congressional Accountability," in *Congress Reconsidered*, 5th ed., edited by Lawrence C. Dodd and Bruce I. Oppenheimer, 375-97 (Washington: CQ Press, 1993), 386.

buy"—just like any corporation confronted with the possibilities of outsourcing. Other than a formalistic understanding of separation of powers, along the lines of the Supreme Court's decision in *Bowsher*, there is no clear reason why Congress could not enforce the terms of the agreement through CBO analysis and related legislation. Although actual budgets forged from this agreement and its subsequent ones can be reconciled with majority party spending and tax priorities on some level, the process reforms themselves do not appear to have been designed for easy majority control. In their 1993 discussion of the reform, Thurber and Durst argue that potential institutional changes from the act are decidedly anti-Congress, and Table 5.8 is summarized from their account. While these changes do not preclude budget outcomes favored by any one majority party, the reforms seem to substantially limit the dominant party's potential to pursue its substantive agenda.

However, these estimates are not universally accepted. Other budget-watchers disagreed on exactly how much power the BEA really gave the president. Penner writes:

the new process has greatly enhanced the executive branch's power in the budget process. In bargaining over emergency legislation, the president's power bears some resemblance to having an item veto. So far, the power has been used judiciously, but problems at the edges have created tensions with Congress that far exceed the quantitative importance of the relevant issues. But Congress has little choice. If Congress writes rules that crucially depend on estimates and definitions, the Constitution gives it little choice but to let the executive branch administer those rules.[80]

While Schick makes a very different assessment of the procedural changes:

The Budget Enforcement Act has devalued, at least for the next few years, OMB's scorekeeping role. With BEA on the books, the legislative market for revenue and spending measures has shrunk. . . . Moreover, on important matters such as the extension of unemployment benefits, the scoring of legislative impacts has been negotiated by the two branches. At the 1990 budget summit, Congress did not concede any lasting institutional advantage to the executive branch. BEA made significant changes in Congress's institutional capacity to deal with the budget, but it did not adopt any of the president's reforms, such as enhanced rescission authority.[81]

And Wildavsky and Caiden give a middle-ground perspective on the power shift in their 1997 update of the budget process:

In order to make them play their assigned parts, presidents, through the OMB, were given stronger procedural powers. It is they who must submit a certain kind of budget according to their own calculations; who must alter their budget proposal according to the state of the economy; and whose findings must or must not trigger sequestrations of various kinds. This is a lot of procedural clout. . . . But Congress has the means, namely, the power of the purse, to compel OMB and through it the president to back down.[82]

As much as the OMB scoring and enforcement power question dominated the delegation issue, this aspect of the BEA may not have been the most restrictive component of the new rules. The extensive and detailed annual spending limits, discretionary spending caps, and enhanced compliance rules, most of which expired at the end of 2002, severely restricted majority power to manipulate the process as well as general congressional prerogatives to pursue other budgeting goals.

Granting that the push for the reform certainly reflected election-year political motivations on both sides, and even granting that the BEA was very important to the recent, if short-lived, elimination of the deficit, the question still remains—why have deficit control and reduced congressional budgeting powers gone hand-in-hand?

Institutional Self-Diagnosis and Reform

In the legislative action and rhetoric behind the 1990 Budget Enforcement Act, the focus was on restricting Congress's ability to act on its majority preferences. Even though there is little doubt that partisan agendas and strategies were behind these behaviors on some level, the principles and structures of the actual reform resemble the two GRH laws in being a shift away from the pro-Congress reforms of 1974. The nature of this shift has received attention from various other Congress- and budget-watchers from *Congressional Quarterly Weekly Report:*

Under the new law, with tax and spending limits set for 1991–95, Congress is relegated to its pre-1974 role. It will continue to adopt and send spending and tax bills to the White House, but it will lack the power to change the fiscal framework. Although Congress will continue to draft budget resolutions, the key numbers for those resolutions are dictated by the recent budget deal.[83]

The undertow of political fear, coupled with Congress's system of diffuse power, makes it tough to impose the discipline needed to solve the deficit problem. Throughout the 1980s, members bridled when they lost power under efforts to impose greater fiscal discipline—through the Budget Committee, high-level groups such as the summit or the automatic spending cuts of the Gramm-Rudman deficit law. That exposes the central contradiction of the contemporary Congress: Despite their craving for political cover on controversial issues, lawmakers resent being left out of decision-making.[84]

Yet Congress remained involved in budgeting and helped forge tough budget decisions with the president in 1993 and 1997, which were in part extensions of the principles of the 1990 agreement. While the booming 1990s economy also deserves much credit for the temporary elimination of the deficit, the BEA represented a more fiscally realistic approach to deficit reduction than GRH and the next major reform of the 1990s—the line-item veto. But the political success of all these delegation-based actions leads back to the fundamental question of why Congress needed to be restrained in the first place. The nature of representative government and the problems of imposing discipline on a fragmented institution received continual attention throughout the 1990s.

6

STOP US BEFORE WE SPEND AGAIN

The Line–Item Veto Act of 1996

The line-item veto is about eliminating wasteful spending. We are not talking here about some highfalutin principle of Constitutional powers. I just don't go along with the idea of making a fetish out of legislative prerogatives. The issue here is not the separation of powers; the issue is the sharing of responsibility and accountability.

—*Senator Ernest Hollings (D-SC), 1994[1]*

The public perceives Congress as being incapable of addressing the deficit without this kind of outside control, and they are right.

—*Representative Peter Blute (R-MA), 1995[2]*

What real effect will it have on the deficit—is it worth the possible political problems? Is it worth the constitutional shift of power—why should the President's spending priorities be substituted for those of Congress? What is wrong with the current rescission process?

—*Senator Barbara Boxer (D-CA), 1995[3]*

Movements to reduce Congress's budgetary power continued through the mid-1990s, even as annual deficits began to decline and the parties switched their institutional dominance. After Republicans gained a majority in the House and Senate in the 1994 off-year elections, a balanced-budget constitutional amendment came closer to congressional passage than it had under the Democrats, but it failed to gain the necessary two-thirds support in 1995 and 1997 by a hair's margin in the Senate. By contrast, the so-called line-item veto, a milder but still controversial form of congressional delegation, won passage in the Republican Congress after ten years of legislative effort. Although it is not difficult to explain why President Clinton also supported the enhancement of his rescission powers, as did almost every president since the Civil War, why did the Republican majority give it to him? In this chapter, I argue again that federal fiscal policy related to spending and deficits brought a harsh Republican-led attack on Congress's particular representative structures and challenges as a national body composed of local interests.

Although political and electoral calculations by members and leaders are unquestionably an important part of this legislative history, the principal-agent approach to delegation cannot make complete sense of the item veto. Years of legislative action and rhetoric by both parties do not match the expectations of a strategic party power shift where power to pursue substantive goals is given to an agent over whom the principal has formidable sanctioning potential. Although Congress did not pass a "true" item veto allowing the president to delete items *before* signing an appropriations bill, which would require a constitutional amendment, it also explicitly rejected various statutory versions that would better preserve majority power. Of course, the most pro-Congress alternative to the item veto was already on the books in the form of the 1974 impoundment provisions of the Congressional Budget Act, but it was regularly criticized for "tilting the process" toward Congress too much.

Along similar lines, Epstein and O'Halloran's "make or buy" calculus for delegation does not apply well to the line-item veto.[4] In light of their general argument that Congress is loathe to delegate distributive powers under conditions of divided government, they acknowledge the Line–Item Veto Act is "puzzling" for their transaction-cost politics theory and give this reform a straight political narrative, which is compelling on the surface. Since Republicans had long argued for the item veto, they would appear inconsistent not to pass it after gaining power, especially when it was listed at the top of the 1994 Contract with America signed by all Republican House incumbents and challengers. Although Senate Republicans were less enthusiastic about the reform, according to Epstein and O'Halloran, Senate majority leader Bob Dole was looking for a legislative victory as he ran for president in 1996, and he would wield the item veto if victorious. Finally, the particular version that passed would likely not pass judicial scrutiny so the delegation to Clinton would be short-lived, which is exactly what happened two years after passage. In other words, Epstein and O'Halloran argue that Republicans were sincere when they pushed for the item veto before Clinton took office but insincere afterward. While there is evidence of some partisan ambivalence on both sides during the 1980s and early 1990s, depending upon who was president, the line-item veto was ultimately not attractive to a majority of Democrats when Clinton was president so the reform makes little partisan sense, in addition to its limited fiscal potential and the fact the Congress already had a majority-friendly rescission power in its hands.[5]

As is detailed below, Congress rescinded more federal funding than all presidents requested after the 1974 impoundment process was put into place. Congress certainly has representation challenges when it comes to balancing budgets, despite pressure for local projects and tax breaks, but it had long used its own mechanism to rein in some excess spending. In addition, studies of gubernatorial use of the item veto showed it merely substituted executive spending preferences for legislative ones, rather than really cutting the budget significantly overall. Nevertheless, the Republican Congress determined the 1974 rescission process was broken, *precisely because it was written and used to increase congressional fiscal powers.* The 1974 act specified two kinds of presidential withholdings and congressional oversight of their use. The president could defer appropriations unless either chamber disapproved the action (*INS v. Chadha* nullified this option after 1983), and he could permanently rescind spending if the Congress passed a bill of approval within forty-five days. In other words, a lack of congressional action allowed deferrals but stopped rescissions, meaning Congress still retained a lot of power in this process.

After 1974, presidents had varying success using the new process, but total impoundments during this period amounted to a fair amount of outlay reductions (see Table 6.2).[6] In President Reagan's first two years in office, for example, the Congress passed more than 75 percent of his rescission requests, which ultimately withheld more than $20 billion of funds previously approved by Congress.[7] As we would expect, presidential rescission success rates dipped under conditions of divided government and Congress often denied presidential requests while rescinding different appropriations through new legislation (see

Table 6.3). Although Congress ultimately rescinded more dollars than presidents' requests called for, the Republican minority during the 1980s and 1990s pushed for greater presidential power in this process.

The three most prominent statutory versions of the item veto emerging in the 1980s and 1990s all tilted the process more toward the president but differed on what kind of a congressional majority was necessary to stop a rescission from taking effect. Under a proposed "expedited rescission" process, the Congress would be mandated to quickly vote up or down on presidential rescission proposals. Although this idea does not seem radically different from the 1974 provisions, its point was to force members to stand and vote on suspect projects instead of burying them in appropriations bills and then ignoring the president's calls to rescind. But similar to the 1974 reform, expedited rescission could be disapproved by a simple majority of members. This relatively pro-Congress alternative proved to be less popular than the following two kinds of rescission, which both required a supermajority to override the president.

Under a "separate enrollment" process, appropriations would be broken down by the enrolling clerk into "billettes" (to use Senator Byrd's disparaging phrase) prior to being presented to the president. The president would then be able to sign or veto each as separate bills, with two-thirds of Congress necessary to override any specific veto. With "enhanced rescission," congressional inaction would automatically allow the president's rescissions to take effect. However, if the Congress wished to stop any one or all of the rescissions, it could pass a disapproval bill, which would be subject to the normal veto and override procedures. As veto overrides are very rare, the enhanced rescission alternative was as close to a real item veto as Congress could get. In 1995, the House approved an enhanced rescission bill and the Senate approved a separate enrollment bill as a last-minute substitute over expedited rescission. After a year-long conference, the Line–Item Veto Act of 1996 took the enhanced rescission form. The fact that the Republican majority in both chambers rejected the expedited rescission alternative, in addition to the even more pro-Congress 1974 provisions, makes the principal-agent explanation less persuasive in this delegation case, unless, as Epstein and O'Halloran write, its sponsors assumed it would be unconstitutional so little harm would be done.

But the item veto cannot be so easily dismissed. Even if it was a short-term gimmick, the item veto has much in common with the congressional budget reforms that preceded it. All these reforms, even in 1974, diagnosed serious institutional capacity problems stemming from Congress's inherent challenges in balancing local and national interests. As the deficit rose through the 1980s, blame was successfully placed on Congress's shoulders, as it was constantly portrayed as a spendthrift institution by the president and many of its own members and leaders. While the line-item veto was a more symbolic reform than the process changes enacted under GRH and the Budget Enforcement Act, it was still a real power that the president could use against members in all kinds of deal making.

With the Congress's basic representative and legislative power at issue, members on both sides often took publicly institutional, rather than partisan, positions. Many Republican members and leaders said they trusted President Clinton to decrease pork more than their own Congress, and many Democrats said the opposite. Those who argued for reducing congressional spending power did so by emphasizing the institutional components and incentives of pork-barrel spending and how the norms of representation and fragmentation in Congress lead to parochial actions, which are hard to reconcile in a "responsible" budget. Those opposed to the strictest item veto alternatives argued that ceding this kind of power put individual members at risk of virtual presidential blackmail, which would be a major institutional blow to Congress's budgeting and legislative prerogatives.

Background of the 1996 Act

To fully understand why deficits and other spending issues led to calls for congressional delegation of budgetary power again in the mid-1990s, and why most members of the majority party in Congress once again supported delegation to the opposition party president, we must figure out why Congress is not considered, and does not consider itself, up to the task of responsible budgeting. As in the 1974, 1985, 1987, and 1990 reforms, deficits and party differences on fiscal policy served to highlight institutional challenges that ultimately dominated the debates. The main institutional dilemma has long been the same: how can Congress satisfy local demands for federal money and national needs for fiscal discipline? Through the 1980s and 1990s, growing anti-Congress sentiment looked for the answer in external entities rather than shoring up its own item-reducing processes or creating new ones. Congress opted to once again disadvantage itself in the legislative process rather than defend its place in the national government.

Fiscal Issues

In light of the high deficits of the 1980s and early 1990s, supporters of a presidential line-item veto argued that it could be a useful tool for reducing certain kinds of pork-barrel spending and targeted tax breaks. However, many supporters also acknowledged that by itself the item veto would not be a potent anti-deficit weapon, unless the deficit was very small, because the kinds of spending the item veto would target are a small minority of the annual budget. For these reasons, supporters of an item veto often also favored a balanced-budget constitutional amendment and cited a similar combination in many states as evidence that sound fiscal policy has a strong relationship to both of these legislative restraints. Nevertheless, one of the themes of the 1996 act's legislative background is how the political revival of the line-item veto in the time of high deficits in the mid-1980s through the mid-1990s highlighted its usefulness as a symbol of budget-process reform in addition to being a minor tool for fiscal discipline.

The item veto was unlikely to target large federal spending commitments for legal and political reasons. After Reagan called for one in his 1984 State of the Union address, a brief study of potential item veto reductions by the Democrat-dominated House Budget Committee showed that only a small amount of the budget would realistically qualify for such a veto during the Reagan administration. According to this study, up to 9 percent of the budget technically could be eliminated by Reagan if he had some kind of item veto. If done completely, these reductions would almost equal half of that fiscal year's projected deficit. But the study argues further that, due to stated policy commitments by the administration in addition to its well-known preference to protect discretionary defense funding, only about 1 percent of the budget would be eligible realistically.[8] By contrast, the next year, the Republican-dominated Senate Rules and Administration Committee said about 11 percent of the federal budget, at most, would be eligible for line–item veto cuts.[9]

In 1992, a GAO study reiterated the point that a line-item veto would not significantly reduce the deficit, but nevertheless argued that over a period of several years, the savings could have made a small but noticeable dent in the amount the federal government borrowed over a six-year period—roughly $70 billion.[10] But a Congressional Research Service report disagreed with the methodology of the GAO report and argued that the more realistic savings would have been $2 billion to $3 billion over a six-year period "and probably less."[11] Also in 1992, Congressional Budget Office Director Robert D. Reischauer testified before a House subcommittee investigating various item-veto proposals that this kind of reform would have primarily an impact on policy outcomes rather than overall spending totals.

The crux of my message is that the item veto would have little effect on total spending and the deficit. . . . First, since the veto would apply only to discretionary spending, its potential usefulness in reducing the deficit or controlling spending is necessarily limited. Second, evidence from studies of the states' use of the item veto indicates that it has not resulted in decreased spending; state governors have instead used it to shift states' spending priorities. Third, a presidential item veto would probably have little or no effect on overall discretionary spending, but it could substitute presidential priorities for Congressional ones.[12]

In the same set of hearings, Assistant Comptroller Harry S. Havens made a similar argument that the line-item veto's ultimate impact would be the balance of power between the branches regarding discretionary spending priorities.[13] And in 1998, after the 104th Congress passed the Line–Item Veto Act, Senator Robert Byrd (D-WV) still argued it would have a very small fiscal impact: "When you strip away all the spending that is indisputably necessary from the discretionary budget, you are left with a small fraction of that budget—itself a third of the overall budget—in which 'pork' supposedly resides. Even if this 'pork' could be identified and surgically removed by some form of budgetary liposuction, federal spending levels would be virtually unchanged."[14]

Many supporters of the line-item veto consistently acknowledged that such a change in the federal budget process was not going to cure deficits and therefore asserted that such criticism of the item veto was a straw-man argument. President Reagan's Secretary of the Treasury, Donald T. Regan, made this point in 1984: "The Administration agrees

Table 6.1: Federal Budget Deficit and Debt, Fiscal Years 1990–1997

Fiscal Year	Deficit (in billions)	Deficit as % of GDP	Total Public Debt (in billions)	Debt as % of GDP
1990	221	3.9	2,412	42.0
1991	269	4.5	2,689	45.4
1992	290	4.7	3,000	48.2
1993	255	3.9	3,248	49.5
1994	203	2.2	3,433	49.4
1995	164	2.2	3,604	50.2
1996	108	1.4	3,734	48.5
1997	22	0.3	3,772	46.0

Source: Congressional Budget Office Historical Tables; www.cbo.gov.

that, by itself, the grant of line-item veto authority to the President would not cause federal budget deficits to disappear. . . . It is a tool that would be targeted at the most wasteful and unnecessary programs. . . . Although a line-item veto amendment would not be a panacea for excessive spending, its adoption would be an important step toward bringing spending under control."[15] In light of this acknowledgment of the limited potential of the item veto, it is curious that the line-item veto was ultimately passed when the deficit seemed to be coming under control, as is shown by Table 6.1.

But even as the deficit was decreasing, the fiscal symbolism of the line-item veto remained potent in the 104th Congress in 1995. Senator Dan Coats (R-IN), a longtime supporter of enhanced presidential rescission power, implied that the relatively small totals of potential cuts were not the entire issue.

There are currently 4,000 American families that dedicate their entire Federal tax burden to pay for research on the screwworm, a pest that has been totally eradicated from the United States. And yet those 4,000 families every year contribute their entire tax burden to an unnecessary process because a single Member or a few Members want to perpetuate a mode of spending. And the only way they can do it is to attach it to an otherwise necessary and supported appropriations bill.[16]

. . . [Discretionary spending] is symbolically very large. It portrays a Congress that cannot discipline itself. It portrays a Congress that is selfish and greedy and out of touch with the American people, that cannot put the national interest ahead of parochial or special interests.[17]

Senator John McCain (R-AZ) made a similar point in his repeated criticism of defense appropriations bills. McCain often cited a Congressional Research Service study that showed that $50 billion in six years of defense appropriations bills "had nothing to do with defense." (The CRS study, however, said that the items' relevance to military operations could be debated.[18])

These supporters of the item veto also made a larger argument that the rescission processes established in 1974 were not strong enough to give the president the power to reduce or eliminate suspect spending projects. Supporters of the item veto argued that Congress disagreeing with so many presidential rescission requests proved that the process was far too tilted toward Congress and away from saving federal dollars. At the same time, critics of the line-item veto frequently invoked two decades of rescission data to demonstrate that Congress's own rescission proposals, plus those they did accept from the presidents, showed the institution's existing intent and ability to shrink wasteful spending, as is detailed in Table 6.2.

Although the conclusion of the 1995 GAO report on this debate indicates that Congress has demonstrated its willingness to cut even more targeted spending than the presidents asked for, CBO Director Robert D. Reischauer's point is underscored in Table 6.3. Perhaps the overall fiscal impact of the item veto is not as important as the policy differences between the presidents and Congress on discretionary spending. As the minority party in the 1980s, Republicans also championed the item veto in part as a method of giving their party's presidents more power over discretionary spending.

Partisan Issues

Perhaps the real partisan issue was not simply reducing federal spending but reprioritizing it. Although public finger-pointing by item-veto supporters was largely directed at Congress as a whole rather than one party or another, there is little doubt that the Democrats' "tax and spend" stereotype was at issue for many Republican lawmakers when they were in the minority, and Presidents Reagan and Bush made such

Table 6.2: Proposed and Enacted Rescissions—Fiscal Years 1974–1995 (Dollars in Millions)

Fiscal Year	# of Pres. rescission requests	$ of Pres. rescission requests	# of Pres. rescission Congress accepted	$ of Pres. rescission Congress accepted	# of Cong. rescission proposals passed	$ of Cong. rescission proposals passed	Total # of rescission for fiscal year	Total $ of rescission for fiscal year
1974	2	496	0	0	3	1,400	3	1,400
1975	87	2,722	38	386	1	5	39	391
1976	50	3,582	7	148	0	0	7	148
1977	20	1,927	9	814	3	173	12	986
1978	12	1,290	5	518	4	67	9	586
1979	11	909	9	724	1	48	10	771
1980	59	1,618	34	778	33	3,238	67	4,016
1981	133	15,362	101	10,881	43	3,736	144	14,617
1982	32	7,907	5	4,365	5	48	10	4,414
1983	21	1,569	0	0	11	311	11	311
1984	9	636	3	55	7	2,189	10	2,244
1985	245	1,856	98	174	12	5,459	110	5,632
1986	83	10,126	4	143	7	4,409	11	5,553
1987	73	5,836	2	36	52	12,359	54	12,395
1988	0	0	0	0	61	3,889	61	3,889
1989	6	143	1	2	11	326	12	328
1990	11	554	0	0	71	2,305	71	2,305
1991	30	4,859	8	286	26	1,420	34	1,707
1992	128	7,897	26	2,068	131	22,527	157	24,594
1993	7	356	4	206	74	2,205	78	2,412
1994	65	3,172	45	1,293	81	2,374	126	3,668
1995	0	0	0	0	12	572	12	572
Totals	1,084	72,801	399	22,879	649	70,061	1,048	92,940

Source: Adapted from Enclosure I, Report by Comptroller General, Joint Hearing, House Committee on Government Oversight and Reform and Senate Committee on Governmental Affairs, January 12, 1995, 122–23.

charges quite explicit in their annual budget fights with opposition Congresses. Of course, both the president and Congress are technically responsible for deficits when they occur, and the Congress has often funded discretionary programs below the presidents' budget requests. But in the fiscal symbolism debate, the term "profligate Congress" could easily have been a code phrase to describe the spending patterns of the Democrat-dominated legislature.

Between the Ninety-eighth and 104th Congresses, dozens of bills were introduced to increase the president's impoundment powers, and the issue was largely a Republican one. As mentioned above, the line-item veto began to receive renewed legislative attention after President Reagan called for an amendment version of it in his third State of the Union address in January 1984: "As Governor, I found this 'line-item veto' was a powerful tool against wasteful or extravagant spending. It works in 43 States. Let us put it to work in Washington for all the people. It would be most effective if done by constitutional amendment. The majority of Americans approve of such an amendment just as they and I approve an amendment mandating a balanced Federal budget."[19] In 1988, the Republican Party platform included a pledge under the category "Controlling Federal Spending" that read: "We will use all constitutional authority to control congressional spending. This will include consideration of the inherent line-item veto power of the president."[20] After the election, various members of the Congress, most visibly Senator Arlen Specter (R-PA), urged President Bush to test the constitutional possibility that he already had such veto powers without waiting for congressional authority to do so. And, of course, the 1994 House Republican Contract with America included the line-item veto along with the balanced-budget constitutional amendment as top-priority campaign pledges.

In light of this history, many institutionally focused arguments during the line–item veto debates can be read as partisan jabs in disguise. The following comments by Representative William J. Martini (R-NJ) in support of the line-item veto in the first month of the 104th Congress can be seen as the Republican view of the institution's recent history from the perspective of a new majority party.

The Congress as an institution has proven itself to be incapable of fiscal restraint when it polices itself. We need to implement tough institutional

Table 6.3: Percentage of Approved Presidential Rescission Requests by Each Administration, Fiscal Years 1974–1995

Fiscal Years	President	% number of proposed rescissions allowed	% dollar amount of proposed rescissions allowed
1974–77	Ford	34%	16%
1977–81	Carter	56%	46%
1981–89	Reagan	36%	36%
1989–93	Bush	20%	17%
1993–95	Clinton	68%	43%

Source: Adapted from Enclosure II, Report by Comptroller General, Joint Hearing, House Committee on Government Oversight and Reform and Senate Committee on Governmental Affairs, January 12, 1995, 124–26.

measures to pull in the reins of a runaway budget, and the line item veto is the place to start. We need this reform to empower the Federal Government to keep itself in check and act prudently with taxpayer money. The people demand that much from us. But this is also a reform that will show the public that they can place their trust in us again. The people deserve that much from their elected officials.[21]

And there is little doubt that partisan differences on the nation's fiscal priorities were an important reason that Presidents Ford, Reagan, and Bush had a lower overall rate of approved rescissions facing Democrat-majority Congresses than did Presidents Carter and Clinton, although Reagan enjoyed overwhelming success in his first set of rescission proposals in 1981, as seen in Table 6.3.

Despite these partisan overtones to the act's background, several prominent Republican leaders publicly maintained their support for the line-item veto after President Clinton was elected. In a 1993 hearing before the Legislation and National Security Subcommittee of the House Committee on Government Operations, House Minority Leader Robert H. Michel (R-IL) explained why he still supported this delegation of power.

Many will argue that giving the President this type of enhanced rescission authority will tip the balance of power in favor of the executive branch and will dilute Congress's power of the purse. . . . I guess my response has been that, over these 36 years now that I have been around here—although it's gotten considerably worse in more recent years—we just haven't done the job. I'm willing to trust a President, any President—as I would Jimmy Carter at that time, our Republican Presidents, and now President Clinton—to give him much more of a hand to get spending under control.[22]

Along similar lines, it is noteworthy how House Speaker Newt Gingrich (R-GA) praised his chamber for giving up power as the House passed the first round of item-veto legislation in 1995: "I think of this evening as a very historic evening. We have a bipartisan majority that is going to vote for a line item veto. For those who think that this city has to always break down in partisanship, you have a Republican majority giving to a Democratic President this year without any gimmicks an increased power over spending, which we think is an important step for America. . . . It is an important step on a bipartisan basis to do it for the President of the United States without regard to party or ideology."[23] And majority leader Bob Dole (R-KS) agreed when he added "the line-item veto is not about partisan politics, as the minority leader said on Friday, as I said on Friday, and as the President said today. . . . It is about our economic future."[24]

Why would the economic future of the country benefit from greater presidential power? What was wrong with the way Congress budgeted?

Institutional Issues

Calls for a presidential line-item veto began after the Civil War, and states began to give such powers to their governors around the same time.[25] President Grant asked for the authority to veto individual items in 1873 in response to the congressional practice of attaching nongermane riders to appropriation bills begun in the 1860s. Members of Congress proposed over eighty line-item veto constitutional amendments between 1876 and 1936 and even more between the New Deal and the 1980s.[26] In a 1936 *Georgetown Law Journal* legislation note, Vernon L. Wilkinson cited several arguments both for and against the line-item veto that largely lay out the institutional issues that dominated debates on the subject for the next sixty years. Wilkinson argued the item veto would "reduce extravagance in public expenditures," "discourage 'pork-barrel' appropriations," "curb 'log-rolling,'" and "restore to the President his veto power." On the other hand, such a veto would also "lessen the responsibility of Congress," "increase the influence of the Executive whose powers have already been much expanded," "destroy the system of checks and balances established by the Constitution," "violate the principle of separation of powers embodied in the Constitution," and "defeat the legislative intent of Congress."[27]

In light of these arguments and the growth of the administrative state, presidents had long utilized some discretion related to dispersing appropriated funds to executive agencies. Congress gave the president formal impoundment powers in the Anti-Deficiency Act of 1905 and renewed those powers twice afterward. However, traditional congressional deference to these rescissions was dramatically reduced after Nixon's impoundments. During the ensuing budget reform process in the early 1970s, the presidential line-item veto was raised by some Republicans as an alternative to the near-unilateral impoundment power at that time. But in light of numerous interbranch conflicts during the Nixon years, the item veto was not yet popular among majority members investigating budgeting reforms:

REP. BROYHILL (R-NC): . . . [an item veto] would be better than impoundment. At least it would give the Congress the right to debate and have a vote on it.

SENATOR HUMPHREY (D-MN): Yes. I suppose diarrhea is better than scarlet fever, but I prefer not to have either one.[28]

These institutional issues and questions of legislative prerogatives were again raised in 1984 hearings before the Senate Subcommittee on the Constitution of the Judiciary Committee as it considered two constitutional amendment proposals and one statutory-based proposal intended to give the president the line-item veto. Senator Alan Dixon (D-IL) explained why he favored the amendment route: "Congress often attaches controversial items to 'must' bills in an effort to make it more difficult for a President to use his veto power. Logrolling, and packaging good and bad projects and programs into a single omnibus bill, has become a way of life."[29] Yet Dixon argued that statutory versions of the line-item veto, in the form of enhanced rescission authority, would "unconstitutionally breach the separation of powers, and put the President in the heart of the lawmaking process."[30] Since enhanced rescission allowed the president to approve a law and then effectively repeal a part of it, Dixon argued that it would give the president almost unilateral lawmaking powers. Separate enrollment, Dixon argued, is also constitutionally faulty because it would stretch the long-held definition of what a "bill" is. By contrast, a true constitutionally designated line-item veto "builds on the role the Constitution has already assigned the President in the legislative process. It permits a President to indicate his or her approval of individual items of spending before they become law, not after. It gives the President only one bite at the apple, not two."[31]

Despite Senator Dixon's explanation that his simple-majority congressional override provision would protect legislative power more than other proposals requiring two-thirds for overriding an item veto, Senator Mark Hatfield (R-OR), chairman of the Senate Appropriations Committee, still maintained that legislative prerogatives were threatened by such changes to the budget process. Although the Senate and the White House were held by Republicans at that time, Senator Hatfield reminded his colleagues that history has shown that presidents will threaten programs and pull support from legislators, even of the same party, who did not agree with the administration. In addition, Hatfield lamented the fact that such proposals would be popular at all ten years after the Congress attempted to take back budgetary power from the president.

[The Congressional Budget Act's] principal goal was to make Congress more effective in its discharge of its constitutional role to control the purse strings of the Treasury. It is indeed ironic that 10 years later, when confronting the largest and most challenging budgetary problems ever, we find proponents of a scheme to diminish the responsibility of the Congress over the budget. It is a self indictment. . . . I am not arguing that the budget process we now employ in Congress is the best or the most effective in terms of assuring responsible spending decisions. Our difficulty in grappling with the current deficit is evidence enough of its shortcomings. But I am equally certain that the answer to our problems is not to delegate further responsibility to the Chief Executive.[32]

In contrast to Hatfield's institutional defense, in 1985 Senator Mack Mattingly (R-GA) submitted a bill—co-sponsored with forty-six other Senators, forty of whom were Republicans—which would provide for separate enrollment of appropriations bills, which the president could veto separately and the Congress could override by the normal two-thirds. The bill defined an "item" as any paragraph and numbered section contained in an appropriation bill. In addition, the bill included a sunset provision so that the separate enrollment rule would expire after two years unless Congress renewed it. According to Senator Mattingly, this sunset was added to mitigate the fears of runaway presidential powers, but the overall point of the statutory proposal was still to rein in excessive congressional spending powers. Mattingly cited various parts of the Federalist Papers that warned of the aggrandizing nature of legislatures and argued that

It was in recognition of this tendency of the legislative branch to intrude on, or usurp, the legitimate rights of the other branches and in recognition of the ineffectiveness of mere parchment barriers that the President was given the power to veto legislation. As a critical element of the originally envisioned balance-of-power distribution by the Constitution among the three branches of our Government, it becomes imperative to rehabilitate or restore the veto—and S. 43 accomplishes this purpose. View it, if you will, as an historical preservation project to the U.S. Constitution.[33]

At the hearing, congressional and budget-process scholars Louis Fisher, Allen Schick, and Norman Ornstein, all frequent contributors to budget-reform hearings, disagreed with Mattingly. They responded that the line-item veto is a political vehicle that would give the president enormous advantages in budgetary negotiations while being of little help in reducing large deficits. Separate enrollment specifically is not only constitutionally suspect, they argued, but would encourage backdoor spending to circumvent the appropriations process and might therefore exacerbate the growth of entitlement spending.[34]

The chairman of the Senate Rules and Administration Committee, Charles Mathias Jr. (R-MD) concluded at the last of the three meetings on the proposal that although he was very skeptical of the power transfer in a constitutional amendment for a line-item veto and opposed greater centralization in the Office of Management and Budget, he would be willing to support a temporary provision to test the reform.[35] Nevertheless, the hearings ended with the committee's unanimous decision to report the bill unfavorably. The subsequent committee report summarized two constitutional "tests" related to S. 43. The "procedural test" was in light of the *Chadha* decision concerning the legislative veto and the committee report concluded that "were the procedural strictures of *Chadha* applied to this consequence of an enacted and implemented S. 43, its constitutionality would fall on procedural grounds alone."[36] However, the second and "more serious" constitutional test was that of the "intended balance of power between the legislative and executive branches of the federal government." This test, the report argued, would depend on the degree to which a particular president executed the power, but the bill was presumed to have failed on this count as well.[37]

The additional views of Senators Dole (R-KS), Warner (R-VA), and Garn (R-UT) included in the committee's report pointed out that the benefits of separate enrollment over traditional impoundment authority was that "the line-item veto rightfully 'tilts' toward savings not spending."[38] In effect, this proposed tilt was also against congressional power to override presidential action: "There now exists within the Congress an institutional bias that makes it easier and more profitable politically to spend the taxpayers' dollar than to save it. . . . We do not contend that President Reagan, or any other President, has a greater concern than Members of Congress do for our Nation's economic health and general welfare. But it is true that only the Chief Executive is elected by the entire Nation, is responsible to a national constituency, and is free from the district, State, or regional considerations with which every Member of Congress must contend."[39]

In the spring of 1989, the line-item veto received attention in the Senate once again as new budget-process-reform proposals were debated two years after GRH II was passed and the deficit was still rising. Ultimately, the deliberations culminated in the 1990 Budget Enforcement Act (see chapter 5) and did not include enhanced rescission proposals for the president. Nevertheless, the usual institutional arguments on both sides of the line–item veto debate were reiterated that year in committee hearings and reports concentrating on some of the twenty proposals submitted in the 101st Congress. In April 1989 the Subcommittee on the Constitution of the Senate Judiciary Committee heard testimony related to three joint resolutions proposing constitutional amendments allowing the president item-veto and item-reduction powers.[40] Democratic sponsors of two of the proposals, Senators Alan Dixon (D-IL) and Paul Simon of Illinois (D-IL), heard testimony against the transfer of power to the president from Republican Senators Orrin Hatch (R-UT) and Mark Hatfield (R-OR), among others. Senator Hatfield argued that Congress has unfairly been given the reputation as wild spenders compared with presidents.

During the Reagan administration we in Congress were bashed many times in public by the President as being the fiscally irresponsible body. More Presidents than Mr. Reagan—all the Presidents in fact—have used that kind of an argument against the Congress. For 36 of the past 38 years, the Congress has underappropriated the President's requests. In 8 years of the Reagan administration, we underappropriated $25 billion to what President Reagan had requested of the Congress. We are giving ammunition to those Presidents who love to bash the Congress as having no fiscal restraints, who declare that only the President has fiscal responsibility; that is simply not borne out by the facts.[41]

Republican congressman Mickey Edwards (R-OK) argued that his severability proposal for continuing resolutions would be a better statutory response to the argument that appropriations bills are not sufficiently separated for presidential review. In addition, Edwards argued that the "pork in the riders" argument for the line-item veto is misplaced: "why doesn't the Senate, if it is concerned about riders, merely adopt the same germaneness rules that the House has. . . . That is a lot easier than changing our system of government."[42] Edwards also argued that "the truth is that none of the arguments for the line-item veto work, except for the most honest one, which is to provide the President with greater control over congressional decision-making."[43]

In October 1989 the line-item veto was also debated in joint hearings before the Senate Governmental Affairs and Budget Committees. Senator Dan Coats (R-IN) testified in favor of his statutory proposal for enhanced rescission, co-sponsored with Senator John McCain (R-AZ) and thirty-one other Senators, which had a companion bill in the House and was endorsed by President Bush. Senator Coats explained that this statutory provision was designed to be a compromise version of what had been previously proposed in the Senate in order to meet the previously stated objections to such legislation. His bill would have amended the 1974 impoundment provisions to allow current presidential rescission power to remain but with additional power to rescind, in whole or in part, budget authority not previously rescinded in the previous fiscal year. His bill had a clear presidential tilt because rescissions would go into effect unless Congress passed a bill of disapproval within twenty days and the president could use such a power both at the beginning and end of each legislative budget cycle. Coats cited President Reagan's difficulties getting his rescissions approved by Congress in his second term as evidence that real savings mandated stronger rescission powers.[44]

Governmental Affairs Committee Chairman John Glenn (D OH) asked Senator Coats to explain why the fiscal ramifications of his proposal were worth the potential political costs.

SENATOR GLENN: . . . if you had a very politically oriented President, one of the things against a line item veto is he could use that politically unfairly against particular members of Congress that he wanted to take some action against for whatever reason. . . .

SENATOR COATS: . . . One, I think if it became clear that a President was utilizing his rescission power for political purposes, members would rally to the support of their colleague. . . . Secondly, I guess I would ask the question, if we don't now do that in reverse? Don't we politically blackmail the President to some extent by attaching our favorite little projects that we know we could never successfully move through the body were it to stand on its own, by attaching that to a bill we know the President has to sign at midnight or 11:59 before the Social Security checks are stopped[?][45]

The next set of major hearings on the item veto occurred three years later, in September 1992 before the Subcommittee on the Legislative Process of the House Rules Committee. The hearings were held in response to over two dozen bills proposed in both chambers in the 102nd Congress and concentrated on statutory line–item veto proposals. In light of the pending presidential election, Representative David Dreier (R-CA) joked that one such proposal was informally called the "Bush-Clinton amendment." On a related note, a bill sponsor, John J.

Duncan Jr. (R-TN), argued that his support for enhanced rescission was neither anti-Congress nor overtly partisan.

Now, I am not one who bashes the Congress, even though I know it is popular to do so. But I go back home and I tell the people I represent that I think almost everyone in this Congress is among the most hard-working, most patriotic, dedicated people that I know. But I will say that the Congress for the last several years has apparently been unable or unwilling to bring Federal spending under control on its own. . . . Almost every appropriations bill has many, many good things in it, but it also has many ridiculous things, and I think there are things that any President, be he Democrat or Republican, would take out.[46]

The public image of Congress was also of concern to some members. Speaking in favor of a separate, expedited rescission bill that had over two hundred co-sponsors, Representative Tim Johnson (R-SD) acknowledged that the fiscal impact of executive rescission of some pork-barrel projects would be minimal but helpful toward deficit reduction as a general goal. At the same time, other institutional considerations were important as well:

Perhaps as importantly, it would introduce greater accountability to Congress, and I think this is something that the American public, with their frankly frustrated, exacerbated views towards this Institution, feels that these spending patterns are a real contributory cause to that problem, and I think it is a reform that would be met well to restore some confidence that the American public has in this Institution.[47]

Representative Dan Glickman (D-KS) agreed:

The issue of unauthorized projects is one that becomes a personal political burden to all Members of Congress. It hurts the institution of Congress beyond the budget issue. . . . We all individually have our own ideas about things that help our own district. And I think what this bill tries to do is improve the process to make sure that collectively it can pass scrutiny so that none of us get personally embarrassed about it, so that it does meet some national interest test as well.[48]

Similar themes regarding Congress's institutional image surfaced in the first set of item-veto hearings of the Clinton administration before the Legislation and National Security Subcommittee of the House Government Operations Committee. The three bills under scrutiny all related to expedited rescission, which would strengthen presidential powers over impoundment because Congress would have to explicitly re-vote on the spending measures in question rather than have the option to ignore the request as the 1974 measure allowed.[49] However, most expedited rescission proposals left more power to congressional majorities than other line–item veto proposals because most of these bills required that Congress vote up or down on the rescission package by a simple majority rather than vote on a bill of rescission disapproval, which the president could veto.[50]

In his opening statement, Representative Al McCandless (R-CA), ranking member of the subcommittee, argued that fiscal impact is not the only reason for supporting the line-item veto: "even if the impact on the deficit was only marginal, the elimination of special interest government spending through line item rescissions would help reassure the American people that wasteful spending on sometimes useless projects would be eliminated. Building the public trust in the Congress and in the federal government is also a worthy goal. Giving the President, whether he be a Republican or a Democrat, the authority to [rescind] immoderate spending would be a step in the right direction."[51]

New OMB Director Leon E. Panetta, former chairman of the House Budget Committee, expressed his support for an expedited rescission bill, which he noted he also supported as a member in the previous Congress. Panetta said although he shared opponents' concerns regarding transfer of power between the branches, presidential expedited rescission powers were not harmful to Congress's institutional prerogatives to control spending. This process change would increase both branches' accountability, Panetta argued. The president would no longer be able to blame Congress for putting him in a position of choosing between eliminating wasteful spending and shutting the government down. The Congress would be more accountable by explicitly voting on suspect individual programs that probably had not received much attention in the first round of votes relating to the entire appropriations or omnibus bill.[52]

House Minority Leader Robert H. Michel (R-IL) added that special tax benefits should also receive additional scrutiny through an item veto. Michel explained that his interest in item vetoes for tax expenditures grew after a careful review of H.R. 11 (the Revenue Act of 1992), which was passed in the aftermath of the Los Angeles riots to enact new enterprise zones. In this tax bill, over fifty special tax provisions were added to the bill as it moved through the Congress. These tax benefits, if passed, would have cost over $2.5 billion over five years—much more than the original enterprise zone provisions. Although President Bush vetoed the bill in 1992, Michel foresaw "President Clinton faced with a take-it-or-leave-it situation later this year when a tax bill or the reconciliation bill is presented to him. I can guarantee that many of these provisions will again be in that legislation as sweeteners to help pass the more difficult provisions. The President should have a tool to avoid being held hostage to all the special interest provisions that are tacked onto legislation, including those in revenue bills."[53]

Testifying before the subcommittee, Louis Fisher again disagreed that such measures would increase congressional spending discipline. In response to a question from the subcommittee chairman regarding decreasing pork-barreling through process reform, Fisher argued that it is possible that congressional budgetary discipline could worsen as a result of any kind of line-item veto. Knowing that the White House and OMB would be searching to cut items, why wouldn't Congress members simply add on all that they wanted and see what would be cut? If a pet project were ultimately eliminated, arguably it would be the president, not the member, who would "take the heat."[54]

But at that time, the public continued to blame Congress more than the president for real or potential problems in deficit reduction, as the opinion sample in Table 6.4 shows. Although the Republicans appeared to receive more responsibility—which had not happened in similar polls through the 1980s (cited in chapters 4 and 5)—note that the question was really about future obstruction of legislation, a typical tactic of the minority, rather than past performance.

A related issue of institutional responsibility for "wasteful" spending was raised again in a 1994 Senate hearing that approached the line-item veto from another angle—the possibility that the president already had the power. As noted earlier, Senator Arlen Specter, a longtime advocate of the item veto, pushed for a "sense of the Senate" resolution stating the president need not wait for legislative authorization to veto individual appropriations items because the Constitution allowed a veto for essentially everything Congress voted on—even parts of an appro-

Table 6.4: Sample of Public Opinion on Responsibility for the Deficit

If Congress does not pass a bill to reduce the federal budget deficit in the near future, who do you think would be more responsible—the Democrats in Congress, the Republicans in Congress, or President Clinton?

	8/93
Democrats	20%
Republicans	38%
Clinton	25%
Not Sure	17%

Source: *Time,* CNN, Yankelovich, Roper Center Public Opinion Online (Question ID: USYANKP.080693, R26, accessed through Lexis-Nexis).

priations bill that received only one overall vote but contained hundreds of items.[55] In defense of such a relatively unorthodox take on the issue, Senator Specter cited and expanded upon many previous institutional arguments for this kind of presidential power. He also explained that having long been a supporter of line–item veto constitutional amendments, and statutory versions as well, he had been frustrated by the failure of both legislative avenues and thus began to research whether legislative authorization was truly necessary at all. Specter explained his strong support for the item veto by arguing that such authority was necessary for reducing wasteful spending that was not in the national interest, improving congressional control of the budget by creating disincentives to add unauthorized programs, and improving the image of the institution generally: "The line item veto is not a partisan issue. It is a good government issue. . . . Beyond the specific savings, the presence and use of the line item veto by the President could give the public assurances that tax dollars were not being wasted. Each year the media reports many instances of Congressional expenditures which border . . . the frivolous . . . [which] creates a general impression that public funds are routinely wasted by the Congress. The line item veto could eliminate such waste and help to dispel that notion."[56]

Also in June 1994 the House Rules Committee voted to report a two-year expedited rescission bill with a favorable recommendation. Although expedited rescission seemed to call for swift and definite action by Congress in response to a presidential rescission message and draft bill, some feared that congressional inaction could still thwart the process and allow the release of the funds in question.[57] The minority view included in the committee report, signed by Representatives Gerald B. Solomon (R-NY), James H. Quillen (D-TN), David Dreier (R-CA), and Porter Goss (R-FL), argued that this bill was a pale and unworthy substitute for a "real" line-item veto, or its best legislative equivalent—enhanced rescission: "H.R. 4600 suffers from the same deficiencies as the current rescission process. While it may expedite the consideration of rescissions, it is still prone to either blockage or substitution by alternative rescissions, thereby thwarting the President's recommendations either way."[58]

In October 1994, a month before the off-year election and two days before the legislative session was scheduled to end, the Senate Budget Committee held hearings to assess H.R. 4600 and over twenty other bills pending in Congress on a statutory line-item veto, in addition to the eighteen amendment proposals and Senator Specter's resolution before the Judiciary Committee.[59] The usual arguments in favor of expedited and enhanced rescissions came out, and Senator Robert C. Byrd (D-WV) lamented a lack of concern for Congress's power of the purse: "Over the past dozen years, we have been plagued with process worship as a way of dealing with controversial problems, the balanced budget amendment, the line-item veto . . . all have been advanced as automatic solutions to the dilemma of budget deficits. In fact, I believe that such process changes would be damaging to the institution's constitutional purpose and functions."[60]

Byrd accused his fellow House and Senate members of being more interested in procedural cure-alls than the actual budget actions themselves and cited recent instances in which deficit-reducing budget bills went unsupported while procedural remedies were championed. Byrd pointed out that in March 1993 forty-five Senators voted to waive Budget Act rules to permit enhanced rescission, but only four of them voted for the 1993 reconciliation bill that arguably would ultimately achieve $400 billion in deficit reduction. And in 1994, sixty-three Senators voted for the "much vaunted" balanced budget amendment, but only seventeen had voted for the previous year's reconciliation bill. Byrd concluded—"Is it any wonder . . . that the American people hold this institution in such low esteem [?]"[61]

Budget Chairman Pete V. Domenici (R-NM) asked Senator Byrd why he maintained these institutional objections to even expedited rescission power, which would merely ask for an up-or-down vote on the president's proposed rescission package. Byrd responded, "I think it is up to the Congress to determine whether or not it wants to vote on his bill up or down, or whether it wants to make some changes. . . . I do not consider us to be under any obligation to any President, Mr. Clinton, Mr. Reagan or any other President, to be mandated by law to vote a second time on appropriations that have already been sent to the President, which he may have vetoed and the Congress may have overridden, and then he gets a second bite at those."[62]

In response to another question from Senator Domenici about the possible institutional harm done in an experimental two- or four-year trial of these new powers, Byrd argued that presidents might behave in a falsely restrained way in a short window of time, and such a one-president experiment would not show much since every president would respond to the power in slightly different ways: "But after it becomes permanent, then it is open to abuse, and once we do that, once we give that power to any President, we will never get it back, never." Byrd added his concern that the courts, not the American people, would tell Congress that it cannot delegate certain legislative powers. In light of these kinds of proposals and public reactions, Byrd concluded that Senators and citizens needed to be better educated on separation of powers and checks and balances.[63]

Passage of the Act

After the Republican off-year victory in 1994, reflecting the House Contract with America campaign pledge, three line–item veto bills were proposed immediately after the 104th Congress convened. An enhanced rescission bill was introduced on January 4, 1995, in the House and referred to both the Committee on Governmental Reform and Oversight and the Rules Committee.[64] Both House committees reported the amended measure at the end of the month. In the Senate, two line–item veto bills were introduced the same week, one expedited and one enhanced rescission, and referred to both the Senate Budget Committee and the Governmental Affairs Committee.[65] Both Senate committees reported the bills, without recommendation, and Senate floor debate began in March.

Before these relatively quick committee decisions to report occurred, a joint hearing before the House Committee on Government Reform and Oversight and the Senate Committee on Governmental Affairs examined some old and new institutional concerns. The House Committee chairman who presided over the hearing, Representative William F. Clinger Jr. (R-PA), a co-sponsor of the House bill, noted the uniqueness of the joint hearing between these committees and said it also signified the "great cooperation we are finding between the two committees to deal with some of the items that were included in the Republican contract and some of the items we want to move."[66] Representative Clinger defended the component of his bill that would allow the rescissions if Congress failed to act and the requirement of a congressional supermajority to spend the money in case of a disagreement between the president and Congress by citing the growing national debt related to a decade and a half of deficit spending. In short, the line-item veto was necessary to change "the tilt of the game from one which favors spending to one which favors saving."[67]

Representative Constance A. Morella (R-MD) and Representative Peter Blute (R-MA) agreed with Clinger, and their comments were typical of those of the bill's supporters:

REPRESENTATIVE MORELLA: I have long felt that the current rescissions process—in which Congress may (and often does) choose to completely ignore Presidential requests to cut spending—is a guardian of gridlock. The current process invites inaction and makes a mockery of efforts to enact meaningful spending cuts. . . . I have come to believe that granting the President line-item veto authority may be a prudent and responsible means of overcoming the inadequacy of the rescissions process. While I do have some concerns about the potential implications of a line-item veto on the balance that we have established in the power of the executive [and] legislative branches, I believe that these issues can be adequately addressed.[68]

REPRESENTATIVE BLUTE: Last November the American people spoke out with perfect clarity against business as usual in the United States Congress. First and foremost they demanded change in the way Congress spends their hard-earned tax dollars. . . . This is not a radical proposal. Giving the President the line-item veto authority would restore power to the President that has been usurped by Congress over the last two hundred years. And at the same time we give budget discipline to the President we give fiscal responsibility to the taxpayers.[69]

While the Democrats were by no means uniformly against the enhanced rescission bill, the following arguments by Cardiss Collins (D-IL), the ranking member of the House Committee, and Edolphus Towns (D-NY) were typical of opponents of the bill. Collins pointed out that in twenty years of the rescission provisions devised in 1974 Congress had rescinded twenty billion more than the president had requested. And the deficit did not explode in growth merely for the lack of stronger presidential rescission powers.

This bill is aimed at the wrong end of Pennsylvania Avenue. This bill seems to be based on the mistaken assumption that Congress is preventing the President from cutting unnecessary federal spending by failing to act on rescissions he proposes. . . . This legislation would, however, better enable the President to spend taxpayer dollars in the way he chooses rather than as Congress provides in the legislation it passes.[70]

And Towns agreed:

The question before us today is whether we should disrupt one of the cornerstones of American government: the checks and balances established between the Legislative, Executive, and Judicial branches of the federal government. The Constitution placed the "power of the purse" with the Congress. Yet, there are those who argue that we are incapable of carrying out our budgetary responsibilities. Recent history, however, disputes that argument . . . giving away our constitutional powers will not result in any real savings.[71]

The use of the line-item veto by the president as an arm-twisting devise was also raised in an exchange between Senators William V. Roth Jr. (R-DE) and Dan Coats (R-IN), both of whom were longtime, strong supporters of presidential rescission power.

SENATOR ROTH: . . . Do you see this legislation enabling the Chief Executive to use it for partisan advantage? In other words, he can threaten to line-item veto something if the Senator or Congressman doesn't vote right on another issue. How great a problem do you see that?

SENATOR COATS: I don't see that as a significant problem. While the president could use it for that purpose, I think certainly it would not be good policy, nor would it be good politics for a President to do that. He might do it once, but I think it would quickly erode the President's credibility in terms of the value of the power that we have given him, and he realizes he can quickly lose if it is abused.[72]

Perhaps as one would expect from their current institutional vantage points, OMB Director Alice M. Rivlin was much more sanguine on the prospect of the presidential line-item veto than was CBO Director Robert D. Reischauer, although Rivlin herself had previously served as CBO Director. Rivlin expressed the administration's strong support for the enhanced rescission bill, and although she acknowledged that such proposals would probably enhance presidential powers over Congress, she argued the more important outcome would be increased accountability in both branches for budget outcomes.[73] While not overtly expressing his disapproval of such proposals, Reischauer downplayed the fiscal potentials of the proposals while emphasizing the potential shifts in the balance of power between the branches: "If a President cared more about reducing spending in the deficit and not in pursuing his own spending priorities, an item veto at the Federal level could decrease spending and it could reduce the deficit. But history suggests that Presidents who support reductions in one area in the budget often favor increases in other areas. They would then be expected to use the item veto to free up resources provided in appropriations bills and redirect them to spending on their own priorities."[74]

Almost a week after the joint hearings, the Senate Budget Committee also met to discuss the enhanced and expedited rescission bills. Chairman Domenici and Ranking Member James Exon (D-NB) favored the expedited approach (S. 14) with a "lock box" for deficit reduction while also allowing rescissions for new direct spending and a four-year sunset provision. Senators John McCain (R-AZ) and Dan Coats (R-IN) favored enhanced rescission with no sunset.[75] The majority agreement on the committee appeared to be for some kind of rescission bill, but a few Senators strongly opposed both measures.

Despite the pending success of this effort to delegate to her party's president, Senator Patty Murray (D-WA) explained that her opposition stemmed from a sense of representative responsibility for her state:

I served in the Washington State Senate before coming here. I was a member of the minority party. Our Governor was a Democrat and he did have the line-item veto. And I know from personal experience how that power can be used for all sorts of purposes. It can be used to horse-trade votes for bills. It can be used to threaten votes against members. I know that we have to lower the deficit, and we have begun to do that. But I really fear that the bills before us . . . are going too far and I cannot support, frankly, something that might leave any part of my own State vulnerable to line-item attacks.[76]

Senator Barbara Boxer (D-CA), after citing Federalist 48 and 58, expressed her fears for the legislative prerogatives of the Congress: "neither of the proposals we are considering would allow Members of Congress to substitute their spending cuts with the ones proposed by the President. In effect, part of the power of the purse is being handed over to the President. It is interesting to me, Mr. Chairman, because I think it is a power grab to the executive branch, and I must say that I did not come to the Congress to abdicate my responsibility. I take it very seriously."[77] And Republican Senator Mark Hatfield reiterated his long-held aversion to institutional power transfers:

If there is one lesson that we should learn from the elections that have caused such significant changes here in Washington, it is that we are held accountable to the voting public. At a time when new Members of Congress have been elected to come to Washington to enact the will of the people, why would we want, or need, to shift additional powers to the President? The idea of a line-item veto may be popular, but not for the procedure that it is. Rather, I suspect its appeal is in the spending cuts that it purports to represent. We have the power to make these cuts, and we will be held responsible. A line item veto does not make us more responsive to the will of the people, it makes us more responsive to one person: the President.[78]

But some Senators admitted they had once opposed the item veto for similar reasons, but came around to support it. In her opening statement, Senator Olympia J. Snowe (R-ME) said when she was in the House, she was "wary of granting broad authority to the President" in a line-item veto. But, she ultimately determined that it was in "the long term best interests of this country."[79] Similarly, Senator Bill Bradley (D-NJ) explained that he did not support the line-item veto until 1992, after watching the quintupling of the deficit, the "shameless" pork-barrel spending in appropriations and tax expenditures, and "our Presidents again and again denied responsibility for their role in the decisions that led to these devastating records."[80]

And one supporter of the item veto was openly wary about how this power would be used in practice. Senator Frank Lautenberg (D-NJ) said he would ultimately vote for a line-item proposal, so long as it included tax expenditures but that "all of us have to be aware of the fact that political extortion might take place." He explained this fear specifically in terms of how presidents view the Electoral College and the importance of partisan victories in a few key states. "And I think it makes for a pretty easy opportunity for someone in the White House, especially in the second go-round or perhaps trying to protect the party's position, to deal with this in a less than objective way."[81] Senator Domenici responded that his bill's four-year sunset provisions would help the Congress to assess these kinds of power and favoritism issues.

But Senator Coats responded to Lautenberg's concerns with criticism of Congress's political spending tendencies: "You talk about political extortion. It is the Congress that is politically extorting. The Congress is sending to the President legislation which it knows the President has to accept or if he vetoes, it will be an extraordinarily unacceptable veto to the American people, and yet it contains item after item of measures and expenditures which are not relevant to the bill, which are not in the National interest but which provide some little benefit to a particular member, his or her State, his or her congressional district."[82] Rather than shifting power unnecessarily to the executive, Senator Coats argued that his bill was redressing the shift toward the Congress engendered by the 1974 bill. Senator McCain agreed and added that a sunset provision is not necessary because the 1974 act showed that presidential abuse of budgetary power could be corrected by Congress through process reform legislation. McCain also said fears of "extortion" were not merited because they are an insult to the forces that truly check presidents—Congress and the American people.[83]

In the last week of January, two constitutional amendment line-item veto proposals received a hearing in the Senate Subcommittee on the Constitution, Federalism, and Property Rights of the Judiciary Committee.[84] Subcommittee Chairman Hank Brown (R-CO) expressed his support for a constitutional line-item amendment, noting that "amending the Constitution should be taken very seriously." Brown said the original presidential veto power was essentially meant to be a line-item veto, but Congress's utilization of bundled legislation damaged this presidential power. Brown argued that "amending the Constitution to provide for the Line Item Veto isn't a radical shift in the balance of power. It actually returns the veto power of the President closer to its original place in the legislative process."[85]

Senator Joseph R. Biden Jr. (D-DE), ranking member of the Judiciary Committee, agreed the item veto would be a positive force to reduce wasteful spending, but argued that a statutory approach is much more sensitive to the balance of power than a constitutional item veto. Biden stated Constitutional amendments were meant to be a "last resort" kind of change that would only be necessary if statutory item veto experiments failed. Furthermore, the practical permanence of an amendment would "commit the citizens and the Government . . . to an unknown and practically unalterable course and fundamentally shift the balance of power."[86] Keeping in mind the end goal, Biden said that a separate enrollment statutory item veto would reduce the unnecessary spending in large omnibus spending measures and continuing resolution and would allow better presidential and congressional budgetary scrutiny.

Senators Brown, Biden, Jon Kyl (R-AZ), and Russell D. Feingold (D-WI) also discussed the reality of how pet projects are inserted into budgets for the benefits of districts and members but concluded they would accept the possibility that such spending in their districts could easily be targeted by an item veto. Senators Biden and Simon especially acknowledged that they would probably not be able to save one of their own state's projects if it were item-vetoed, but if they could not muster the legislative support to keep the library or bridge, then they should not get it.[87]

The various House and Senate committees given the line–item veto bills each reported favorably on at least one of the versions, with the exception of the Senate Budget Committee, which proposed a substitute but without recommendation. The House Rules Committee, which held an informal briefing rather than a hearing on January 24, favorably recommended H.R. 2, the enhanced rescission bill, with amendments. The subsequent Rules report stated its support: "H.R. 2 is a milestone in the budget reform process. For all the rhetoric in the past years, the House has never demonstrated its commitment to an effective line item veto—until now. H.R. 2 marks the beginning of a monumental effort to change the way Congress does business and restore public confidence in its ability to manage the nation's finances."[88] However, the committee's four Democratic dissenters, Joe Moakley (D-MA), Anthony C. Beilenson (D-CA), Martin Frost (D-TX), and Tony P. Hall (D-OH), argued H.R. 2 unnecessarily tilted the process toward the president's rescissions by allowing congressional inaction to be an approval of the reductions and cuts. The current rescission process, the dissenters argued, which required positive congressional action to approve a rescission, "preserves the integrity of the prerogative of the Congress to control the purse which funds the activities of the Federal Government." The dissenters believed that "the grant of authority to the Congress found in Article I should not be cast aside in haste. The tension between the Executive and Legislative branch, while difficult and sometimes burdensome, has essentially worked since it was designed by the Founding Fathers. We see no compelling reason to tamper with it at this time."[89]

The House Committee on Government Reform and Oversight also reported H.R. 2 favorably and with amendments. Its report specifically cited that this bill "keeps faith" with the Republican Contract with America, which asked for a balanced budget amendment and a line item veto "to restore fiscal responsibility to an out-of-control Congress."[90] The report also specifically addressed the balance-of-power issue: "Will enhanced rescission authority give the President too much power and tilt the balance toward executive control of the purse? We think that will not be the case. Greater presidential authority to rescind funds will create a better balance between executive and legislative interests. The Impoundment Control Act of 1974 was too restrictive. Enhanced rescission will protect the public's interest by providing a tool for eliminating wasteful, unnecessary spending and for terminating unfair, narrow special tax benefits."[91]

The minority views included in the report, similar to the Rules dissenters, asserted that the transfer of power to the executive was too "extreme" and perhaps unconstitutional. The minority disagreed with the majority's perspective on which branch is most to blame for deficits and added that this particular version of line–item veto authority did not specify enough the parameters of this presidential power.[92] Other additional views feared the impact of the line-item veto on appropriations for the judiciary and argued for a stronger tax expenditure-reduction feature.

Floor debates on the various line–item veto proposals began in the House on February 2, and an amended bill passed on February 6 by a partisan margin of 294 to 134.[93] The passed bill was H.R. 2, the enhanced rescission bill almost identical to S. 4. The supporters and opponents of the bill made statements on the floor that largely mirrored the institutional criticisms and defenses discussed earlier in committees. While proponents of the item veto argued that Congress had to be restrained from spending opponents retorted that congressional institutional prerogatives had to be protected. Gerald Solomon (R-NY), chairman of the Rules Committee, summarized the proponents' argument:

I am not under any delusion that this is some kind of panacea for deficit reduction. It is not. But it can make a significant difference in our spending habits and our deficit situation. And gosh knows, we need it. I think one of the greatest benefits will be the deterrent effect by discouraging us from slipping pork into our appropriations bills in the first place. I understand the concerns of those who feel the line-item veto shifts too much authority to the President, and that it might somehow be abused or used for political or partisan purposes. . . . No President in his right mind would want to create a major confrontation with the entire Congress by grossly abusing this authority. . . . He would surely realize Congress would find ways to retaliate. And we know we can do that.[94]

And Representative Robert Torricelli (D-NJ) expressed a main concern of opponents to the item veto.

Our national debt has increased by fourfold not because of a Congress, but because of the very executive power that you are using today to control spending. It was, after all, during the Reagan and Bush administrations where they proposed spending in excess of the spending proposed by budgets within this Congress. . . . The proper power of this country with regard to appropriations belongs in the People's House. If that power is not handled well, the people have a remedy with elections. It is best not taken away from the people themselves.[95]

On February 22, the Senate Budget Committee voted to report both S. 4 and an amended S. 14 without recommendation. Chairman Domenici said although he opposes the extent of power granted to the president in S. 4, he did not want to prevent the Senate from voting on enhanced rescission. Citing Federalist 58's passage on the power of the purse, Domenici expressed a fear that "once we, the Congress, concede this power to the executive branch, it will never be restored."[96]

On February 23, the Senate Committee on Governmental Affairs met again to discuss the merits of the enhanced and expedited measures, and the amended version of enhanced rescission passed in the House. In his opening statement, ranking member John Glenn (D-OH) argued against the "magic" number of one hundred as the number of people affected by a tax break for the break to qualify for an item veto.[97] Senator Bradley (D-NJ) agreed that there should not be a limit on which tax items should qualify and he argued this "gimmick" should not be endorsed by the Senate.[98]

Allen Schick agreed with the Senators about the need for reduced restrictions on which tax expenditures would qualify for a veto but had much harsher words for the bill the House passed overall and its version in the Senate.

I must apologize for the strong language I use here. I have never encountered in 30 years a bill that is so ill-advised and so constitutionally-defective as S. 4. It may not be defective in the legal sense. The courts will decide that. But certainly in the political sense, for it would fundamentally change the constitutional arrangement for how laws are made and unmade, and it would strip much of the power of the purse from Congress. Mr. Chairman, Presidents have extraordinary veto powers, and it is their choice alone whether to exercise that power. George Bush vetoed 36 bills in a row that Congress failed to override. It overrode only the 37th.[99]

Schick objected to the language in the bill allowing presidential rescissions on nonappropriations bills and reports and various forms of direct spending, including entitlements. In addition, the bill seemed to allow for presidential rescissions of budget authority related to substantive laws passed in prior years. Schick also emphasized that although Congress could override such presidential action, it would take three votes for Congress to work its will and as many as nine sets of actions, including House and Senate votes and probable conferences committees: "Talk about legislative gridlock." Schick concluded that expedited rescission was more acceptable regarding both balance of power and the legislative process.[100]

On March 7, the Senate Committee on Governmental Affairs voted to report both bills without recommendation, with an amendment to S. 14. In addition to criticizing Chairman William V. Roth and the rest of the majority members' decision to vote down any amendments for S. 4, Senators David Pryor (D-AR), John Glenn (D-OH), Sam Nunn (D-GA), Daniel K. Akaka (D-AK), and Carl Levin (D-MI) all argued that the balance-of-power shift was too extreme in S. 4, but Glenn, Levin, and Akaka also added that the Budget Committee's amendment of tax expenditure vetoes only for one hundred taxpayers or more in S. 14 was too narrow a requirement.[101] On March 23, on the fourth day of debate on the line-item veto, the Senate passed an amended S. 4 by a margin of 69 to 29. Senators Dole, McCain, Coats, and Domenici offered an amendment in the form of a substitute, which gave the president line–item veto authority through a separate enrollment procedure.[102] Dole explained his support for separate enrollment as a better way of ensuring that "items" are clearly defined in each piece of legislation: "Is this substitute perfect? Probably not. There may be some good ideas on change, maybe here, maybe in the conference. But it moves us in the right direction. And in my view it does not change the balance between the legislative branch and the executive branch. Both sides have the opportunity to lay out their priorities and subject them to the review of the other branch. The President retains his authority to veto, and we retain our authority to override such a veto."[103]

By contrast, Senator Byrd asserted that even the separate enrollment option, which theoretically retained more congressional power than enhanced rescission, reduced the Senate's representative power in a very negative way. The small "billettes" created by a separate enrollment process would be very vulnerable to a veto because many would be local or state issues unlikely to be considered a "national interest" and thus muster the necessary two-thirds to override. By contrast, vetoing an entire bill does generally affect enough representatives to be connected to the national interest. Therefore, Byrd argued, the separate enrollment option reduces the amount of representation given to the states, even in the Senate, which was designed as the states' fo-

rum.[104] On the floor, Senator Daniel P. Moynihan (D-NY) also criticized the item veto in institutional terms and cited the recent March 2
vote in which the Senate failed to muster the two-thirds necessary to
send the balanced budget amendment to the states by one vote: "the
separate enrollment bill would have Congress surrender fundamental
constitutional prerogatives to the Executive. I hope the Senate will recognize the constitutional and practical defects of this proposal, and I
hope we will again have the wisdom to say no."[105]

Despite Moynihan's argument, the separate enrollment substitute
passed the Senate soon after, but conferees to iron out the differences
between the chambers were not named until September 7 and only
met twice in 1995. Senate majority leader (and presidential candidate)
Bob Dole and Speaker Newt Gingrich were believed to be responsible
for initially slowing the line-item veto's progress due to hesitance to
give the new power to President Clinton, as well as other issues regarding the choice of conferees, especially in the Senate.[106] By spring
1996, however, Dole pushed for a compromise among fellow Republicans regarding the conference report. The important issue of when
the bill would take effect (before or after Clinton's first term) was also
left to Dole and Gingrich.[107] Differences between the chambers on the
Line–Item Veto Act are highlighted in Table 6.5.

The conference committee also specifically addressed the balance-of-
power question that had been so prevalent in the act's legislative history.

The conferees note that while the conference report delegates new powers
to the President, these powers are narrowly defined and provided within
specific limits. The conference report includes specific definitions, carefully
delineates the President's cancellation authority, and provides specific limits
on this cancellation authority. The delegation of this cancellation authority
is not separable from the President's duties to comply with these restrictions. To the extent the President broadly applies this new cancellation
authority or reaches beyond these limits to expand the application of this
new authority, the President will be reaching beyond the delegation of
these authorities. Given the significance of this delegation, the conference
report includes a sunset of this authority.[108]

Within a week of receiving the conference report, both chambers

Table 6.5: Conference Report for the Line–Item Veto Act—Comparison of House and Senate Positions on Major Issues

Issue	House	Senate	Conference
Form of item veto	Enhanced rescission	Separate enrollment	House version
New direct spending and/or targeted tax breaks open to veto	Targeted tax breaks included for 100 or fewer taxpayers	Both included without limits	House version plus new dir. spending
Cong. disapproval of presidential action necessary to stop veto	2/3	2/3	2/3
Sunset provision	None	5 years for bill; 10 for tax changes	7 years
Fast-track judicial review and severability	Expedited review only	Both included	Expedited review only

Source: House Report 104-491, to accompany S. 4, March 21, 1996, 16–42.

approved it (in the House in tandem with a debt-limit extension, similar to the way the GRH reforms were approved). This quick agreement reflected the new bill's compromise between the enhanced rescission approach of the House and the broader coverage of eligible items from the Senate. The Senate passed the conference report by a margin of 69 to 31, after a 58 to 42 vote to kill Senator Byrd's motion to recommit the measure to the conference committee with instructions to substitute the bill with S. 14, the expedited rescission proposal. The House passed the report by a margin of 232 to 177, with almost no floor statements. In both chambers, the votes were along party lines, with nearly complete party unity within the Republicans and Democrats in the House.[109]

In contrast to such clear party differences seen in this bill and the entire legislative history of the line-item veto, on the Senate floor once again, institutional self-consciousness dominated the arguments of both sides. This theme was evident in Senator Domenici's remarks when he commended Senator Stevens's hard work in support of the bill and then explained his own position, especially regarding the need for a sunset provision on the bill to help Congress evaluate the president's use of the veto power.

Obviously, there is no Senator here who is more dedicated to our prerogatives as a Senate and our prerogatives as individual Senators, and there is no Senator more concerned about maintaining that power [than Senator Stevens]. . . . I think the objectives of this legislation are correct. We should enact legislation that facilitates our ability to extract lower priority spending from legislation and to devote that to deficit reduction. However, I share the concerns of others about this bill's impact on the balance of power between the legislature and executive branch.[110]

Senator Hatfield still disagreed with the premise of the reform: "Call it by any other name, it is still a transfer of power and an enhancement of power in the hands of the President. I think it is a sad commentary on the responsibility and the history and the constitutional duties of the U.S. Congress to say to the President, 'We don't have the capability to exercise this, so we're going to dump it in your lap.'"[111] And, notably, future majority leader Senator Trent Lott (R-MS) defended the transfer: "I am in the Congress. I guess I should be jealous of ceding authority to the President, but I really do feel the President should have this authority. We can only have one Commander in Chief at a time. He is the ultimate authority. He should have the ability to go inside a bill and knock out things that are not justified, that have not been sufficiently considered, that cost too much—whatever reason—without having to veto the whole bill."[112]

Clinton signed P.L. 104-130 on April 9, 1996, and it became effective January 1, 1997.

Major Provisions of the 1996 Act

Two crucial themes are evident in the line–item veto conference report. First, the line-item veto was meant to be an important response to public dissatisfaction with federal budgeting practices and wasteful spending: "the American people consistently cite run-away federal spending and a rising national debt as among the top issues of national concern."[113] Although the report authors acknowledge potential savings from this legislation could not by itself eliminate the deficit, supporters had long asserted that an accumulation of savings from small items could be significant over a several-year period. The second principle, related to the first, is that much of the responsibility for the wasteful spending the item veto would target is Congress's. The report states that the purpose of the legislation "is to promote savings by placing the onus on Congress to overturn the President's cancellations of spending and limited tax benefits."[114] This new onus on Congress partially mitigates the one supporters have long argued the president bears—to sign a bill that includes wasteful spending or to veto the entire bill.

As the legislative history shows, the fragmented structures of Congress and related incentives of members to add pork-barrel projects almost unnoticed have long been behind the drive for the item veto in its various guises. But it was the strong anti-Congress sentiment that seems to have driven the victorious version of the bill, which ensured that any presidential rescission could be upheld by only one-third plus one of either the House or the Senate. The most majority-friendly item veto alternative, known as expedited rescission, was explicitly rejected at the last minute in the Senate.

This powerful, Republican-led anti-Congress sentiment overcame the most often repeated arguments against the item veto. While opponents did not deny Congress engages in pork-barrel practices, they argued an item veto would not shrink the deficit substantially, could be used to extort votes from members, and inflated the powers of the president, who had his own targeted constituencies to please. Furthermore, Congress had demonstrated its capacity to approve presidential rescission requests while adding its own through the 1974 processes. Granted, Congress did not always agree with the president's requests, but that is how members can protect their districts, through checks and balances. And Congress had used the 1974 process to rescind more money than the presidents even proposed.

How the Item Veto Worked

Under P.L. 104-130, the president could cancel in whole any dollar amount of discretionary spending, any item of new direct spending, or any limited tax benefit if he determines that such a cancellation will reduce the Federal budget deficit, not impair any essential Government functions, and not harm the national interest. In making the decision of what to cut the president shall consider the "legislative history, construction, and purpose of the law . . . and consider any specific sources of information referenced by such law."[115] The savings would be "lockboxed" into deficit reduction, and these cancellations would take place after an appropriations bill is signed.

In addition, the president must notify the Congress in a special message within five calendar days (excluding Sundays) of the law's enactment detailing the cut items. The special message must specify: the dollar amount canceled; the reasons for the cancellation; the estimated fiscal, economic, and budgetary effects of the cancellation; issues and estimated impact related to the cancellation in light of the purpose and programs for which the original spending was provided; and the adjustment to the discretionary spending caps current at the time. In the case of cancellation of new discretionary budget authority or new direct spending, the special message shall also include: the account and specific project or governmental function involved; the specific states and congressional districts affected by the cancellation; and the total number of cancellations imposed during the current session of Congress on these above states and congressional districts.[116]

The president's cancellation would be in effect until a disapproval bill was enacted into law. The special message detailing the cuts would be referred to both chambers' budget committees, as well as the relevant substantive committees. Under specified expedited procedures, the entire time allowed for congressional review is thirty days beginning on the day the Congress receives the special message. A disapproval bill must be introduced no later than five days after the thirty-day period begins. In the House, the law mandates that the referred committee report the bill within seven days of receiving it with or without recommendation but without amendment. Failing to report the disapproval bill could result in a highly privileged discharge motion by a supporter of the disapproval. The bill would then be considered by the Committee of the Whole in a general debate not to exceed one hour without extraneous debate and equally divided between supporters and opponents of the disapproval.

Amendments striking various parts of the disapproval bill shall be in order only if there are fifty members in agreement and, at most, an hour may be allotted for debate over this amendment.[117]

Consideration for the disapproval bill in the Senate must also begin with the committee(s) in charge of the disapproval bill reporting the measure within seven days or the committee shall be automatically discharged from considering the bill. When the Senate receives the House's disapproval bill, the bill would go right on the calendar instead of to a committee. On the floor, the only amendment that would be in order would strike an item from the disapproval bill or include an item that was included in the president's message but not in the disapproval. These rules can only be suspended with a three-fifths vote. Debate on the disapproval bill is limited to ten hours equally divided between the majority and minority leaders and their designees and an additional five hours of debate is possible. Amendments are limited to an hour of debate and no motion to recommit the bill would be in order (the rules restrict debate and amendment time if the House disapproval bill is on the floor). In case of a conflict, a conference committee must be named and convened "promptly" and each chamber given limited times for debate (one hour in the House, four in the Senate), and neither can vote to recommit the conference report.[118]

As was the case in GRH I, an expedited judicial review procedure was included in the act that said that any member of Congress or any individual adversely affected by the act "may bring an action . . . for declaratory judgment and injunctive relief on the ground that any provision of this part violates the Constitution." An appeal from the District Court for the District of Columbia, named as the court for such suits, shall go right to the Supreme Court. "It shall be the duty" of both courts to expedite the matters.[119]

Finally, the act created an incentive for President Clinton if he wished to wield the power in his current term. The act allowed the item-veto power to take effect on the day after a law entitled "An Act to provide for a seven-year plan for deficit reduction and achieve a balanced Federal budget" was passed or January 1, 1997, whichever came first. Either way, the line-item veto would sunset on January 1, 2005.[120]

Clinton v. City of New York

The first Supreme Court decision handed down in connection with the 1996 Line–Item Veto Act was *Raines v. Byrd*, which was first filed in U.S. District Court by Senator Robert Byrd and five other members of Congress the day after the item veto became effective. The lower court held the members had sufficient standing to file the suit, even though President Clinton had not yet used the power, because they were in a position of "unanticipated and unwelcome subservience to the President before and after their votes on appropriations bills."[121] The District Court granted summary judgment, and U.S. District Judge Thomas Penfield Jackson held that the act violated the presentment clause of Article I, section 7, clause 2, and constituted an unconstitutional delegation of legislative power to the president.[122] On appeal from the District Court, the Supreme Court disagreed and said the members of Congress lacked standing to bring the suit because there was no particularized, concrete, and otherwise judicially cognizable injury "and [because] their claim is based on a loss of political power, not loss of something to which they are personally entitled."[123]

The following term, two cases claiming specific injury under the 1996 act were filed after President Clinton utilized his new rescission authority, and the Congress did not pass a disapproval bill for either action. One suit was filed by the City of New York (along with two hospital associations, one hospital, and two unions representing health care employees) and the other by the Snake River farmers' cooperative and one of its members.[124] The District Court consolidated the cases, determined that at least one of the plaintiffs in each case had standing, and again ruled that the act's rescission procedures violated the presentment clause. The Supreme Court quickly took the case under the expedited review requirements of the act and affirmed the lower court decision.[125]

Justice Stevens delivered the opinion of the Court and was joined by Chief Justice Rehnquist, Justices Souter, Thomas, and Ginsburg, and Kennedy in part. Stevens argued that, in "both legal and practical effect, the President has amended two Acts of Congress by repealing a portion of each." And according to *INS v. Chadha*, "repeal of statutes, no less than enactment, must conform with Art. I."[126] According to Stevens, two major differences between the president's constitutional ability to return a bill under his veto power and the cancellation authority under the 1996 act were, first, that the constitutional return of a bill takes place before the bill becomes law, whereas the item-veto cancellation takes place afterward, and second, the constitutional veto power entailed a whole bill while the item veto entails only a part. Justice Stevens was not persuaded by the government's contention that the item veto was a similar power to the president's impoundment powers, which enable him to decline to spend appropriated funds. He argued that the critical difference between these powers is that impoundment does not allow the president to change the "duly enacted" text of statutes, whereas the item veto does.[127]

Justice Stevens concluded by emphasizing three other points. First, the Court did not express an opinion on the "wisdom" of the item-veto procedures. Acknowledging the long legislative history of the act, as well as its support by many people of both parties and in both the legislative and executive branches, Stevens added that the Court did not "lightly" conclude that the act is unconstitutional. Second, the Court did not consider the District Court's holding that the act "impermissibly disrupts the balance of powers among the three branches of government," even though that issue was raised by the appellants, because the only constitutional question the Court need decide is the "narrow" issue of the legislative procedures altered by the act. Third, a constitutional amendment is the only permissible way for the president's role in the legislative process to be changed.[128]

Although delegation issues related to the item veto were raised more thoroughly by other justices, they were still found to be relatively inconsequential overall. In Part III of Justice Scalia's part-concurring and part-dissenting opinion, which Justices O'Connor and Breyer joined, he argued the item veto did not violate the presentment clause. On the contrary, the presentment requirements had been satisfied prior to the president's use of the line–item veto power. Although the more relevant constitutional question of the act surrounds the nondelegation doctrine, Scalia found that the actual delegation of power in the act was insufficient for the item veto to be disallowed on this ground. The item veto may have been technically different from traditional presidential spending discretion, but it was essentially an equivalent power transfer from Congress: "Insofar as the degree of political, 'lawmaking' power conferred upon the Executive is concerned, there is not a dime's worth of difference between Congress's authorizing the President to cancel a spending item, and Congress's authorizing money to be spent on a particular item at the President's discretion. And the latter has been done since the Founding of the Nation."[129]

Justice Breyer also explained why he did not think that the Line–Item Veto Act violated either the presentment clause or any separation of powers principles. Specifically, he found the act did not give the president "non-Executive power," nor did it give the president the power to "encroach" upon Congress's constitutional territory in a way that violated the nondelegation doctrine. In other words, the act did not conflict with any significant separation of powers objective. Breyer argued the act maintained separation between the branches by allowing Congress to disapprove the president's actions and, as Scalia agreed, was really a kind of spending power long-given to presidents under their executive authorities. And the Congress was delegating to an elected official rather than someone more hidden from the voters as they assess the consequences of the act.

> In sum, I recognize that the Act before us is novel. In a sense, it skirts a constitutional edge. But that edge has to do with means, not ends. The means chosen do not amount literally to the enactment, repeal, or amendment of a law. Nor, for that matter, do they amount literally to the "line item veto" that the Act's title announces. Those means do not violate any basic Separation of Powers principle. They do not improperly shift the constitutionally foreseen balance of power from Congress to the President. Nor . . . do they threaten the liberties of individual citizens. They represent an experiment that may, or may not, help representative government work better. The Constitution, in my view, authorizes Congress and the President to try novel methods in this way.[130]

Conclusions on the Line–Item Veto Act

Even if the Line–Item Veto Act was an "insincere" reform, a mere symbolic gesture, and/or a presumptively unconstitutional alteration to the legislative process, it still deserves to be taken seriously in light of the pattern of delegation that preceded it. As the background of the act conforms to patterns and arguments laid out in earlier decades, the item veto is an important component to understanding Congress's self-diagnosis of its capacity to budget. Although it was held unconstitutional by the Supreme Court two years after its enactment, the legacy of the item veto seems to be a deep disgust with the way Congress conducts legislative business.

Strategy and Reform

As in 1985, 1987, and 1990, the majority party did not pursue a "principal-agent" strategy in the Line–Item Veto Act of 1996. In each case, the ultimate choice of agent and ability to override executive actions were among the least amenable to congressional majority power among the viable alternatives debated in committees and on the floors. Even if Congress enacted these reforms because they could deliver the substantive outcome of deficit reduction, not because they were most likely to heed the principals' wishes, why couldn't Congress achieve these ends with delegations to internal agents? In other words, even if Congress does have a pork-barreling tendency, perhaps it could retain power while also addressing the problem.

This question arose in 1973 when Arthur Burns (then chairman of the Federal Reserve Board of Governors) testified before the Joint Study Committee investigating reforms of the federal budget process and the president's impoundment powers.

SEN. BENNETT (R-UT): Suppose we give the Budget Committee in each House, or possibly consider a Joint Budget Committee, and give them an item veto before the bill finally goes to the President. Force them to review each bill and give them an opportunity to recommend a change to the Congress which would bring the bill back in line, with the idea that by a two-thirds majority they could be overridden before the bill goes to the President. That would put another layer of review and strengthen the powers of the Congress to control itself.

DR. BURNS: . . . If the Congress were willing to entrust the kind of power that you suggested to a committee of its own and then if the Congress were further willing, in order to protect itself, to require a two-thirds vote to override that committee, that might make for greater efficiency. But I am not sure the Congress is psychologically prepared at this time to entrust that much power to one of its committees.[131]

In the mid-1970s, Congress was concerned with both reining in the president and democratizing its internal processes. In the 1980s and 1990s, Congress seemed to be far more concerned with just reining itself in. After decades of deficit-related anti-Congress rhetoric and the specific promise of the 1994 Contract with America, it is reasonable to assume members of both parties, particularly Republicans, who drove the reform effort, supported an item veto because they believed their constituencies would reward such a step toward budget control. Despite the persistence of divided government, the fact that the president already had rescission power, and the acknowledgment even by supporters of the reform that it would not substantially impact annual deficits, the lure of this symbolic reduction was broad and deep. But that does not mean the behavior of members and leaders made strategic sense.

If institutional power is necessary to fundamentally protect the delivery of goods and services to home districts via individual legislator power, the item veto is very curious from a strategic perspective, as discussed by Patrick J. Fett and Jeffrey S. Hill:

If the line-item veto allows presidents to eliminate special tax exemptions or special expenditures, then it will increase the president's ability to control the formation of supporting coalitions on other proposals. By threatening to veto the side deals on which a coalition is based, the president can prevent the passage of policy he opposes. If eliminating the side deals prevents the creation of the coalition, then the policy opposed by the president will fail. In this way, the president's ability to control the legislative agenda is vastly increased. As long as his opponents cannot muster the two-thirds majority to override, a minority party president who is poor and unpopular would have significant bargaining power.[132]

Against this assumption, supporters of the item veto argued that Congress would still retain significant powers to retaliate against a president that used the veto power to extort support for his positions from members, and the final version of the reform included a sunset provision. In the end, the policy results and constituency rewards for deficit and spending control likely controlled the assumed risks of power loss for members. Perhaps the likelihood of a member's project being cut was small and perhaps it was a foregone conclusion that the federal courts would knock it down. Granting these points, there are still more fundamental issues at stake.

Institutional Self-Diagnosis and Reform

Even short-lived, gimmicky delegations can highlight deep institutional problems, and the line-item veto is a case in point. In over a century of debate on the line-item veto, supporters consistently cited inherent problems with congressional budgeting related to pork-barreling, log-rolling, and fragmented budget processes. While these challenges are arguably sewn into the procedures and norms of Congress because they give individual members representative power, anti-Congress sentiment among members was steadily high through the 1980s and 1990s, as measured by support for delegation movements. This vocal institutional criticism gave the final push to reforms designed to legislate the widely held, and quite possibly erroneous, belief that Congress alone is driven by parochial concerns leading to unbalanced budgets.

Like the two GRH laws in 1985 and 1987, as well as the 1990 Budget Enforcement Act, the item veto was grounded in the notion that the congressional budget process begun in the mid-1970s had failed to control federal spending. As these case studies show, the favored solutions to this problem, as articulated by members, leaders, and presidents of both parties, largely entailed delegating important aspects of congressional spending power to automatic processes and outside institutions. In this vein, the line-item veto is an example of the congressional majority of one party allowing a president of the other party to gain potentially significant leverage in the legislative process over individual members and coalitions. And also like the earlier cases, Congress did not choose the version of the reform that was most likely to preserve congressional prerogatives. Although Congress did not seriously pursue an amendment-based item veto, the House chose the enhanced rescission alternative and the Senate chose separate enrollment, both of which required a congressional supermajority to override the president's will.

Is the problem that Congress really cannot control its spending because it is unwilling to do so? Or is this "problem" actually an outgrowth of the extraordinary legislative power granted to the institution and its members to further their representation of individual districts? Proponents of the item veto persistently maintained that Congress's budget processes are designed to accommodate members' particularistic spending interests at the expense of sound fiscal policy in the national interest. Only by the president's drawing attention to and forcing members to vote on suspect spending projects and tax expenditures can Congress determine whether or not the item is truly in the national interest. Simply burying these items in appropriations bills and forcing the president to sign or veto the entire bill encourages bad budgeting. Many members also expressed embarrassment over media attention to silly-sounding federal spending projects, like a Lawrence Welk museum, that were buried in large budget bills and harmed Congress's public image when found.

Opponents of the item veto also argued in largely institutional terms, emphasizing the protection of congressional spending and representative prerogatives, as well as the separation of powers design. Many opponents acknowledged the perceived problems with congressional budgeting but argued that ceding such powers to the president could put individual members' projects at risk if they did not vote favorably on other presidentially supported issues. Not only did these members argue that an item veto was a poor institutional move, but also that presidents are not necessarily better than Congresses at budgeting responsibly in the first place. In addition, presidents have ample political and partisan incentives (such as garnering Electoral College votes as well as helping or thwarting the reelection of certain members of Congress) to spend or withhold federal dollars in specific regions and interests despite the stereotype of being elected by "the nation." Finally, some outside experts argued that there are major institutional differences between state governments and the federal government, which should discourage applying a typical governor's powers to the president.[133]

All this is not to say that Congress is never institutionally protective, nor that partisan strategies have little to do with budgetary reform. At the same time that the existence of divided government makes all these episodes of delegation curious, it is important to consider whether these delegations were a reflection of the need for Congress to negotiate with an opposition president to resolve budgetary conflicts. In addition, the longtime Republican support of the item veto may be traced to the frustrations of a minority party eager to shore up the powers of Presidents Reagan and Bush or to the aspirations of a majority party hoping to give power to Dole after 1996. The year of delays between the chambers' passing their versions and the vote on the conference report was presumed to be due to Dole and Gingrich's hesitation to give President Clinton the item-veto power.

And, as was said earlier, Congress is actually more ambivalent about its powers than these reforms might lead us to believe—delegation on paper does not mean abdication in subsequent budget battles. The distinction is made clearer by the actual use of the item veto by President Clinton and congressional reaction to it. In the short period of time Clinton had the item veto, he successfully rescinded almost $600 million, which is a small fraction of total appropriations over a multiyear period. Despite the supermajority requirement and other restrictions on disapproval legislation, Congress in 1997 successfully overrode one of the cancellation packages and the administration retreated on another, after getting a lot of criticism for its actions. The rescission package Congress disallowed entailed thirty-eight military construction projects, which Clinton estimated would save around $290 million over five years. After hearings in the Senate Appropriations Committee featuring three branches of the military, a bipartisan supermajority passed the disapproval bill and overrode Clinton's veto of it. After congressional outrage on a separate cancellation involving the federal retirement system, the administration backed down.[134]

Louis Fisher's description and analysis of these incidents and Clinton's relatively modest attempts to use the item veto on eligible tax benefits shed light on the so-called national interest the president brings to the budget process. Following is Clinton's response (as quoted by Fisher) to a reporter's question about why he only used the item veto to eliminate 2 of 79 possible tax breaks affecting the requisite one hundred taxpayers or fewer: "Well, it's certainly the definition of a special interest group, but not all special interests are always in conflict with the general interest. If that were true, our country would not have survived for over 200 years." Fisher's response summarizes the commonly held differences on how the perceived vices of one branch can be assumed to be the virtues of another.

Put another way, a limited tax benefit is a special interest if a legislator wants it and a matter of general interest if the president wants it. While it is true that Clinton made modest use of cancellation authority, the political impact of the statute was not modest. Far more damaging to the legislative prerogatives was the message that Congress sent in enacting this law: "We are irresponsible and unable to control ourselves. We need to depend on the president to protect the national interest." The abdication of spirit and institutional self-respect was much greater than the transfer of statutory authority.[135]

But in contrast to Fisher, I characterize the line–item veto case as one of institutional ambivalence rather than abdication. Such ambivalence was dramatically demonstrated by the 104th Congress. After gaining power in 1995, the Republican-dominated Congress twice shut the government down in protest of Democratic President Bill Clinton's budget priorities yet also advocated the reduction of its institutional powers arsenal with the balanced budget amendment and line-item veto. One can argue both sets of actions were toward the same end of deficit reduction, but members were unsure whether Congress's legislative prerogatives were the problem or the solution.

UNDERSTANDING DELEGATION OF POWER

Twenty years have transpired since [the 1974] act was passed and the tenor of the debate has shifted dramatically. We have gone from a sense of urgency to restrict an imperial President to a sense that the President needs to restrict, if not an imperial Congress, at least a spendthrift one.

—*Senator William Cohen, (R-ME) 1995[1]*

In the 1980s and 1990s, the policy problem of the deficit became fodder for a Republican-led attack on Congress as the symbol of an irresponsible federal government. Even though presidents put their own spending and taxation pressures on the federal budget, they often blamed Congress for unpopular fiscal policies, and the public appeared to agree. Congress became the center of debate over the causes of, and solutions to, imbalanced budgets as members and leaders engaged in a range of curious public behaviors from diffidence to outright self-flagellation, even under conditions of divided government. Such rhetoric and action undoubtedly reflected short-term electoral and policy goals but more deeply served to highlight, if not resolve, the core budgetary challenges faced by the nation surrounding how to reconcile local spending demands with a national consensus against large amounts of deficit spending. In the past two decades, Congress was viewed as a collection of greedy "special interests," while presidents were assumed to be protectors of the "national interest." Regardless of whether recent decades of Congress-bashing originated with members' and challengers' anti-government philosophies, weak congressional leaders, or dissatisfaction in the electorate, its results contributed to the success of delegation-based reform movements that continued to threaten Congress's place in the separation of powers system, already much reduced throughout the twentieth century.

While certain kinds of process reform may promote temporary spending restraint and reconciliation of revenues and appropriations, they cannot replace the fiscal and political reality that should be faced equally by Congress, the president, and the public: we want more than we wish to pay for. Delegation of Congress's budgeting power to automatic processes and the president will not resolve this fundamental challenge to the nation's fiscal policies, and such power shifts can harm broader constitutional values intertwined with representation, such as deliberation and power balance. In these ways, a new look at the delegation question is needed because recent rational choice–based explanations do not deeply question the significance of this institutional trend. These approaches emphasize delegation's electoral and policy benefits to members and majority parties but not the larger possibility of how representation and legislative goals can be severely harmed at the same time. Delegation can rob Congress of its most fundamental responsibility: deliberation over important ideas from a variety of perspectives. Our federal system was based in part on the notion that intra- and interbranch conflict mitigates the most pervasive problems in democracy—aggressive interests that want quick satisfaction of policy agendas. As we continue to demand more government services while avoiding taxation as much as possible, perhaps the public, educative struggle to reconcile our desires is as important to our nation's health as the goal of balanced budgets in any one year.

Even so, recent episodes of delegation can be seen on a continuum of constitutional and fiscal responsibility. Extremely automatic mechanisms meant to dictate balanced budgets and/or cut programs across-the-board at the expense of simple majority control and extended debate, such as both Gramm-Rudman-Hollings reforms and various balanced budget amendment proposals, can be dangerous to both the president's and Congress's representative roles as well as the nation's fiscal health. The line-item veto proved to be a relatively harmless short-lived experiment, but one that could have been a serious threat to legislative power on the member and institutional levels even as its supporters conceded it would have little impact on deficit reduction in the first place. The rules and spending caps put into place by the 1990 Budget Enforcement Act can be deemed a fiscal success, as they helped eliminate the deficit within the decade, but such accomplishments would not have happened without the economic boom and tough political choices by Presidents George H. W. Bush and Bill Clinton, as well as the slim majorities that signed on to the budget deal of that year and in 1993 and 1997. Although Congress's powers were still explicitly under attack in the 1990 reform, and the reform disadvantaged the Congress relative to the executive branch, representation and accountability were still preserved more than under GRH. Of course, Congress's staunchest defenders would say the complex process built in 1974—which provided low deficits and an overdue blow to the imperial presidency—proved to be the best of both worlds, at least temporarily.

Is Process the Fundamental Problem?

Although perceived and real fiscal problems are not necessarily tied to structure, it is reasonable to assume that executives are inherently better at budgeting than legislatures for several basic reasons. Legislatures and executives are organized in very different ways that impact accountability and efficiency. Legislatures are usually decentralized and collegial and often need to tolerate the minority party, while executive branches are usually hierarchical, unitary, and peopled with relatively like-minded appointees. In part due to these differences, most western countries have almost complete executive-dominated budgeting, as do our states to a lesser degree. Congress has long wondered whether its structures harm fiscal responsibility, and, along these lines, the Joint Study Committee on Budget Control organized prior to the 1974 Congressional Budget Act explored the correlation between state fiscal stringency and governors' budgeting power. Arthur Burns, then chairman of the Board of Governors of the Federal Reserve System, testified that states have a greater tendency for a balanced budget because one or more of the following is true: a balanced budget is constitutionally mandated in the state (or at least is a consistently important issue in gubernatorial elections), the governor can exercise a line-item veto (as well as a pocket veto in states with short legislative sessions), and/or state laws mandate that new spending and revenue be matched. With these differences in mind between state legislatures and the national government, Representative Herman Schneebeli (R-PA) and Burns had this exchange:

SCHNEEBELI: . . . the State executive has more power generally in his budgetary controls than the Federal Executive, and State governments do a much better job in budgetary control. Doesn't it follow we should give our Executive a little more power in order to achieve the same results?

BURNS: It follows that we ought to think about that as one possibility among others. I would hope that a good answer can be found in other ways.

SCHNEEBELI: You also make a statement that Congress is better equipped than are State legislatures to play a strong role in fiscal policy. To what degree do you mean this?

BURNS: By that I mean that Members of Congress have by and large a greater knowledge about economic and fiscal problems than I believe members of our State legislatures have. Speaking in terms of averages, that is my impression. . . . They are on the job longer. This is their full-time job and they deal with these questions on a national level and in the process are better educated in a wide range of problems.[2]

In the 1974 act, Congress created and revised internal procedures and resources at the same time as it augmented institutional power, and it can do so again. Measured by deficit and debt at least, the Budget Act worked relatively well until early in the Reagan administration. In subsequent budget reforms, Republicans successfully made congressional power synonymous with an irresponsible process, even though both branches were responsible for the nation's fiscal problems. Despite the fact that recent delegation-based reforms have chipped away at many powers and prerogatives developed by the 1974 act, Congress still retains significant budget power potential with its information resources (the nonpartisan Congressional Budget Office), personal expertise (members, leaders, and staff of the budget, appropriations, taxation, and authorization committees), and constitutional accountability (every two years for the entire House and one-third of the Senate).

So while Congress's lawmaking processes are extremely untidy, even if in a principled way, both branches deserve responsibility when their representative and legislative powers create large deficits, and the public is culpable as well. Old and new deficit burdens can be traced to an unrealistic electorate that has little interest in paying for what it wants or naively goes along with seemingly painless tax and spending plans often promoted by presidents and presidential candidates. After the failure of the Gramm-Rudman-Hollings reform, former CBO Director Rudolph G. Penner made this point so well that it is worth quoting at length.

Whenever I examine the history of the process, I am struck by a profound paradox. Looking at the situation in the late nineteenth century and early twentieth century, before there was a presidential budget, the process looked incoherent and disorderly, but the outcome was highly disciplined. The budget was close to balance or in surplus unless there were very good reasons for a deficit. The budget process reforms of the early 1920s and 1970s were applauded by most public policy analysts and appeared to provide a more coherent approach to Administration and Congressional decision making. The addition of Gramm-Rudman was more controversial, but its supporters felt that it would provide extra discipline and quickly reinvigorate the old rule that budgets should be balanced. Yet, a process that appears orderly on paper has now led to extremely disorderly and dishonest results with only modest improvements in the deficit outlook, most of which, I would argue, occurred despite the budget process and not because of it. Unfortunately, I cannot easily explain this paradox. It is my strong hunch, however, that the fundamental problem is only tangentially related to process and has more to do with basic public attitudes toward spending and taxation. The nation has committed more resources to the public sector than taxpayers are willing to pay for.[3]

Majority leader George Mitchell (D-ME) echoed a similar sentiment when Congress was considering the Budget Enforcement Act, another process-based solution to the deficit problem: "nobody likes to pay taxes. As a result, in a legislative body, in a representative democracy, nobody likes to vote to raise taxes. It is equally true that nobody likes to see cuts in popular spending programs. And as a result, in a representative legislative body, nobody likes to vote to cut popular spending programs. But we all know that the reality we confront is that a budget deficit can be closed by one or both of two ways. We must either raise revenues or reduce spending, or do both."[4]

If Congress is at all responsible for helping the electorate confront these difficult budgetary choices, then delegation of power can indeed become irresponsible abdications of legislative duty, especially as automatic processes and executive power have not proven to be magic bullets in the deficit wars. Budget discipline should not mean disconnection between member and institutional ambition, which can lead to a further demise of Congress's role in countering the president as the centerpiece of public attention and policy formation. A vibrant separation of powers system is necessary to foster deliberation and accountability, although it could also result in neither at times. A step in the right direction can be educating citizens about the difficult decisions and sacrifices that are part of responsible budgeting, rather than artificially taking public voices out of the process, which has not proven to last for long anyway. Congress needs to remember, and articulate, the virtues of its unique organization and place in representative democracy. It is hard and messy to reconcile particular interests with the general interest. But the president often makes his case for helping certain areas, industries, and tax brackets, and the Congress should find its own voice to do the same, even if both require follow-up questions regarding how we can afford it all.

In these ways, Congress could do a much better job of explaining to citizens the real challenges, if not all the intricacies, of federal budget-making and the role of the chambers. Instead of bashing their own institution, already held in low esteem by the public, members and leaders of both parties can express the local-national tensions inherent in fragmented budget processes and pork-barreling but not necessarily make such criticism the basis for delegation of power. While it may be naive to think citizens would ever sacrifice a local bridge to help the nation balance its budget, at least members could defend themselves for being responsive to their constituents and (gently) explain the difficulties of delivering greater federal goods and services to the district, along with low taxes, broadened and/or new national entitlements, and a balanced budget too. And since it is possible that presidents can make grave fiscal miscalculations, with or without public mandates, institutional protectiveness can be in the interest of national fiscal policy and responsiveness.

Representation requires leadership for, not fear of, the electorate, which Congress displays more than the other branches. The executive and judicial branches do not suffer from widespread, public self-loathing, and thus, in contrast to the Congress, have not had a working philosophy of "restraint" since the dawn of the modern administrative state. When Congress repeatedly endures external allegations of obstruction and irresponsibility when it exercises its powers and prerogatives without adequately explaining or defending itself and then veers from utilizing its powers to institutional insecurity about its ability to legislate, it diminishes itself in the separation of powers system and can no longer function as a counterweight to the other branches' visions of what is best for the country. While presidents and federal courts have been accused of excessive arrogance at times, especially when making controversial decisions, Congress could still learn much about public institutional self-confidence from them.

The point of separation of powers and checks and balances is not just fighting for its own sake but a public hashing out of constitutional and political tensions through different institutional perspectives and behaviors: Congress deliberates through the representation of many local and ideologically mixed voices; the president has institutional "energy" and perhaps a national mandate, which public opinion polls may broaden or restrict between elections; and the federal courts reconcile the actions of these branches and the states with constitutional values sometimes separated from majority power. Today, Congress remains a potentially powerful institution for legislative ideas and interbranch oversight, but it does not get the institutional respect it deserves for its necessary role in the national government and too often and too easily steps aside when asked.

Ambivalence, not Abdication, for Now

At the same time that Congress has disadvantaged itself both formally and informally, in recent years it has investigated numerous executive scandals and utilized its oversight powers regarding the federal bureaucracy's interpretation and enforcement of law and, during the Clinton years especially, took many opportunities to criticize the president's policy agenda. In these and other ways, the contemporary Congress is riddled with institutional ambivalence. Despite the recent pattern of budgetary delegation emphasized here, in the 1980s we witnessed extraordinary inter-institutional clashes over the budget, in the 1990s we witnessed government shutdowns, and until the presidency of George W. Bush, executive budgets were often "dead on arrival" in Congress. Yet, Congress has paradoxically failed to champion its institution's prerogatives, even as it has simultaneously fought for particular spending and tax outcomes. In this way, the significance of recent budgetary history surrounds not only the balance of power between the Congress and president, but also the public, and often contradictory, struggles within Congress over what kind of institution it should be. And such struggles do not always make clear partisan sense.

As was said in chapter 6, such ambivalence was visible in the 104th Congress, which fought for and against its institutional budgeting powers, and is also seen in the repeated, if narrow, rejections of various balanced budget amendment and biennial budgeting proposals in the past decade. In addition, annual budget-cycle skirmishes between presidents and Congresses, even under unified government, as well as the media's gleeful exposure of various kinds of fine-print pork, indicate that members are still working hard to represent their constituents' interests. The fact that Congress has often found creative ways to circumvent its own deficit and spending ceilings may even be heartening to Congress's champions. While such contradictory behavior can indicate how institutions develop at cross-purposes due to overlapping individual and partisan strategies, such conflicts can also be recast as deeper dilemmas in representation and institutional place.

From budgets to wars, all of these pressures have made Congress's institutional defenders a small and sometimes inconsistent group. Democratic Senator Robert Byrd has long defended his method of representing West Virginia through the procurement of federal dollars and is arguably the most prominent current advocate of the prerogatives of the Congress as an institution. Former Republican Senator Mark Hatfield of Oregon, famous for preventing the necessary two-thirds of congressional support for the balanced-budget amendment to go to the states in 1995, long argued, contrary to common assumptions in his own party, that Congress often under-appropriated presidential budget requests and was *the more fiscally responsible branch* in the 1980s and 1990s. Along these lines, during the line–item veto debates, several members drew upon two decades of rescission data to show

how Congress peeled back more unnecessary federal spending than presidents asked for, all the while retaining institutional powers and choices the line-item veto would diminish. Over the decades, sometimes the partisan leaders of Congress held their noses during episodes of delegation to an opposition president, such as the Democratic House leadership in the mid-1980s, while at other times delegated with great fanfare, as seen when Robert Michel, Newt Gingrich, Bob Dole, and Trent Lott all said separately, while Clinton was in office, that presidents are inherently better at looking out for the national interest.

Although it may be difficult at times for both parties in Congress to take on the usually more popular president, it is far from clear in the nation's history whether the executive branch is inherently better at taking a national perspective on the budget or any other policy issue free from its own interest in satisfying narrow regional, economic, and ideological demands. In both branches, representation of constituents' diverse, and even maddeningly contradictory, desires requires politicians to express ideas, debate them, and, if deemed necessary, exercise institutional powers against other parts of government, even as all these actions can make the political system so messy and time-consuming that it becomes a frustrating distraction to problems at hand. Although policy controversies can be swept under the legislative rug through broad delegations of power, often they will resurface.

However, despite the dramatic return of high deficits in recent years, thus far process-based budgetary reforms have not gotten the same attention from the president and Congress that they did in the 1980s and 1990s. Unlike those decades, the current budget deficit has grown under conditions of unified government, which complicates the kinds of presidential finger-pointing used by former Presidents Reagan, Bush, and Clinton that contributed to Congress's past delegations of power to the executive and automatic processes. This current political and institutional awkwardness has been noted by commentators, such as George Will: "Republicans are swiftly forfeiting the perception that they are especially responsible stewards of government finances. It is surreal for a Republican President to submit a budget to a Republican-controlled Congress and have Republican legislators vow to remove the 'waste' that he has included and that they have hitherto funded."[5] Along these lines, both branches have shared budgetary criticism on a variety of issues recently, including new spending from the Heritage

Foundation on the right, Bush's tax-reduction policies from the Center on Budget and Policy Priorities on the left, and both aspects of fiscal policy from the centrist Concord Coalition.[6] In response, while constitutional amendment proposals to grant the president an item veto and force a balanced budget have not garnered the national attention they once did, the Congress and president have recently begun to consider different ways of reviving some of the expired Budget Enforcement Act's pay-as-you-go processes.

Of course, since September 11, 2001, the budget has often taken a lower place in media, public, and political agendas. But there are definite similarities between the war on the deficit in the 1980s and 1990s and the country's current war on terrorism at home and abroad: all have been waged at the expense of Congress's traditional prerogatives to debate and craft legislation, while the president is perceived as having a monopoly on "the nation's interest."

NOTES

Introduction

1. Joint Study Committee on Budget Control, *Improving Congressional Budget Control*, 93rd Cong., 1st sess., 7 March 1973, 110.
2. *Congressional Record*, 104th Cong., 1st sess., 1995, 141: S 4308.

1. Origins and Significance of Delegation of Power

1. Publius, *The Federalist Papers*, ed. Clinton Rossiter (New York: New American Library, 1961), 322.
2. Ibid., 359. The context of this quotation is Publius's defense of the structures and powers of the House of Representatives.
3. David R. Mayhew, *Congress: The Electoral Connection* (New Haven: Yale University Press, 1974).
4. See R. Kent Weaver, "The Politics of Blame Avoidance." *Journal of Public Policy* 6, no. 4 (1986): 371.
5. See Stephen R. Weissman, *A Culture of Deference: Congress's Failure of Leadership in Foreign Policy* (New York: Basic Books, 1995); and Gordon Silverstein, *Imbalance of Powers: Constitutional Interpretation and the Making of American Foreign Policy* (New York: Oxford University Press, 1997).
6. See Douglas R. Arnold, *The Logic of Congressional Action* (New Haven: Yale University Press, 1990).
7. See Charles H. Stewart III, *Budget Reform Politics: The Design of the Appropriations Process in the House of Representatives, 1865–1921* (New York: Cambridge University Press, 1989).
8. See Patrick J. Sellers, "Fiscal Consistency and Federal District Spending

225

in Congressional Elections," *American Journal of Political Science* 41, no. 3 (1997): 1024–41.

9. See Richard F. Fenno, *Home Style: House Members in Their Districts* (Boston: Little, Brown, 1978).

10. Mayhew, *Electoral Connection*, 145.

11. Kenneth R. Mayer and David T. Canon, *The Dysfunctional Congress? The Individual Root of an Institutional Dilemma* (Boulder, CO: Westview Press, 1999).

12. Allen D. Hertzke and Ronald M. Peters Jr., eds., *The Atomistic Congress: An Interpretation of Congressional Change* (Armonk, NY: M.E. Sharpe, 1992); Eric M. Uslander, *The Decline of Comity in Congress* (Ann Arbor: University of Michigan Press, 1993); and Barbara Sinclair, *Unorthodox Lawmaking: New Legislative Processes in the U.S. Congress* (Washington: CQ Press, 1997).

13. D. Roderick Kiewiet and Matthew D. McCubbins, *The Logic of Delegation: Congressional Parties and the Appropriations Process* (Chicago: University of Chicago Press, 1991).

14. Ibid., 170.

15. David Epstein and Sharyn O'Halloran, *Delegating Powers: A Transaction Cost Politics Approach to Policy Making under Separate Powers* (New York: Cambridge University Press, 2000).

16. Ibid., 5.

17. Ibid., 9.

18. Bruce I. Oppenheimer, "Abdicating Congressional Power: The Paradox of Republican Control," in *Congress Reconsidered*, 6th ed., ed. Lawrence C. Dodd and Bruce I. Oppenheimer (Washington: CQ Press, 1997).

19. Howard E. Shuman, *Politics and the Budget: The Struggle between the President and Congress*, 3rd ed. (Englewood Cliffs, NJ: Prentice Hall, 1992).

20. Louis Fisher, *Congressional Abdication on War & Spending* (College Station, TX: Texas A&M University Press, 2000).

21. Lawrence C. Dodd,. "Congress and the Cycles of Power," in *The Presidency and the Congress: A Shifting Balance of Power?*, ed. William S. Livingston, Lawrence C. Dodd, and Richard L. Schott (Austin: LBJ School of Public Affairs, 1979); and Lawrence C. Dodd, "Congress, the Constitution, and the Crisis of Legitimation," in *Congress Reconsidered*, 2nd ed., ed. Lawrence C. Dodd and Bruce I. Oppenheimer (Washington: CQ Press, 1981).

22. According to Dodd ("Cycles of Power" and "Crisis of Legitimation"), since national service would be a substantial burden in early American agrarian society and because most political issues were handled at the local and state levels, long-term service in Congress was presumed to be unusual and undesirable. In this context of weak ambition in the general membership, the fear was that a few careerist legislative leaders, specifically the presiding officers of the House and Senate, would grow extremely powerful and aggressively pursue institutional

prerogatives. This fear was partly based on the colonial experience with state legislatures described in Federalist 48. See also Woodrow Wilson, *Congressional Government* (1885; repr. New York: World Publishers, 1954), who lamented congressional dominance in the nineteenth century precisely because, he argued, Congress was too fragmented to effectively lead.

23. Samuel P. Huntington, "Congressional Reponses to the Twentieth Century," in *The Congress and America's Future*, 2nd ed., ed. David Truman (Englewood Cliffs, NJ: Prentice Hall, 1975).

24. James L. Sundquist, *Decline and Resurgence of Congress* (Washington: Brookings Institution, 1981).

25. Lawrence C. Dodd, "Congress and the Quest for Power," in *Congress Reconsidered*, ed. Lawrence C. Dodd and Bruce I. Oppenheimer, (New York: Praeger Publishers, 1977). For an alternative analysis of the institutional powers of committee government, see Joseph Cooper, *The Origins of the Standing Committees and the Development of the Modern House* (Houston: Rice University Press, 1970); and Joseph Cooper, *Congress and Its Committees* (New York: Garland Press, 1988) on how the specialization and policy expertise of committees can actually be counterweights to executive dominance.

26. Huntington, "Congressional Responses," 7.

27. Ibid.

28. Ibid., and Eric Schickler, *Disjointed Pluralism: Institutional Innovation and the Development of the U.S. Congress* (Princeton, NJ: Princeton University Press, 2001).

29. Sundquist, *Decline and Resurgence of Congress*.

30. Steven S. Smith and Gerald Gamm, "The Dynamics of Party Government in Congress," in *Congress Reconsidered*, ed. Lawrence C. Dodd and Bruce I. Oppenheimer, (Washington: CQ Press, 2001); and John H. Aldrich and David W. Rhode, "The Logic of Conditional Party Government: Revisiting the Electoral Connection," in *Congress Reconsidered*, ed. Lawrence C. Dodd and Bruce I. Oppenheimer (Washington: CQ Press, 2001).

31. Allen Schick, *Congress and Money: Budgeting, Spending, and Taxing* (Washington: Urban Institute, 1980).

32. See Joseph White and Aaron Wildavsky, *The Deficit and the Public Interest: The Search for Responsible Budgeting in the 1980s* (Berkeley: University of California Press / New York: Russell Sage Foundation, 1989) and Allen Schick, *The Capacity to Budget* (Washington: Urban Institute, 1990), among others.

33. John R. Hibbing and Elizabeth Theiss-Morse, *Congress as Public Enemy: Public Attitudes Toward American Political Instiututions* (New York: Cambridge University Press, 1995).

34. Dodd, "Quest for Power"; Dodd, "Cycles of Power"; and Lawrence C. Dodd, "The Rise of the Technocratic Congress: Congressional Reform in the

1970s," in *Remaking American Politics*, ed. Richard A. Harris and Sidney M. Milkis, (Boulder: Westview Press, 1989).

35. Nelson W. Polsby, "The Institutionalization of the House of Representatives," *American Political Science Review* 62 (1968): 144–68; Roger H. Davidson and Walter J. Oleszek, "Adaptation and Consolidation: Structural Innovation in the U.S. House of Representatives," *Legislative Studies Quarterly* 1 (1976): 37–65; Joseph Cooper, *Congress and Its Committees*; Sinclair, *Unorthodox Lawmaking*; David W. Rhode, *Parties and Leaders in the Postreform House* (Chicago: University of Chicago Press, 1991); and Elaine K. Swift, *The Making of an American Senate: Reconstitutive Change in Congress, 1789–1841* (Ann Arbor: University of Michigan Press, 1996).

36. Schickler, *Disjointed Pluralism*.

37. Sotirios A. Barber, *The Constitution and the Delegation of Congressional Power* (Chicago: University of Chicago Press, 1975).

38. Theodore J. Lowi, *The End of Liberalism: Ideology, Policy, and the Crisis of Public Authority* (New York: W.W. Norton, 1979); and David Schoenbrod, *Power Without Responsibility: How Congress Abuses the People through Delegation* (New Haven: Yale University Press, 1993).

39. Jeffrey K. Tulis, *The Rhetorical Presidency* (Princeton, NJ: Princeton University Press, 1987), and "The Politics of Deference," unpublished manuscript, 2004.

40. See Sarah Binder, "Congress, the Executive, and the Production of Public Policy: United We Govern?," in *Congress Reconsidered*, ed. Lawrence C. Dodd and Bruce I. Oppenheimer (Washington: CQ Press, 2001).

41. Clinton Rossiter, ed., *The Federalist Papers* (New York: Mentor/Penguin, 1961), 268.

42. Ibid., 342.

43. Hanna F. Pitkin, *The Concept of Representation* (Berkeley: University of California Press, 1967); and Joseph M. Bessette, *The Mild Voice of Reason: Deliberative Democracy and American National Government* (Chicago: University of Chicago Press, 1994).

44. Tulis, *Rhetorical Presidency*.

45. Fisher, *Congressional Abdication*, xiv.

2. Reforming the Reforms

1. Aaron Wildavsky, *The Politics of the Budgetary Process* (Boston: Little, Brown, 1964), 4.

2. These two pro-Congress episodes and their outcomes may also reflect related cyclical intra- and interbranch reform dynamics. See Dodd, "Quest for Power"; Dodd, "Cycles of Power"; and Dodd, "Rise of the Technocratic Congress."

3. Schickler, *Disjointed Pluralism*.

4. Dodd, "Cycles of Power"; and Dodd, "Rise of the Technocratic Congress."

5. This summary was compiled with information from the following sources, as well as others cited in the chapter: Louis Fisher, *Presidential Spending Power* (Princeton: Princeton University Press, 1975); Fisher, *Congressional Abdication*; James P. Pfiffner, *The President, the Budget, and Congress: Impoundment and the 1974 Budget Act* (Boulder, CO: Westview Press, 1979); Shuman, *Politics and the Budget*; Aaron Wildavsky and Naomi Caiden, *The New Politics of the Budgetary Process*, 3rd ed. (New York: Longman, 1997); and two congressional reports related to the consideration of the 1974 Congressional Budget and Impoundment Act, U.S. Congress, House Committee on Rules, *Budget and Impoundment Control Act of 1973*, 93rd Cong., 1st sess., 1973, H. Rept. 658 to accompany H.R. 1541, and Senate Committee on Governmental Affairs, *Federal Act to Control Expenditures and Establish National Priorities*, 93rd Cong., 1st sess., 1973, S. Rept. 579 to accompany S. 1541.

6. For a detailed history and additional citations related to this aspect of the appropriations committees' history, see Kiewiet and McCubbins, *Logic of Delegation*, 63–77; Stewart, *Budget Reform Politics*, chapters 3 and 4; and David Brady and Mark A. Morgan, "Reforming the Structure of the House Appropriations Process: The Effects of the 1885 and 1919–20 Reforms on Money Decisions," in *Congress: Structure and Policy*, ed. Matthew D. McCubbins and Terry Sullivan (New York: Cambridge University Press, 1987).

7. The 1905 act allowed agency heads to waive the apportionment requirements, and their extensive use of that provision prompted Congress to impose tighter restrictions in 1906. An amendment to these laws in 1950 strengthened the executive branch's power over agency apportionment. The amendment originated in 1947, when the Post Office spent all but one percent of its budget in the first three-quarters of the fiscal year, and threatened to stop delivering the mail without more funds (Fisher, *Presidential Spending Power*, 28 and 155). It is important to note that Nixon defended the legality of his impoundments partly through provisions of the 1950 amendment to the Anti-Deficiency Acts that allow for executive adjustment of agency funds for greater efficiency or altered requirements. For more on this issue, see chapter 3 on the background of the 1974 Congressional Budget and Impoundment Act.

8. Senate Committee, *Federal Act to Control Expenditures and Establish National Priorities*, 5.

9. Congress had sent a similar act to President Wilson in 1920, but he vetoed it because Congress could remove the new Comptroller General and his deputy through a concurrent resolution that did not require the president's signature. The 1921 act allowed for removal only by a joint resolution, initiated by Congress and requiring presidential approval (Fisher, *Presidential Spending Power*, 31–35).

10. See Sundquist, *Decline and Resurgence of Congress*, 39. Both the House and Senate gave more power to their appropriations committees, but the need for specialization, subsequent increases in subcommittee autonomy, and action on each appropriations bill as it was finished instead of the entire budget all reduced the centralization effort in practice (Fisher, *Presidential Spending Power*, 31–34, 36–37). See also Stewart, *Budget Reform Politics*, chapter 5.

11. See Fisher, *Presidential Spending Power*, 37.

12. See ibid., 44–46.

13. Sundquist points out that the money allocated in the Employment Act to the new CEA and Joint Economic Committee indicated their relative importance. The CEA received $345,000 for staff and member salaries, and the Joint Committee received $50,000 (*Decline and Resurgence of Congress*, 66). Nevertheless, Congress dominated fiscal policy after the 1946 act during divided government in the Truman years (69–74).

14. House Committee, *Budget and Impoundment Control Act of 1973*, 27.

15. Senate Committee, *Federal Act to Control Expenditures and Establish National Priorities*, 12. For more on the 1946 act, see also Avery Leiserson, "Coordination of Federal Budgetary and Appropriations Procedures Under the Legislative Reorganization Act of 1946," *National Tax Journal* 1, no. 2 (June 1948).

16. Schick, *Congress and Money*, 51.

17. Pfiffner, *President, the Budget, and Congress.*

18. Senate Committee, *Federal Act to Control Expenditures and Establish National Priorities*, 15.

19. See also James Savage, *Balanced Budgets & American Politics* (Ithaca, NY: Cornell University Press, 1988).

20. See Sondra Nixon, "Budget Amendments: An Idea that Never Goes Out of Style," *Congressional Quarterly Weekly Report* 53, no. 2 (14 January 1995).

21. See Andrew Taylor, "Senate Again One Vote Short; GOP Says House Will Act," *Congressional Quarterly Weekly Report* 55, no. 10 (8 March 1997): 577.

22. See Senate Committee on Judiciary, *Balanced-Budget Constitutional Amendment*, 105th Cong., 1st sess., 1997, S. Rept. 103-3, 7.

23. Ibid., 33.

24. Ibid., 54.

25. See Louis Fisher, "Annual Authorizations: Durable Roadblocks to Biennial Budgeting," *Public Budgeting and Finance* 27 and 38 (Spring 1983). Fisher points out that, although the 1974 act emphasized multiyear authorizations and planning, as the first budget resolution became more binding over the years, committees began to compete in order to have their programs included.

26. Meanwhile, in 1979, the State Department moved to a two-year authorization, and in 1988 the Coast Guard did the same. In 1981, the international affairs functions of the Treasury Department went to a permanent authorization,

and Congress also passed a two-year authorization for foreign assistance (Senate Committee on Rules and Administration, *Improving the Operations of the Legislative Branch of the Federal Government*, 103rd Cong., 2nd sess., 1994, S. Rept. 297, 11).

27. For more on the Study Group on Senate Practices and Procedures (Pearson-Ribicoff study) and Temporary Select Committee to study the Senate Committee System (also known as the Quayle Committee), see Senate Committee, *Improving the Operations of the Legislative Branch of the Federal Government*, 4.

28. Senate Committee on Energy and Natural Resources, *Great Smoky Mountains Wilderness Act*, 100th Cong., 2nd sess., 1988, S. Rept. 297, 5–6, 9.

29. House Committee on Rules, *Budget Responsibility and Efficiency Act of 2001*, 107th Cong., 1st sess., 2001, H. Rept. 200, Part 2, 5.

30. House Committee, *Budget Responsibility and Efficiency Act of 2001*, Part 2, 11. Although Byrd remains opposed to biennial budgeting, he pledged not to mount a filibuster against it, arguing that this proposal did not offend the Constitution in the same manner as the line-item veto and balanced-budget amendment. See Eric Pianin, "Biennial Budgeting Moves Closer to Reality," *Washington Post*, 23 February 2000, sec. A, p. 19.

31. Senate Committee, *Great Smoky Mountains Wilderness Act*, 10.

32. See Sinclair, *Unorthodox Lawmaking*.

33. House Committee, *Budget Responsibility and Efficiency Act of 2001*, 4.

34. Senate Committee on Governmental Affairs, *Activities of the Committee on Governmental Affairs*, 107th Cong., 1st sess., 2001, S. Rept. 20, 3.

35. Senate Committee, *Improving the Operations of the Legislative Branch of the Federal Government*, 7 and 9.

36. House Committee, *Budget Responsibility and Efficiency Act of 2001*, 2.

37. Senate Committee, *Improving the Operations of the Legislative Branch of the Federal Government*, 9. Kliman and Fisher also support multiyear authorizations for administrative planning while opposing biennial appropriations.

38. House Committee, *Budget Responsibility and Efficiency Act of 2001*, Part 2, 6.

39. Ibid., 42.

3. 1974 Budget Act

1. Joint Study Committee on Budget Control, *Improving Congressional Control over Budgeting Outlay and Receipt Totals, Interim Report*, 93rd Cong., 1st sess., 1973, H. Rept. 93–13, 2 (to be cited as "JSC Interim Report").

2. Hearings Joint Study Committee on Budget Control, *Improving Congressional Budget Control*, 93rd Cong., 1st sess., 7 March 1973, 108.

3. House Rules Committee, *Budget and Impoundment Control Act of 1973*, 93rd Cong., 1st sess., 1973, H. Rept. 93–658, 30.

4. Epstein and O'Halloran, *Delegating Powers.*

5. For criticism of the bill by both chambers' Democratic leaders, see *Congressional Record*, 92nd Cong., 2nd sess., 1972, 34612, 34591, and 34603, as cited in Sundquist, *Decline and Resurgance of Congress*, 3.

6. See Public Law 599, 92nd Cong., 2nd sess. (27 October 1972). The JSC was composed of mostly senior members of the revenue and appropriations committees in both chambers. It had thirty-two members—twenty-eight came from the House and Senate Appropriations, House Ways and Means, and Senate Finance Committees; four other members of the House and Senate were members-at-large; no members of either party's leadership were on the JSC; the co-chairmen were the ranking Democrats on the House Appropriations and Ways and Means Committees. The Joint Study Committee submitted two reports of its hearings, investigations, and recommendations regarding budget-process reforms. JSC Interim Report. *Recommendations for Improving Congressional Control over Budgetary Outlays and Receipt Totals*, 93rd Cong., 1st sess., 1973, H. Rept. 147 will be cited as "JSC Final Report."

7. Schick, *Congress and Money*, chapter 2; the following legislative history relies heavily on Schick, chapter 3.

8. Ibid., chapter 2. Between 1966 and 1972 consumer prices rose 3 to 6 percent and producer prices from 2 to 4 percent. In 1973 the rates were 8.8 and 11.8 percent, respectively, and in 1974 they were 12.2 and 18.3 percent (Shuman, *Politics and the Budget*, 215). For analysis of how congressional spending affected interest rates, the value of the dollar, inflation, and revenue needs see also Arthur Burns, Chairman, Board of Governors of the Federal Reserve System in testimony before the Joint Study Commission on Budget Control, *Improving Congressional Budget Control*, 93rd Cong., 1st sess., 7 March 1973, 21–27, and Representative John R. Rousselot in testimony before the Joint Study Commission on Budget Control, *Improving Congressional Budget Control*, 93rd Cong., 1st sess., 13 March 1973, 195.

9. The JSC Final Report explains "relatively uncontrollable" programs to be social insurance trust funds (old age and survivors insurance benefits, Medicare payments, and unemployment benefits) and nontrust fund programs (interest on the public debt, farm price support payments, veterans benefits, and public assistance), 12. See also Charles Schulze's testimony before the JSC, 18 January 1973.

10. The JSC Interim Report maintains that any "meaningful" overall spending and authority control must also apply to all such backdoor appropriations, 2. Although Congress ostensibly has control over the qualifications for these entitlements, the extent of their benefits, and the kinds of adjustments to make to compensate for inflation, Congress is well known to be hesitant to pare down or otherwise reduce these programs, as the most expensive have politically important constituents.

11. See JSC Final Report, 1, 8.

12. JSC Interim Report, 10.

13. For a detailed history of the use and legality of presidential impoundment, see James P. Pfiffner, *President, the Budget, and Congress*, chapters 3 and 4, and Fisher, *Presidential Spending Power*, chapters 7 and 8.

14. As chapter 5 discusses in greater detail, the line–item veto debates are closely related to controversy over presidential impoundment powers.

15. See Schick, *Congress and Money*, chapter 2.

16. See Shuman, *Politics and the Budget*, 223–26, and Fisher, *Presidential Spending Power*, 177–97, for details on some of the impoundment arguments related to HUD grants, water pollution funds, and farm programs.

17. In the Anti-Deficiency Act of 1905 and its amendments in 1906 and 1950, the president was given power to impound funds already appropriated to executive agencies for two main reasons: to prevent agency manipulation of Congress regarding supplemental funds to prevent agency shutdowns, even if the original funds were misused, and to adjust appropriations if agencies performed their tasks before the full budget cycle was complete. As discussed earlier, traditional congressional deference to presidential discretion on impoundments essentially evaporated during Nixon's broad interpretation of the 1950 amendments, allowing fund decreases for "changes in requirements," "greater efficiency of operations," or "other developments." This vague wording was changed in 1974 by clearly stating the conditions and kinds of presidential action and creating two kinds of congressional oversight of this executive power. See references to presidential documents related to impoundment defenses in Fisher, *Presidential Spending Power*, 158.

18. Joint Study Committee, *Improving Congressional Budget Control*, 6 March 1973, 25.

19. Ibid., 9 March 1973, 168.

20. The original impoundment control bill, H.R. 8480, was reported by Committee on Rules on 27 June 1973 (House Committee on Banking, Finance, and Urban Affairs, *Extension for the President's National Commission on Productivity Report*, 93rd Cong., 1st sess., 1973, H. Rept. 366). As incorporated into House Bill 7130, which ultimately became the foundation of the 1974 act, the impoundment provisions were made more permanent than they had been under H.R. 8480, the role of the Comptroller General in bringing suits to enforce the impoundment provisions was altered, and the spending limits in H.R. 8480 for Fiscal 1974 were excluded.

21. For more on the history of OMB, the confirmation controversy, and the results of Senate appointment involvement, see Fisher, *Presidential Spending Power*, 47–55, and Larry Berman, *The Office of Management and Budget and the Presidency, 1921–1979* (Princeton, NJ: Princeton University Press, 1979), 10–130.

22. Senate Committee, *Federal Act to Control Expenditures and Establish National Priorities*, 4.

23. William Moorhead, Joint Study Committee, *Improving Congressional Budget Control*, 6 March 1973, 82.

24. House Committee, *Budget and Impoundment Control Act of 1973*, 6.

25. *Weekly Compilation of Presidential Documents*, Vol. 8, 1498, cited in Schick, *Congress and Money*, 44.

26. Senate Committee on Finance, *Public Debt Limitation*, 92nd Cong., 2nd sess., 1972, S. Rept. 1292, 9. For earlier studies on the perceived need for reconciliation of spending and revenue prior to the 1974 act, see also JSC Interim Report, 4–10; Arthur Smithies, *The Budgetary Process in the United States* (New York: McGraw-Hill, 1955), Joseph P. Harris, *Congressional Control of Administration* (Washington: Brookings, 1964); John S. Saloma III, *The Responsible Use of Power: A Critical Analysis of the Congressional Budget Process* (Washington, American Enterprise Institute, 1964); Robert Ash Wallace, *Congressional Control of Federal Spending* (Detroit: Wayne State University Press, 1960); William A. Niskanen, *Structural Reform of the Federal Budget Process* (Washington, American Enterprise Institute, 1973).

27. For more details on fiscal 1974 outlays, see also JSC Interim Report, 7, 11–12, and JSC Final Report, 10.

28. This total included nineteen appropriation bills, fifty-two actions on legislative budget proposals, twenty-four actions on mandatory or backdoor legislation, fifty-six actions on authorizing legislation, and nine actions on revenues. In addition, there were eighty-two other actions that had a potential impact on the 1973 budget and/or subsequent fiscal years. See JSC Interim Report, 7, 11–12 and JSC Final Report, 10.

29. House Committee, *Budget and Impoundment Control Act*, 31.

30. Schick, *Congress and Money*, 16.

31. House Committee, *Budget and Impoundment Control Act*, 24–25.

32. Senate Report 92–1292, 8. For instance, in 1969, despite $8.4 billion in program reductions covered by the ceilings, Congress failed to meet the overall spending reduction of $6 billion because of growth in exempted programs. The overall actual savings was only $1.5 billion. Senate Committee on Finance, *Public Debt Limitation*, 8. The exemption issue arises again in the Gramm-Rudman-Hollings laws discussed in the next chapter.

33. JSC Final Report, 15–17.

34. As discussed earlier, backdoor spending is any kind of budget authority that is provided outside the Appropriations Committee, and it exists in borrowing authority, contract authority, and permanent appropriations. Borrowing authority is the ability of the Treasury and federal agencies and corporations to spend money borrowed from the public. For example, there is no limit on bor-

rowing from the Treasury and public to back up student loan guarantees. Contract authority is the authority granted to executive departments to enter into contracts that obligate the federal government to pay. Technically, the appropriations committees must subsequently pass bills to "liquidate" these obligations, but at that point there is little or no control over the original contract since the obligation must be met. Permanent appropriations are a kind of backdoor authority because these obligations exist by law but fluctuate in actual yearly appropriations and are not annually reviewed by all relevant committees. Examples of permanent appropriations are interest payments on the public debt, Social Security, general revenue sharing, and various kinds of public assistance. Some permanent authority, like Social Security, does not contribute to larger deficits in the long run because they are usually accompanied by tax increases. The JSC notes that the social security tax increases have actually helped mitigate annual deficits in the unified budget because of surpluses in the trust fund. See JSC Interim Report, 7–8, and JSC Final Report, 11–12.

35. JSC Final Report, 16–31.

36. Rivlin recommended reducing the number of stages, hearings, bills, presentations, and time allotted to the budget process, most of which is dedicated to debating small items and programs. For better congressional information, she argued a professional budget-analysis staff be installed. Rivlin also argued that a new budget-process calendar and three-year appropriations cycle would help Congress control future impacts of spending decisions and lessen time spent on reviewing programs each year. With multiyear commitments, the entire appropriations process could be further simplified with a combined authorization-appropriation process in a single committee, without the addition of the JSC's recommended budget committees: "It seems to me essential to reduce, not increase, the current complexity of the process." "Improving the Congressional Budget Process," Select Committee on Committees, Working Papers on House Committee Organization and Operation, June 1973, 5.

37. For instance, the Ways and Means and Finance Committees dominated in the legislation of entitlements, which were technically backdoor items. This prerogative of the tax committees was ultimately protected, except for new backdoor measures. However, the appropriations committees were granted their wish that authorization committees stop slowing down the annual budget process through a new rule mandating that authorizations take place in the fiscal year before they would take effect. See Schick, *Congress and Money*, 57, 59.

38. Schick, *Congress and Money*, 60–71; and Pfiffner, *President, the Budget, and Congress*, 134–35.

39. An additional assurance for rank-and-file members was a proposed rule mandating the entire House Budget Committee's membership to rotate, with no member serving more than four years in any ten-year period. The Rules Com-

mittee also recommended that party caucuses appoint all the members of the Budget Committee and that ten members, instead of fourteen, come from Appropriations and Ways and Means. In addition, the chairmanship would be open to non-Appropriations and non–Ways and Means members, and two positions would be held by representatives of each party's leadership. House Committee, *Budget and Impoundment Control Act of 1973*, 30.

40. Ibid., 30.

41. House Report, 93rd Cong., 2nd session, 93–652, accompanying House Resolution 715, 20.

42. Schick, *Congress and Money*, 65–66.

43. Hearings before the Senate Subcommittee on Budgeting, Management and Expenditures of the Government Operations Committee, 92nd Cong., 1st sess., 1973, 137–38.

44. Ibid., 9 April 1973, 171. Schulze argued that only a reconciliation process at the end of the legislative budget cycle could ensure that appropriations are in line with ceilings.

45. Ibid., 177.

46. See Hearing before the Senate Committee on Government Operations, 93rd Cong., 1st session, on S. 1214, 27 April 1973. This bill, introduced by Senators Ervin and Muskie, would require that each time an official or employee of a federal agency or department submits a budget request to the president or OMB, a copy must be submitted to the Senate and House. OMB Director Roy Ash testified against the bill.

47. Congress could exceed spending levels mandated by the budget resolutions, but the amounts could not be spent until Congress enacted specific "triggering" legislation, which could be considered only if the actual amounts to be spent were within the resolutions' guidelines. See Senate Committee, *Federal Act to Control Expenditures and Establish National Priorities*, 17–72.

48. For more on the composition and outcomes of the working group, see also Senate Committee on Rules and Administration, *Congressional Budget Act of 1974*, 93rd Cong., 2nd sess., 1974, S. Rept. 688, 2–3.

49. The SBC would be a "Category A" committee, meaning its members would only be allowed one other committee membership. Since the new SBC would mandate that its members resign another committee post starting in 1979 (changed to 1977 in the conference report), the report acknowledged that experienced members might be hard to recruit, Senate Committee, *Congressional Budget Act of 1974*, 7–9.

50. For details on the differences between S. 1541 as reported by the Goverment Operations Committee and the Rules Committee, see the comparative analysis in Appendix II, ibid.

51. An earlier version of impoundment control, S. 373, would have automatically stopped an impoundment, unless Congress approved the action within sixty days, whereas H.R. 8480 would have allowed the impoundment unless one chamber of Congress disapproved the action within sixty days. The compromise reached by the conferees designated that rescissions would follow the procedure of the Senate's bill and deferrals would follow the procedure of the House's bill. See Schick, *Congress and Money*, 71, and discussion of Title X in Senate Committee on Governmental Affairs, *Congressional Budget and Impoundment Control Act of 1974*, 93rd Cong., 2nd sess., 1974, S. Rept. 924. See also Consideration of House Committee on Rules, *Congressional Budget and Impoundment Control Act of 1974*, 93rd Cong., 2nd sess., 1974, H. Rept. 1101.

52. For remarks on the House floor and the vote, see *Congressional Record*, 93rd Cong., 2nd sess., 1974, 120, Pt. 15: 19671–98. For remarks on the Senate floor, see *Congressional Record*, 93rd Cong., 2nd sess., 1974, 120, Pt. 15: 20464–86 with the vote on 20500.

53. In the House, the vote breakdown was Democrats 224 to 4 (Northern Democrats 145 to 4 and Southern Democrats 79 to 0) and Republicans 177 to 2. In the Senate, the vote breakdown was Democrats 50 to 0 and Republicans 25 to 0. See *Congressional Quarterly Weekly Report* 32, no. 26 (22 June 1974): 1658 for the House vote and (29 June 1974): 1724 for the Senate Vote.

54. The contentious JSC proposal that each budget committee's membership come equally from that chamber's appropriations committee, revenue/tax committee, and the general membership was dropped, as was the requirement that the chairmanship of the two new committees alternate between the appropriations and revenue members only. The final changes were less uniform and restrictive than the JSC's recommendation and ensured that more interests in both chambers would be represented. This emphasis on breadth of interest was also reflected in requirements that all legislative committees with budget-related jurisdiction communicate regularly with the budget committees. But as Schick argues, broad participation may not have been an end in itself as much as it was the necessary means to galvanize institutional support for the outcomes of the new process, *Congress and Money*, 77.

55. Ibid., 73.

56. For details on these recommendations, see JSC Final Report, 5–7.

57. In 1975 the HBC was enlarged from twenty-three to twenty-five members. The extra members were chosen from the other House standing committees. HBC members are now allowed to serve a maximum of six years out of every ten. Other specific instructions from the act were that members could not serve on the HBC for more than two Congresses in any period of five and "all selections of Members to serve on the committee shall be made without regard to

Seniority. Public Law 344, 93rd Cong., 2nd sess. (12 July 1974), section 101, clause a. Schick notes that both the HBC and the SBC have been dominated by senior members despite this clause (*Congress and Money*, 87).

58. The SBC was initially sixteen members but was expanded to twenty by the 96th Congress. For more details on the first five years of the Budget Committee's membership distribution relating to geography, seniority, ideology, and committee representation, see Schick, *Congress and Money*, 86–95. For more details on the early education, socialization, and performance of the budget committees, see Schick, *Congress and Money*, 105–30.

59. Public Law 344, sections 101, clause 5, and sections 102, clause 2.

60. Schick, *Congress and Money*, 119–21.

61. Public Law 344, section 201 (a, 1). According to section b, the Director should appoint all CBO personnel according to the same guidelines.

62. Aaron Wildavsky, *The Politics of the Budgetary Process*, 4th ed. (Glenview, IL: Scott-Foresman, 1984), 143.

63. Public Law 344, section 202 (a–d).

64. The act authorized the Director to procure temporary (or intermittent) assistance from outside experts, consultants, and other organizations as needed. The Director was authorized to secure information, data, estimates, and statistics "which he determines to be necessary in the performance of his duties and functions" directly from executive agencies and departments, as well as from regulatory agencies and commissions in the government (except where disclosure would violate the law). The act also mandated that these agencies and departments cooperate with these requests and other service needs of the CBO and required the General Accounting Office, the Library of Congress, and Office of Technology Assessment to honor CBO information and services requests. Finally, the CBO was specifically mandated to obtain up-to-date computer capability, use the services of computer technology experts and consultants, and to create techniques for evaluating budget requirements using this technology. Public Law 344, sections 201 (c–e) and section 202 (g).

65. The act created a new fiscal year from October 1 to September 30. The old cycle, from July 1 to June 30, was criticized for consistently delaying nine out of the regular thirteen appropriations bills because of the time needs of the authorization process prior to the appropriations process.

66. Public Law 344, section 301 (a).

67. Ibid., section 301 (d). For details on debate and amendment rules after the first resolution has been reported by the budget committees and procedures for action on the conference reports, see section 305.

68. A minor provision in section 304 provided that a new concurrent resolution could be passed to revise spending in the operating fiscal year. This provision was used by Reagan, in addition to the reconciliation requirement, to revamp

the budget resolution already in effect in his first term. For more on the budget-process "revolution" of 1981, see Shuman, *Politics and the Budget*, 249–66.

69. Authorization bills are obligations for the federal government to contract, borrow, or spend immediately or in the future. Appropriations bills are the spending subset of the authorization process and can only be passed after authorization legislation is completed by the committee with jurisdiction over the specific legislative area.

70. However, as Shuman points out, if a committee is dictated to cut a large amount of money, and the discretion of the committee is limited for various reasons, committee control over which program(s) to cut is reduced (*Politics and the Budget*, 241).

71. Public Law 344, section 10.

72. Shuman, *Politics and the Budget*, 242.

73. Public Law 344, section 1001.

74. *Immigration and Naturalization Service v. Chadha*, 462 U.S. 919 (1983), held that a similar one-House "legislative veto" was unconstitutional. After *Chadha*, Congress used appropriation bills and/or joint resolutions to disprove the president's deferral proposals. But in *City of New Haven v. United States*, no. 86–0455 (D.D.C. 16 May 1986), the U.S. District Court for the District of Columbia found the deferral provisions of Title X inseverable from the one-House veto provision and ordered that section 1013 of the act be set aside.

75. Public Law 344, section 1012. See also sections 1011 and 1013–17 for the entire set of procedures for deferral and rescission.

76. John W. Ellwood and James A. Thurber, "The Politics of the Congressional Budget Process Re-examined," in *Congress Reconsidered*, 2nd ed., ed. Lawrence C. Dodd and Bruce I. Oppenheimer, 246–71 (Washington: CQ Press, 1981); and Schick, *Congress and Money*, 98.

77. Schick, *Congress and Money*, 242.

78. Kiewiet and McCubbins, *Logic of Delegation*, 105–7, argue that lessened demand for spots on HBC, likely due to the term limit, gives less discretion to the party leaders and disproportionate seats to less-representative members of each party.

79. Aaron Wildavsky, *The New Politics of the Budgetary Process* (Glenview, IL: Scott-Foresman, 1988), 149.

80. House Budget Committee press release, 2 July 1976, as cited in Schick, *Congress and Money*, 358. For details on the passage of the first two budget resolution cycles, see Ellwood and Thurber, "Congressional Budget Process Re-examined." For a fuller assessment of the first five years of the budget process, see also Schick, *Congress and Money*, 169–579. For an assessment of the first decades of the congressional budget process, see W. Thomas Wander, F. Ted Hebert, and Gary W. Copeland, ed., *Congressional Budgeting: Politics, Process, and Power* (Baltimore:

Johns Hopkins University Press, 1984) and "Congressional Budgeting and Impoundment Control Act—'94 Symposium," in *Public Budgeting and Finance* 17, no. 3 (Fall 1997): 3–73.

4. Congress Attacks Deficits (and Itself)

1. *Congressional Record*, 99th Cong., 1st sess., 1985, 131: S 17438.

2. Paul Taylor, "Antideficit Bill's Backers Among Its Worst Enemies," *Washington Post*, 7 November 1985, sec. A, p. 1, 14–15, cited in John F. Hoadley, "Easy Riders: Gramm-Rudman-Hollings and the Legislative Fast Track," *PS*, 19, no. 1 (Winter 1986), 31.

3. Schick, *Capacity to Budget*, 4. For more on "deficit neutrality" in the 1974 act, see also Schick, *Congress and Money*, 73.

4. See Charles O. Jones, *The Presidency in a Separated System* (Washington: Brookings Institution, 1994), 22–23.

5. See Schick, *Congress and Money*.

6. See Message to the Congress, *Fiscal Year 1982 Budget Revisions*, 10 March, 1981, cited by the House Committee on the Budget, *A Review of President Reagan's Budget Recommendations, 1981–1985*, 2 August 1984, 3.

7. See Shuman, *Politics and the Budget*, and Fisher, *Congressional Abdication*, among others.

8. Hearing before the House Budget Committee, *Budget Process Review*, 97th Cong., 2nd sess., 14 September 1982.

9. According to Penner, in 1985 huge inflows of foreign capital into the U.S. were necessary to avoid domestic problems with investment "crowding-out" and related reductions of corporate productivity. Theoretically, a rise in external debt leads to the diverting of a larger share of domestic output toward interest payments. For Penner, the political and economic problems with too much deficit spending boiled down to "slower growth of Americans' living standards than what could have been achieved with smaller budget deficits." Ruldoph G. Penner, Director of the Congressional Budget Office, in Hearings before the House Budget Committee, *Budget Outlook and Its Economic Implications*, 99th Cong., 1st sess., 10 October 1985, 2. See also full testimony and prepared statement, 4–26. For an overview of economic theories on the pros and cons of deficit spending generally, see also Savage, *Balanced Budgets & American Politics*.

10. Mandatory spending is largely discussed as an institutional issue in chapter 3 on the 1974 act but grew to such an extent in the interim years that it deserves to be equally noted as a fiscal issue prior to GRH. For example, a little more than one-third of income tax revenue went to interest payments on the debt through the 1980s. See Senate Finance Committee, *Increase of Permanent Public Debt Limit*, 99th Cong., 1st sess., 1985, S. Rept. 144, 28.

11. Lance T. LeLoup, Barbara Luck Graham, and Stacey Barwick, "Deficit Politics and Constitutional Government: The Impact of Gramm-Rudman-Hollings," *Public Budgeting and Finance*, 7, no. 1 (Spring 1987): 83–85. See also Harry S. Havens, "Gramm-Rudman-Hollings: Origins and Implementation," *Public Budgeting & Finance* (Autumn 1986): 4–24. See also prepared statement of Elmer B. Staats, Comproller General, Hearings, Task Force on Budget Process before the House Budget Committee, Budget Act Review, 96th Congress, 1st session, 11 December 1979, 86.

12. For more details on spending and related budgetary conflicts during the early Reagan years, see Gregory B. Mills and John L. Palmer, eds., *Federal Budget Policy in the 1980s* (Washington: Urban Institute Press, 1984).

13. *Washington Post*, 22 October 1985, sec. A, p. 18, cited in Shuman, *Politics and the Budget*, 294.

14. Allen Schick, ed., *Crisis in the Budget Process: Exercising Political Choice* (Washington: American Enterprise Institute, 1986), 4 and Table 1.7 on 36–37.

15. Havens, "Gramm-Rudman-Hollings," 7–9, Shuman, *Politics and the Budget*, 281–83.

16. Havens, "Gramm-Rudman-Hollings," 8.

17. See Hearings, Task Force on Budget Process, House Budget Committee, *Budget Act Review*, 96th Cong., 1st sess., 11–12 December 1979, 4.

18. See ibid., 40–45.

19. See prepared statement, ibid., 277.

20. During the budget cycle in 1975, prior to the budget act's first year in use, Congress tested the reconciliation process in a "dry run" (Shuman, *Politics and the Budget*, 257).

21. The first budget resolution was meant to be a general agreement on total numbers, including outlays for each budget function, revenue, deficit, and debt. This resolution, drawn up by the House and Senate Budget Committees, would be approved in floor votes by May 15, but not enrolled as a bill. The thirteen annual appropriations bills debated and passed subsequently would be shaped by these legislative ground rules. The second resolution was to reaffirm or revise the first resolution through a binding vote by September 15, after the authorizing and appropriations committees finished their work, and to serve as the basis for any conference committee negotiations. If needed, the second resolution would call for targeted revenue and spending committees to adjust their bills and submit the changes to their chambers, or to the budget committees if several committees are targeted. The final binding package of changes is the reconciliation resolution and/or bill, and it would have to be passed by September 25, with the new fiscal year beginning October 1. For more details, see chapter 3.

22. Schick, Hearings, Task Force on Budget Process, House Budget Committee, *Budget Act Review*, 96th Cong., 1st sess., 11–12 December 1979, 12.

23. Such an alteration to the 1974 process was proper under sections 301 (a) (7) and 301 (b) (2) of the act, which are considered to be its "elastic clauses." These clauses allow changes in the annual budget resolution "considered appropriate to carry out the purposes of this Act."

24. *Congressional Quarterly Weekly Report* 39, no. 2 (10 January 1981): 63, as cited in Shuman, *Politics and the Budget*, 257.

25. See also Shuman, 249–66, for details on the passage of the resolution and reconciliation package in the House and Senate.

26. In August 1982 the Senate passed Joint Resolution 58—which proposed adding a Constitutional amendment to balance the budget—by a margin of 69 to 31. For summaries of this and other statutory and constitutional proposals, see Congressional Budget Office Study, *Balancing the Federal Budget and Limiting Federal Spending: Constitutional and Statutory Approaches*, September 1982 (Washington D.C.: GPO, 1982). See also Hearings before the House Judiciary Committee's Subcommittee on Monopolies and Commericial Law, *Constitutional Amendments Seeking to Balance the Budget and Limit Federal Spending*, 97th Cong., 1st and 2nd sess., 18–19 March 1981 and 3–5 August 1982.

27. Hearing before the House Budget Committee, *Budget Process Review*, 97th Cong., 2nd sess., 14 September 1982, 2. Although Penner opposed the Constitutional Amendment proposed in the Senate, he did argue that requiring supermajorities to waive spending ceilings would be a positive step (ibid., 12).

28. Hearings, Senate Committee on the Budget, *Proposed Improvements in the Congressional Budget Act of 1974*, 97th Cong., 2nd sess., 14 September 1982, 33–57.

29. Ibid., 17–18.

30. Ibid., 25–26.

31. See Hearings before the Task Force on the Budget Process of the House Rules Committee, *Congressional Budget Process*, 98th Cong., 1st sess., 15 September and 29 April 1983, and 98th Cong., 2nd sess., 8–9 February, 1984.

32. In 1984, the first budget resolution was not adopted until October 1, the same day the fiscal year began.

33. House Committee on Rules, *Congressional Budget Act Amendments of 1984*, 98th Cong., 2nd sess., H. Rept. 1152, 20–84. Although the 1974 act does not require it, aggregate levels of credit activity (direct loan obligations and primary loan guarantee commitments) have been included in the budget resolutions since the fiscal 1981 budget and have been divisions of the credit totals by functional category since fiscal 1982; see 25.

34. The bill would increase the total amount of U.S. debt from $1.848 trillion to $2.079 trillion. For more on the debt-ceiling issue, see Senate Finance Committee, *Increase of Permanent Public Debt Limit*, 144.

35. *Washington Post*, 4 October 1985, cited in Shuman, *Politics and the Budget*, 284–85.

36. The Reagan administration threatened to shut down the government if the debt ceiling was not raised immediately. Instead, the Treasury Department raised funds through various borrowing actions and bond sales, and Congress passed two temporary measures to raise the ceiling until the bill passed. See *Congressional Quarterly Weekly Report* 43, no. 42 (12 October 1985): 2041 and (19 October 1985): 2091.

37. See ibid., 2035–42, for a summary of amendment proposals and floor debate from October 5–6 and 9–10. For more on the unconventional passage of the bill, see Representative John F. Hoadley, "Easy Riders: Gramm-Rudman-Hollings and the Legislative Fast Track," *PS*: Winter 1986, 30–36.

38. Republicans supported the bill 38 to 8, Northern Democrats 8 to 21, and Southern Democrats 5 to 8; ibid., *Congressional Quarterly Weekly Report* 43, no. 42 (12 October 1985), 2073.

39. Hearings before the Joint Economic Committee, *Gramm-Rudman Budget Proposal*, 99th Cong., 1st sess., 21 October 1985, 32.

40. Hearings before the House Budget Committee, *Working toward a Balanced Budget*, 99th Cong., 1st sess., 9 October 1985, 35.

41. Ibid., 18.

42. Ibid., 25.

43. Ibid., 27. For several economists' criticism of Gramm-Rudman-Hollings, see also testimony on October 10.

44. Ibid.

45. Hearings before the Joint Economic Committee, *Gramm-Rudman Budget Proposal*, 99th Cong., 1st sess., 11 October 1985, 1.

46. Ibid., 3.

47. Ibid., 6.

48. Prior-year contracts would be exempted by the Gramm-Rudman proposal, and 40 percent of military expenditures would therefore be exempted. Specifically, weapons systems, considered by Heller to be the heart of pork-barrel military spending, would be almost completely exempted from cuts because almost all operate under prior-year commitments. By contrast, most research and development, maintenance and operating expenditures, as well as personnel expenditures come from current appropriations, which means these basic aspects of "combat readiness" would qualify for cuts. On the civilian side, national parks and Peace Corps expenditures are mostly current, while hospital construction and Export-Import Bank expenditures are not. See ibid., 8.

49. Ibid.

50. For Blinder's testimony, see ibid., 11–16.

51. For Modigliani's testimony, see ibid., 21 October 1985, 32–45.

52. 462 U.S. 919 (1983).

53. Letter, October 16, as printed in Hearings, House Legislation and Na-

tional Security Subcommittee, *Balanced Budget and Emergency Deficit Control Act of 1985*, 99th Cong., 1st sess., 17 October 1985, 60 (emphasis in the original).

54. Ibid., 67.

55. Ibid., 69–70.

56. Ibid., 102. For a fuller discussion of the balance of power between the president and Congress on budgetary matters, see also ibid., Subcommittee testimony and prepared statement of Louis Fisher, 197–224 and 228–32, and ibid., Congressional Research Service Report (American Law Division), 225–27.

57. Ibid., Prepared statement, 122–28. Bowsher also expressed concern for the role of CBO and OMB in making deficit estimates and the proposal's impact on the 1974 Impoundment provisions, which involved the Comptroller General's office.

58. Ibid., 156–57. See also 181–84 for technical problems relating to the averaging proposal.

59. Shuman, *Politics and the Budget*, 284.

60. The Senate's proposed ceiling for fiscal 1986's deficit was about $5 billion higher than the deficit that CBO had predicted in August. Democrats charged that this figure protected Senate Republicans up for reelection in 1986.

61. Quoted in *Congressional Quarterly Weekly Report* 43, no. 45 (2 November 1985): 2191. For details on the first conference report, see House Committee on Ways and Means, *Increase in Debt Limit*, 99th Cong., 1st sess., 1985, H. Rept. 351.

62. *Congressional Record*, 99th Cong., 1st sess., 1985, 131, Pt. 171: 17382.

63. *Congressional Record*, 99th Cong., 1st sess., 1985, 131, Pt. 171: 17383.

64. Senate breakdown of votes: Republicans 39 to 9, Democrats 22 to 22 (Northern Democrats 11 to 20, Southern Democrats 11 to 2). House breakdown of votes: Republicans 153 to 24, Democrats 118 to 130 (Northern Democrats 60 to 108, Southern Democrats 58 to 22), *Congressional Quarterly Weekly Report* 43, no. 51 (14 December 1985): 2645–46.

65. See Statement, *Weekly Compilation of Presidential Documents*, Vol. 21, no. 50 (12 December 1985): 1490–91. Reagan specifically mentioned the possible constitutional problem with congressional officers (the Director of CBO and the Comptroller General) performing executive functions relating to the sequestration procedures, as well as the provision authorizing the president to terminate or modify defense contracts if approved by the CG.

66. Hearings before the Senate Committee on Governmental Affairs, *Possible Legislative Responses to Bowsher v. Synar*, 99th Cong., 2nd sess., 23 July 1986, 1.

67. See *Congressional Quarterly Weekly Report* 44, no. 52 (21 December 1986): 2665–66 and 2669–71.

68. For example, the U.S. Postal Service is by law "off budget." See Sec. 201 (a).

69. Sec. 241 (b).

70. Secs. 251 (a) (1–3).

71. Dozens of programs and outlays were exempt from sequestration, including Social Security, veterans' compensation and pension, net interest payments, the earned income tax credit, and several income-stabilizer and insurance programs such as welfare, food stamps, child nutrition, and Medicaid, among others. Other special rules applied to how other federal programs, such as unemployment, student loans, child support enforcement, and others would be cut. See Secs. 255, 256, and 257. See also Sec. 251 (a) (3) for procedures to reduce other automatic spending programs and (6) (d) for defense sequestion details.

72. President Reagan was given some discretion on fiscal 1986 defense spending cuts if a sequestration was ordered for that year. See Sec. 252 (a) (3) and (5).

73. Sec. 252 (b) (1) and 253.

74. Sec. 254 (a).

75. See changes to Sec. 301 (e) (g) and 302 (a).

76. Bills taking effect the following fiscal year and House Appropriation bills passed after May 15 are exempt from this requirement.

77. See changes to Sec. 301 (c) (f), 303 (a), and 311 (a) for kinds of proposed legislation subject to points of order in the House and Senate, section 308 (a) for reporting requirements, and Sec. 304 (a) for concurrent resolution revision provisions.

78. It would be out of order for budget legislation (including resolutions and reconciliation) to exceed the spending limits; for committee legislation to come to the floor if that committee had not made their required subcommittee allocations from the budget resolution; for legislation to exceed a subcommittee's allocation; for legislation providing new budget authority, increases, or decreases in the federal debt or revenues to come to the floor prior to the completion of a budget resolution; for legislation to exceed the budget resolution; and for legislation establishing new budget authority in addition to actual appropriations.

79. Sec. 302 (b).

80. Sec. 274 (a) (b) (c).

81. Secs. 251 (a) and 274 (f).

82. See also testimony and statements of Charles Bowsher (Comptroller General) and Rudolph Penner (CBO Director), Hearings before the Legislation and National Security Subcommittee of the House Committee on Government Operations, *Impact of the Gramm-Rudman-Hollings Law*, 99th Cong., 2nd sess., 18 and 19 June 1986, and testimony of Budget Committee Chairman William H. Gray, III, House Committee on Government Operations, *Trigger Mechanism of the Gramm-Rudman-Hollings Act*, 99th Cong., 2nd sess., 24 July 1986.

83. Shuman, *Politics and the Budget*, chapter 9.

84. OMB's deficit estimate was almost $15 billion below CBO's. See Report of the Comptroller General of the United States to the Chairman, Committee on

Government Operations, House of Representatives, Budget Reductions for Fiscal Year 1987: Review of Initial OMB/CBO Report Under the Deficit Control Act, as cited in Shuman, *Politics and the Budget*, 292.

85. Shuman, *Politics and the Budget*, and *Congressional Quarterly Weekly Report* 44, no. 39 (20 September 1986): 2179.

86. 626 F. Supp. 1382–90. See 1378–82 for issues relating to the plaintiffs' standing to sue and the consolidation of their cases.

87. Ibid., 1390.

88. As Justice White notes in his dissent in *Bowsher v. Synar*, the removal resolution needs to be signed by the president.

89. Ibid., 1403.

90. For more on constitutional law issues related to *Bowsher*, including the president's removal powers, separation of powers, and budget-law history, see Alfred C. Aman Jr., et al., "Symposium: Bowsher v. Synar," *Cornell Law Review* 72 (1987): 421; William C. Banks and Jeffrey D. Straussman, "Bowsher v. Synar: The Emerging Judicialization of the Fisc," *Boston College Law Review* 28 (1987): 659; Jonathan L. Entin, "The Removal Power and the Federal Deficit: Form, Substance, and Administrative Independence," *Kentucky Law Journal* 75 (1987): 699; Kate Stith, "Rewriting the Fiscal Constitution: The Case of Gramm-Rudman-Hollings," *California Law Review* 76 (1988): 593; and Cass Sustein, testimony and statement before the Senate Committee on Government Affairs, *Possible Legislative Responses to Bowsher v. Synar*, 81–85 and 132–50.

91. For example, Senator Domenici pointed out that the schedule for the fallback Temporary Joint Committee to receive and report the director's sequestration report did not take into account Congress's regular August recess. See prepared statement, Hearing before the Senate Committee on Governmental Affairs, *Possible Legislative Responses to Bowsher v. Synar*, 24.

92. See ibid., 27–28.

93. Ibid., 30–31.

94. Ibid., 36–37.

95. Hearings, House Government Operations Committee, *Trigger Mechanism of the Gramm-Rudman-Hollings Act*, 7.

96. See also Miller's testimony, Hearing before the Senate Committee on Governmental Affairs, *Possible Legislative Responses to Bowsher v. Synar*, 61–69.

97. Hearings, Subcommittee on Legislation and National Security, *Reform of the Federal Budget Process*, 100th Cong., 1st sess., 12 March 1987, 1.

98. For additional issues concerning the congressional budget process from legislators' perspectives, see also ibid., hearings and statements on April 2 and 30 and Committee on Government Operations, *Reform of the Federal Budget Process: An Analysis of Major Proposals*, 100th Cong., 1st sess., June 1987.

99. Two temporary increases on the public debt had already been approved

since GRH I. See Public Law 384, 99th Cong., 2nd sess. (14 August 1986) and Public Law 84, 100th Cong., 1st sess. (10 August 1987).

100. *Congressional Record*, 100th Cong., 1st sess., Vol. 132, no. 150, 1987, H7791–2.

101. Ibid., H7792.

102. Ibid., 23 September 1987, S 12556.

103. Ibid., S 12567.

104. In the House: Republicans 105 to 65 and Democrats 125 to 111 (Northern Democrats 74 to 88 and Southern Democrats 51 to 23). In the Senate: Republicans 32–13 and Democrats 32–21 (Northern Democrats 20 to 16 and Southern Democrats 12 to 5). See *Congressional Quarterly Weekly Report* 45, no. 39 (26 September 1987): 2348 for the House and *Congressional Record*, 100th Cong., 1st sess., Vol. 132, no. 152 (23 September 1987): S 12577 for the Senate.

105. See *Congressional Quarterly Weekly Report* 45, no. 39 (26 September 1987): 2309–10, and *Weekly Compilation of Presidential Documents*, Vol. 23, no. 40 (29 September 1987): 1662–70.

106. The legislation also raised the debt-ceiling limit to $2.8 trillion, which meant the next vote would be in May of 1989, well after the 1988 election. See Shuman, *Politics and the Budget*, 295, and the 1987 act's preamble.

107. See *Congressional Quarterly Weekly Report* 45, no. 39 (26 September 1987): 2310–11; and Public Law 119, 100th Cong., 1st sess. (29 September 1987), 104, 107, 202, 205, and 210.

108. "It is the sense of the Congress that the Congress should undertake an experiment with multiyear authorizations and two-year appropriations for selected agencies and accounts. An evaluation of the efficacy and desirability of such experiment should be conducted at the end of the two-year period. The appropriate committees are directed to develop a plan in consultation with the leadership of the House and Senate to implement this experiment." Title II, Sec. 201.

109. See Kiewiet and McCubbins, *Logic of Delegation*, chapters 4–6 and 8.

110. Louis Fisher, "Federal Budget Doldrums: The Vacuum in Presidential Leadership," *Public Administration Review*, 50, no. 6 (1990): 698.

5. Old Problems and New Tools of Self-Restraint

1. *Congressional Record*, 101st Cong., 2nd sess., 1990, 136, Pt. 150: S 17517.

2. Ibid., S 17520.

3. Ibid., S 17521.

4. James A. Thurber and Samantha L. Durst, "The 1990 Budget Enforcement Act: The Decline of Congressional Accountability," in *Congress Reconsidered*, 5th ed., ed. Lawrence C. Dodd and Bruce I. Oppenheimer (Washington: CQ Press, 1993), 381.

5. For more on the 1993 budget agreement, see Wildavsky and Caiden, *New Politics of the Budgetary Process*, 153–62. For more on the 1997 budget, see Daniel Palazzolo, *Done Deal? The Politics of the 1997 Budget Agreement* (NY: Chatham, 1999).

6. Shuman, *Politics of the Budget*, 305–6.

7. Ibid. For details on the fiscal 1990 "Rose Garden Agreement" between congressional leaders and the administration, subsequent debates regarding appropriations, and the specific cuts made under the sequestration order, see Shuman, *Politics of the Budget*, 306–11.

8. For more on the debate over trust fund surpluses being included in annual deficit calculations under the unified budget, see Hearings before the Legislation and National Security Subcommittee of the House Government Operations Committee, *Budgetary Treatment of Federal Trust Funds*, 101st Cong., 1st sess., 12 October 1989.

9. In this report, OMB stated that before any proposed cuts, the fiscal 1991 deficit would be $168 billion; if the savings and loan bailout were not included, the deficit would be $231 billion; and if the Social Security trust fund surplus were not included, the deficit would be $280 to $300 billion. See Office of Management and Budget, *Mid-Session Review of the Budget* (Washington, D.C.: 16 July 1990), Table 7, 13, as cited in Shuman, *Politics of the Budget*, 315. See also Congressional Budget Office, *The Economic and Budget Outlook: Fiscal Years 1990–1994: A Report to the Senate and House Committees on the Budget—Part I* (January 1989).

10. Rudolph G. Penner, "The Political Economics of the 1990 Budget Agreement," in *Fiscal Politics and the Budget Enforcement Act*, ed. Marvin H. Kosters, 1–19 (Washington, D.C.: AEI Press, 1992), 2.

11. Ibid., 3.

12. See Hearings before the House Committee on Ways and Means, *The Budget Deficit, the State of the U.S. Economy, and Federal Budget Policy for Fiscal Year 1990 and Beyond*, 101st Cong., 1st sess., 7–9 February and 7, 8, and 15 March 1989; Hearings before the House Committee on Ways and Means, *Budget Deficit, the State of the U.S. Economy and Federal Budget Policy, and the Administration's Budget Proposal for the Fiscal Year 1991 and Beyond*, 101st Cong., 2nd sess., 6 February and 8 March 1990; and Hearings before the House Budget Committee, *The Budget and the Economy, Part I*, 101st Cong., 2nd sess., 30 and 31 January and 21, 26, and 27 February 1990.

13. General Accounting Office Transition Series, "The Budget Deficit," November 1988, 4–5, included in a hearing before the Senate Committee on Governmental Affairs, *Critical Issues and Problems Facing the New Administration and Congress*, 101st Cong., 1st sess., 18 January 1989, 101–16. Several other budget experts argued that no deficit reduction occurred if trust fund surpluses were excluded from the calculation. See Hearings before the Legislation and National

Security Subcommittee of the House Government Operations Committee, *Budgetary Treatment of Federal Trust Funds.*

14. See testimony and prepared statement of Alice M. Rivlin before the House Committee, *Budget Process Reform*, 24–27.

15. Schick, "Deficit Budgeting in the Age of Divided Government," in *Fiscal Politics and the Budget Enforcement Act*, ed. Marvin H. Kosters, 20-37 (Washington, D.C.:AEI Press, 1992), 21–22.

16. Hearings, Senate Committee on Governmental Affairs, *Budget Reform*, 100th Cong., 2nd sess., 7 June 1988, 50.

17. See Wildavsky and Caiden, *New Politics of the Budgetary Process*, 136–46, for more details on the inter- and intra-party conflicts, as well as the 1990 budget summit.

18. Shuman, *Politics and the Budget*, 314–16. See also 317–28 for more on the specific manifestations of intra-party conflicts in fiscal 1991's negotiations, including the brief government shutdown over Columbus Day weekend, 1990.

19. For details and roll calls related to the October 5 budget vote, conservative Republican defection led by Minority Whip Newt Gingrich, and the subsequent continuing resolution, see *Congressional Quarterly Weekly Report* 48, no. 41 (6 October 1990): 3173–202 and 3247–49; and House Concurrent Resolution 310.

20. Shuman, *Politics and the Budget*, 309.

21. Senate Committee, *Budget Reform*, 1.

22. Public Law 119, 100th Cong., 1st sess. (29 September 1987), Title II, Sec. 201. In the November 1987 "Budget Summit Agreement," a two-year budget schedule was technically put into operation with set spending totals for the second year. Although budget resolutions since Gramm-Rudman-Hollings I generally include multiyear spending information, generally only the first year has enforceable provisions.

23. Senate Committee, *Budget Reform*, 6–7. See also text of "Biennial Budget Act of 1988," also known as the "Ford–Roth Biennial Budget Bill," inserted in the committee record at 62–105. Ford first introduced biennial budgeting legislation in 1981, as he says in his statement, 57–61.

24. Senator Roth cited a study of Congress members by the Center for Responsive Politics, ibid., 8.

25. Ibid., 8–9.

26. Ibid., 11–13. For more on these proposals, see prepared statement, 107–14.

27. Ibid., 18–26.

28. Ibid., 34. See also prepared statement, 121–62.

29. "Games" Sasser cited involved various kinds of activities to hide deficits through "off-budget" entities (such as the FLSIC bailout), the inclusion of trust fund surpluses to mask "true" deficit numbers, and one-time savings actions to meet deficit ceilings, including pay date shifts and quick revenue enhancers such

as sales of government assets. See Joint Hearings before the Senate Committee on Governmental Affairs and Committee on the Budget, *Budget Reform Proposals*, 101st Cong., 1st sess., 19 October 1989, 2–3.

30. Ibid., 3–4.

31. Prepared statement, ibid., 8.

32. Ibid., 26 October 1989, 70.

33. Hearing before House Committee, *Budget Process Reform*, 1.

34. Ibid., 15–16.

35. See ibid., 2.

36. Ibid., 3.

37. Ibid., 10.

38. Ibid., 3–5.

39. Ibid., 32. See also 7–10 and 28–33.

40. Ibid., 22–23. Penner argues that the Supreme Court's *Chadha* decision taking away the one-house veto lessened presidential power over rescission because it effectively denied the deferral option. See chapter 2 for more on the 1974 impoundment provisions.

41. Shuman, *Politics and the Budget*, 337.

42. For criticism of the budget summit's bypass of conventional legislative and deliberative processes, see Robert W. Merry, "The Budget Summit's Assault on Congress," *Congressional Quarterly Weekly Report* 48, no. 40 (6 October 1990): 3266, and Sinclair, *Unorthodox Lawmaking*.

43. Pamela Fessler, "Provisions Designed to Tighten Clasp on the Federal Spending Purse," *Congressional Quarterly Weekly Report* 48, no. 40 (6 October 1990): 3196–97.

44. Shuman, *Politics and the Budget*, 336.

45. See Fessler, "Federal Spending Purse." Other proposed changes included: presidential-requested emergency funds not being subject to sequestration if Congress consented to its "emergency" status; any mandatory spending or revenue legislation enacted after a budget deal is adopted to be "deficit neutral" with additional mini-sequestrations possible; numerous entitlement programs would continue to be exempt from sequestration (including Social Security) but possible Medicare and veterans' funds cuts would be increased from 2 to 4 percent; and enactment of revenue-losing tax bills would trigger automatic reconciliation instructions to the tax-writing committees, which must provide offsetting savings or revenue increases; the higher spending "cushion" would be reduced by any amounts that the appropriations committees exceeded their spending caps but limited to $2.5 billion each for domestic and defense spending and $1.5 billion for international programs; total budget authority for all categories could exceed the cap by 0.4 percent over the first three years of the deal; laws to increase the debt ceiling would go from annual to five-year votes and credit; credit activities

would be counted through present-value cost of federal subsidies regarding loans and loan guarantees; and new appropriations reporting requirements regarding government-sponsored private entities.

46. Shuman, *Politics and the Budget*, 337.

47. The House and Senate passed different reconciliation instructions for fiscal 1991, which began October 1. See HR 5835 and S 3209, and for details on the House alternative to the budget summit-generated procedural reforms, which the Senate largely adopted, see House Rules Committee Report 101–882 to accompany H. Res. 509, 16 October 1990. For differences between the total deficit caps in the House and summit plans, see Title VI, 31–32.

48. See George Hager, "Deficit Deal Ever So Fragile As Hours Dwindle Away," *Congressional Quarterly Weekly Report* 48, no. 43 (27 October 1990): 3574–75.

49. Ibid., section XII, 2877. See 2877–81 for specific scorekeeping procedures for fiscal 1991. Shuman reports that Senator Byrd directly negotiated the increased powers for OMB with Director Richard Darman while also negotiating for increased powers for his Appropriations Committee. See *Politics and the Budget*, 337.

50. For floor debates in the House and in the Senate, see *Congressional Record*, 101st Cong., 2nd sess., 1990. For details on the budget package and conflicts, see also Shuman, *Politics and the Budget*, 317–30.

51. *Congressional Record*, 101st Cong., 2nd sess., 1990, 136, Pt. 139: H 10113.

52. Ibid., H 10126.

53. Ibid., S 17528.

54. Ibid., S 17521.

55. Ibid., S 17566.

56. Ibid., S 17568.

57. House vote breakdowns: Republicans 47 to 126, Democrats 181 to 74 (Northern Democrats 120 to 54, Southern Democrats 61 to 20); Senate: Republicans 19 to 25, Democrats 35 to 20 (Northern Democrats 23 to 15, Southern Democrats 12 to 5). See *Congressional Quarterly Weekly Report* 48, no. 4 (3 November 1990): 3764 and 3769.

58. Lawrence J. Haas, "New Rules of the Game," *National Journal*, 22, no. 44 (17 November 1990): 2794.

59. Fisher, *The Politics of Shared Power: Congress and the Executive* (Washington: CQ Press, 1993), 197.

60. Public Law 508, 101st Cong., 2nd sess. (5 November 1990), Secs. 253 (g) (1–2) and 13101 (g).

61. See Sec. 13101 (c) (4) (b) and 251 (b) (2) (D). More recent controversies over the "emergency" designation have prompted questions about what should qualify under this label.

62. See Sec. 13101 (b).

63. If during the first half of the calendar year Congress passes appropriations that exceed the caps, a sequester can be ordered to make the corrections within the breeched category. If the breech takes place between July 1 and September 30, sequestration occurs in the next fiscal year in the relevant category. This provision is often referred to as a "look-back" rule. See Shuman, *Politics and the Budget*, 334, and Thurber and Durst, "1990 Budget Enforcement Act," 383, and Public Law 508, Sec. 251 (5) and (6).

64. Sec. 13101 (c) (8) defines direct spending as "budget authority provided by law other than appropriation Acts; entitlement authority; and the food stamp program."

65. PAYGO rules do not require offsetting action if revenue falls due to a weak economy or if spending increases are pursuant to existing law, such as increases in an indexed entitlement. See Sec. 252.

66. Thurber and Durst, "1990 Budget Enforcement Act," 383.

67. Sec. 252 (d).

68. In December 1990 the House Democratic Caucus approved a rule that, if attached to relevant bills, would give the CBO and Joint Committee on Internal Revenue Taxation the power to score tax and entitlement estimates. President Bush vowed to veto any bill that contains such a rule and argued that such a change in scorekeeping procedures would undercut the credibility of the agreement. See Shuman, *Politics and the Budget*, 339, and Thurber and Durst, "1990 Budget Enforcement Act," 387. A confusing point arises since Shuman implies that the Democratic caucus rule never was instated, but Thurber and Durst say it was put into effect.

69. See Part I, section 251 (1) and (2).

70. Haas, "New Rules of the Game," 2794–95.

71. Shuman, *Politics and the Budget*, 340.

72. Ibid., 339.

73. See Thurber and Durst, "1990 Budget Enforcement Act," 385.

74. Thurber and Durst, ibid., and Sec. 258 (B) and (C). For additional point-of-order rules, see Secs. 605 and 606 of the Budget Enforcement Act.

75. As Shuman notes, the former "unified" budget was criticized for using trust fund surpluses to mask the annual deficit (*Politics and the Budget*, 335). But Allen Schick asks "how can the budget's impact on the economy be assessed when one-fifth of the government's revenues and outlays are excluded? In fact, social security is almost always included in both government and news references to the budget. By law, social security is excluded; in practice, it is included." *The Federal Budget: Politics, Policy, Process* (Washington: Brookings Institution, 1995), 28.

76. Sec. 13301, 13302, and 13303.

77. Sec. 13201 and Title V—Credit Reform.

78. Sec. 506 (a) and 13501. Government-sponsored enterprises (GSE) in-

clude the Federal Home Loan Bank System, the Student Loan Marketing Association, the Farm Credit System, the Federal National Mortgage Association, and the Federal Home Loan Mortgage Corporation. Wildavsky and Caiden explain the inclusion of GSE regulation in the 1990 act through their argument that "the savings and loan debacle had made everyone more cautious, thus giving force to concern over the last several decades about the exposure of federal finances to failures of GSEs" (*New Politics of the Budgetary Process*, 149).

79. Sec. 258.

80. Penner, "Political Economics," 16. See also Shuman, *Politics and the Budget*, 338, for an additional explanation regarding how the BEA greatly expands presidential prerogatives.

81. Schick, "Deficit Budgeting," 31.

82. Wildavsky and Caiden, *New Politics of the Budgetary Process*, 152–53.

83. Haas, "New Rules of the Game," 2797.

84. Janet Hook, "Budget Order Poses Question: Why Can't Congress Be Led?," *Congressional Quarterly Weekly Report* 48, no. 42 (20 October 1990): 3471–73.

6. Stop Us Before We Spend Again

1. Hearing before the Senate Budget Committee, *Legislative Line-Item Veto Proposals*, 103rd Cong., 2nd sess., 5 October 1994, 2.

2. Prepared statement, Joint Hearing before the House Committee on Government Reform and Oversight and the Senate Committee on Governmental Affairs, *Line-Item Veto*, 104th Cong., 1st sess., 12 January 1995, 3.

3. Hearing before the Senate Budget Committee, *Concurrent Resolution on the Budget for FY96, Vol. II*, 104th Cong., 1st sess., 18 January 1995, 8.

4. Epstein and O'Halloran, *Delegating Powers*, 227–30.

5. In 1984, the Senate came within one vote of adding a line-item veto to its fiscal 1985 deficit-reduction plan. In 1985, after a weeklong filibuster, the Senate was again unable to push a version of the line–item veto bill known as separate enrollment. In 1992, after a dramatic confrontation between conservative House Democrats and the party's leadership, an expedited rescission measure passed the House by a large margin, but Senate Appropriations Committee Chairman Robert C. Byrd (D-WV) prevented the bill from reaching the floor. Meanwhile, presidential candidate Bill Clinton expressed his support for such a presidential power (as governor he also had line–item veto power). In 1993 and 1994 (before the midterm election) the Senate first rejected an enhanced rescission bill and then allowed a House-passed expedited rescission bill to languish. See Mark T. Kehoe, "History of the Line-Item Veto Effort," *Congressional Quarterly Weekly Report* 54, no. 13 (1996): 867, and the notes for the "Institutional Issues" section in this chapter.

6. For more analysis of the impoundment control aspect of the 1974 act, and how impoundment compares with line-item vetoes in terms of presidential power, see Virginia A. McMurtry, "The Impoundment Control Act of 1974: Restraining or Reviving Presidential Power?," *Public Budgeting and Finance* 17, no. 3 (Fall 1997): 39–61.

7. Ironically, as item-veto proposals were more seriously considered in Congress in the mid-1980s, President Reagan proposed rescissions very sparingly. See House Budget Committee, *Line-Item Veto: An Appraisal*, 98th Cong., 2nd sess., 1984, Committee Print, 7.

8. The House Budget Committee staff estimated that due to the administration's stated commitments in the areas potentially eligible for a line-item veto—such as the FBI, Coast Guard, the DEA, education and training, the National Institutes of Health, various cancer research programs, and Reagan's fiscal 1985 budget—the administration's intent was to reduce these programs by no more than $2.0 billion, 1 percent of the budget. The HBC print goes on to say that not only are these eligible amounts too small to make a major difference in a deficit hovering in the $200 billion range, but the time it would take to pass a constitutional amendment would not be sufficient to test the efficacy of the item veto. See House Committee, *Line-Item Veto: An Appraisal*, 6.

9. Senate Committee on Rules and Administration, *Providing That Each Item of Any General or Special Appropriation Bill and Any Bill or Joint Resolution Making Supplemental, Deficiency, or Continuing Appropriations Shall Be Enrolled As a Separate Bill for Presentation to the President*, 99th Cong., 1st sess., 1985, S. Rept. 92, 11.

10. The GAO report to the House and Senate Appropriations Committees estimated that if the president had had the line-item veto between fiscal years 1984–1989, estimated savings could have been a total of $70 billion, which would have reduced federal borrowing by 6.7 percent over the same time period. The study estimated potential items for reduction by analyzing the policy recommendations and criticisms in Statements of Administrative Policy, which the OMB issues to Congress in light of pending appropriations actions. The study estimated that almost 72 percent of the potential savings would have occurred in five spending areas that account for roughly 20 percent of discretionary spending, including transportation, commerce and housing credit, education, training employment and social services, income security, and natural resources and environment. For more, see GAO, "Line Item Veto: Estimating Potential Savings," January 1992, submitted in Hearings before the Subcommittee on the Legislative Process of the House Rules Committee, *Legislative Line-Item Veto Proposals*, 102nd Cong., 2nd sess., 18 September 1992, 21–31.

11. See "CRS Evaluation of the GAO Line-Item Veto Report," prepared by Louis Fisher, Senior Specialist in Separation of Powers, reprinted from the *Congressional Record*, 30 April 1992, in Hearing before the Senate Budget Committee,

Concurrent Resolution on the Budget for FY96, Vol. II, 20–23. Fisher argued that the GAO report's methods were faulty for six reasons: use of SAPs, "theoretical v. realistic savings," double counting rescissions, double counting program terminations, assumptions that the savings were permanent, overlooking presidential spending initiatives, and misinterpreting studies on state experiences to conclude that the states have enjoyed larger fiscal impacts than they actually have.

12. Robert D. Reischauer, prepared statement before the Subcommittee on the Legislative Process of the House Rules Committee, *Legislative Line-Item Veto Proposals*, 102nd Cong., 2nd sess., 25 September 1992, 260.

13. Ibid., 273–89. Under the 1974 budget act's impoundment title, the Comptroller General performs several roles regarding presidential deferral and rescission powers, including reviewing impoundment messages and classifications, informing Congress of unreported impoundments, and monitoring the status of the impounded funds, among other related duties.

14. Robert C. Byrd, "The Control of the Purse and the Line Item Veto Act," *Harvard Journal on Legislation* 35, no. 2 (Summer 1998): 315.

15. Statement submitted for the record, Hearings on the Line-Item Veto, Senate Subcommittee on the Constitution of the Senate Judiciary Committee, *Line Item Veto*, 98th Cong., 2nd sess., 9 April 1984, 177–78.

16. Joint Hearing before the House Committee on Government Reform and Oversight and the Senate Committee on Governmental Affairs, *Line-Item Veto*, 14.

17. Ibid., 22.

18. See report inserted into Hearing before the Senate Budget Committee, *Concurrent Resolution on the Budget for FY96, Vol. II*, 25–48.

19. House Committee, *Line-Item Veto: An Appraisal*, 1. North Carolina does not allow the executive any veto authority and Indiana, Maine, Nevada, New Hampshire, Rhode Island, and Vermont do not allow line-item vetoes. States that do allow item vetoes generally allow supermajority legislative overrides. See also ibid., 13, and McMurtry, "Impoundment Control Act of 1974."

20. Robert J. Spitzer, "The Constitutionality of the Presidential Line-Item Veto," *Political Science Quarterly* 112, no. 2 (Summer 1997): 261, n. 3.

21. Prepared statement, Joint Hearing before the House Committee on Government Reform and Oversight and the Senate Committee on Governmental Affairs, *Line-Item Veto*, 5.

22. Hearing before the Legislation and National Security Subcommittee of the House Committee on Government Operations, *Expedited Rescission Authority for the President*, 103rd Cong., 1st sess., 10 March 1993, 71.

23. *Congressional Record*, 104th Cong., 1st sess., 1995, 141: H1262.

24. Ibid. 141, S 4189.

25. Proposals or executive actions that are similar to the line–item veto concept are also traced to Presidents Jackson and Tyler. In addition, the Provisional

Constitution of the Confederate States entailed an executive line-item veto in 1861, and from 1902–1954 the U.S. Congress granted the power to the governors of the Territories of Hawaii, Alaska, the Philippines, Puerto Rico, and the Virgin Islands. See House Committee, *Line-Item Veto: An Appraisal*, 11–12.

26. The item-veto power was also requested by Presidents Hays in 1879 and Arthur in 1882 and almost received a floor vote in 1883 but failed to get the support to overcome a rule technicality. In 1884, the Senate Judiciary Committee favorably reported a line–item veto amendment proposal, but the bill was not considered on the floor. Hearings were also held in 1913 but that bill was never reported; see See House Committee, *Line-Item Veto: An Appraisal*. For more details on early colonial, state, and federal history pertaining to the item veto, see Vernon L. Wilkinson, "Federal Legislation: The Item Veto in the American Constitutional System," *Georgetown Law Journal*, 25 (1936): 106–12, and Spitzer, "Constitutionality," 263–79. President Roosevelt proposed a wider legislative veto for appropriation bills as a response to potential presidential line–item veto authority. The House adopted this language as an amendment to the Independent Offices Appropriations Act in 1939, but the proposal failed in the Senate; see House Committee, *Line-Item Veto: An Appraisal*, 12.

27. Wilkinson, 112–36.

28. Hearings before the Joint Study Committee on Budget Control, *Improving Congressional Budget Control*, 93rd Cong., 1st sess., 6 March 1973, 88.

29. Hearing before the Senate Subcommittee on the Constitution, *Line Item Veto*, 12.

30. Ibid., 13.

31. Ibid., 14.

32. Ibid., 21.

33. Hearings before the Senate Committee on Rules and Administration, *Line Item Veto I*, 99th Cong., 1st sess., 14 May 1985, 7.

34. See ibid., testimony and prepared statements, 80–109, and 20 May 1985, 89–204, and appendices.

35. Ibid., 20 June 1985, 217.

36. See "Constitutionality of Empowering Item Veto by Legislation," by Johnny H. Killian, Senior Specialist, Congressional Research Service, Library of Congress, American Law Division, inserted into the Senate Committee Report, *Providing That Each Item of Any General or Special Appropriation Bill and Any Bill or Joint Resolution Making Supplemental, Deficiency, or Continuing Appropriations Shall Be Enrolled As a Separate Bill for Presentation to the President*, 8.

37. The report also specifically reflected the chairman's concern that item veto power would further centralize power within the President's OMB, which had grown particularly powerful in the 1970s and 1980s as a result of Presidents Nixon's and Reagan's various reorganizations of the office. Ibid., 8–9.

38. Ibid., 19–20. These Senators also explain that despite their support for S. 43, they voted for the bill's unfavorable reporting to get the measure to the Senate floor for full consideration as soon as possible.

39. Ibid., 20–21.

40. S.J. Res. 14 proposed item disapproval authority with normal congressional override possible, S.J. Res. 23 and 31 proposed reduction and disapproval authority with a simple-majority override possible. Senators John McCain (R-AZ) and Robert Dole (R-KS) also introduced S. 6, a statutory enhanced rescission proposal with a normal congressional override possible.

41. Hearings before the Subcommittee on the Constitution, the Senate Judiciary Committee, *Line Item Veto*, 101st Cong., 1st sess., 11 April 1989, 212.

42. Ibid., 208. Despite this argument, the Judiciary Committee favorably reported two of the amendment proposals, although the Constitution Subcommittee voted to report without recommendation. Senate Judiciary Committee, *Line Item Veto*, 101st Cong., 2nd sess., 1989, S. Rept. 466, to accompany S.J. Res. 14 and 23, 1. See 9–14 on the substitute statutory proposal submitted by Chairman Joseph Biden (D-DE). Senator Edward Kennedy (D-MA) also argued that the item veto did not require a constitutional amendment; see "additional views," 15. For arguments opposing statutory and amendment-based line-item, see additional views of Senator Howard Metzenbaum (D-OH), Orrin Hatch (R-UT), Dennis DeConcini (D-AZ), Patrick Leahy (D-VT), and Herb Kohn (D-WI), 16–19. In early October 1989 the Senate Budget Committee reported a legislative separate enrollment bill sponsored by Senator Ernest F. Hollings (D-SC), although the Committee did not have formal hearings on the subject. See Senate Committee on the Budget, *Legislative Line Item Veto Separate Enrollment Authority Act*, 101st Cong., 2nd sess., 1989, S. Rept. 518 to accompany S. 3181.

43. Ibid.

44. In 1986 and 1987, Congress approved 3 and 5 percent of Reagan's proposed rescissions, respectively.

45. Joint Hearings before the Senate Committee on Governmental Affairs and Committee on the Budget, *Budget Reform Proposals*, 45.

46. Hearings before the Subcommittee on the Legislative Process of the House Rules Committee, *Legislative Line-Item Veto Proposals*, 102nd Cong, 2nd sess., 18 September 1992, 11–12. Duncan's bill, H.R. 78, was an enhanced rescission bill which had roughly 130 co-sponsors.

47. Ibid., 59. The expedited rescission bill was H.R. 2161. It mandated that the president propose rescissions within three days of signing an appropriations bill and that Congress vote on the proposed rescission package, without amendment, within seven days. The bill would also limit potential rescissions for authorized programs to 25 percent, but unauthorized programs could be rescinded in full.

48. Ibid., 60–61.

49. H.R. 354 and H.R. 1013 provided for expedited presidential and congressional action regarding rescission packages, with 1013 allowing Congress to strike individual items from the package if fifty House members request a vote on such a motion. H.R. 493 provided enhanced rescission authority over appropriations bills and targeted tax benefits in revenue bills.

50. Although an expedited rescission bill (H.R. 2164) passed the House 312 to 97 in the previous session, the Senate took no action on that bill. See House debates and votes on 2 October 1992, *Congressional Record*, 102nd Cong., 2nd sess., 1992, 13: H10805, H10975. Several votes in the Senate in 1989, 1990, 1992, and 1993 rejected various efforts to waive the 1974 budget rules to allow for various kinds of item veto authority. Although the Senate did not debate H.R. 2164 in 1992, an extensive debate on line–item veto issues took place in light of McCain Amendment no. 1698 to S. 479 and McCain/Coats Amendment no. 3013 to H.R. 5677. See *Congressional Record*, 102nd Cong., 2nd sess., 1992, 138: S 2457 and S 13684, respectively.

51. Prepared statement, Hearing before the Legislation and National Security Subcommittee of the House Committee on Government Operations, *Expedited Rescission Authority for the President*, 45.

52. Ibid., 47–48.

53. Ibid., prepared statement, 73. For a list of special-interest provisions in H.R. 11 inserted into the record, see 62–70.

54. Ibid., 154–55. But this was not a common argument raised in any of the line–item veto hearings, even by opponents.

55. Specter's argument, which formed the basis of his S. Res. 195, largely stems from Article I, section 7, clause 3: "Every Order, Resolution, or Vote to which Concurrence of the Senate and House of Representatives may be necessary (except on a question of Adjournment) shall be presented to the President of the United States; and before the Same shall take Effect, shall be approved by him, or being disapproved by him, shall be repassed by two thirds of the Senate and House of Representatives, according to the Rules and Limitations prescribed in the Case of a Bill." (The veto procedures for a bill are laid out in clause 2.) Among other pieces of evidence, Specter argued that this inherent line–item veto power is also supported by the fact that this clause was directly taken from the Massachusetts constitution, which allowed the line-item veto based on it, and by two Anti-Federalist papers that opposed clause 3 because it "made too strong a line item veto in the hands of the President." See Forrest McDonald, "The Framers' Conception of the Veto Power," in *Pork Barrels and Principles: The Politics of the Presidential Veto*, 26-48 (Washington: National Legal Center for the Public Interest, 1988), edited by Stephen Glazier (who is credited with beginning the inherent veto issue during Reagan's second term). The McDonald article is in-

cluded in the record of the hearing before the Subcommittee on the Constitution of the Senate Judiciary Committee, *Line Item Veto: The President's Constitutional Authority*, 103rd Cong., 2nd sess., 15 June 1994, 5–11. For an anti-inherent veto argument, see letter from Laurence H. Tribe and Philip B. Kurland to Senator Kennedy in response to the Senator's question of the inherent veto's constitutionality. Tribe and Kurland cited Madison's notes from the Constitutional Convention as part of their argument that clause 3 does not entail inherent item-veto powers for the president. They argue that Madison explained clause 3's inclusion so that Congress would not try to evade clause 2's presidential veto power by passing congressional acts that were not in bill form (*Congressional Record*, 101st Cong., 1st sess., 1989, 135: S 14387, and cited in the Sidak and Smith reply). For other perspectives, see J. Gregory Sidak and Thomas A. Smith, "Four Faces of the Item Veto: A Reply to Tribe and Kurland," *Northwestern University Law Review* 84, no. 2 (1990): 437–79, and "Why Did President Bush Repudiate the 'Inherent' Line-Item Veto?" *Journal of Law and Politics* 9, no. 1 (Fall 1992): 39–59. Both articles are included in the subcommittee record, 23–87. Earlier encouragement for the president to test the inherent item-veto power came from H.R. Res. 297, 101st Cong., 1st sess. (1989), and H.R. 152, 102nd Cong., 1st sess. (1991), both sponsored by Representative Thomas J. Campbell (R-CA), cited in Sidak and Smith, "Four Faces of the Item Veto," 41–43.

56. Prepared statement, Hearing before the Subcommittee on the Constitution of the Senate Judiciary Committee, *Line Item Veto: The President's Constitutional Authority*, 16–17. While no witnesses explicitly denied Specter's claim of what the line-item veto would provide, the question of its inherent existence in the Constitution prompted fascinating exchanges between the Senators and executive branch officials and scholars on the colonial and constitutional history of the veto powers and constitutional debates on the issue by the Federalists and Antifederalists, among other sources of evidence on both sides. See especially testimony and statements by Assistant Attorney General Walter Dellinger, Office of Legal Counsel, Department of Justice, and his predecessor from the Reagan administration, Charles J. Cooper, both of whom concluded after extensive study of the issue that the president had no inherent item veto powers, 89–106 and 116–95.

57. H.R. 4600 was identical to the previous year's H.R. 1578, and both passed the House but received no action in the Senate. The bills provided that the president may transmit a message and draft a rescission bill within three days after the enactment of an appropriations bill. Within three legislative days either a party leader or member would introduce the bill, which would be reported to the Appropriations Committee. The Appropriations Committee must report the bill or a substitute (with equal or greater savings in the same programs the president designated for cuts) within seven days or the bill would be automatically dis-

charged. Without amendment, the House would vote within ten days of the president's rescission message, and then on the substitute if the president's was rejected, and if the bill and the substitute failed, the funds would be released the next day. See consideration and passage of H.R. 1578 (by a margin of 258 to 157), *Congressional Record*, 103rd Cong., 1st sess., 1993, 139: H2067 and H2138, and the consideration and passage of H.R. 4600 (by a margin of 342 to 69), *Congressional Record*, 103rd Cong., 2nd sess., 1994, 140: H5692.

58. Minority Views, House Committee on Rules, *Amending the Congressional Budget and Impoundment Control Act of 1974 to Provide for the Expedited Consideration of Certain Proposed Rescissions of Budget Authority Report*, 103rd Cong., 2nd sess., 1994, H. Rept. 557, 18, to accompany H.R. 4600.

59. The chairman of the Senate Budget Committee, Jim Sasser, and others noted that, although there was no realistic expectation of Senate action that session, these debates would inevitably continue in the 104th Congress.

60. Hearing before the Senate Budget Committee, *Legislative Line-Item Veto Proposals*, 46.

61. Ibid., 48.

62. Ibid., 54.

63. Ibid., 55 and 56–59.

64. H. 2 stipulated that the president must send a separate rescission message for each proposed reduction or elimination in discretionary budget authority and targeted tax benefits. The Congress would have twenty days to pass a disapproval bill, or the rescissions would go into effect automatically. If Congress did pass a disapproval of the rescission proposals, the president could veto the disapproval, and the normal two-thirds of Congress would be necessary to reinstate the funds. Although the bill included a time limit for congressional review of the proposals, unlike typical expedited review proposals, the Congress was not required to act and vote up or down.

65. S. 4 was the companion bill to H. 2. S. 14 was more similar to a traditional expedited rescission proposal in that the president would send a draft bill with his rescission message and the Congress would have an explicit vote on the proposal, which could be defeated by a simple majority.

66. Joint Hearing before the House Government Reform and Oversight Committee and the Senate Committee on Governmental Affairs, *Line-Item Veto*, 1.

67. Ibid., prepared statement, 2.

68. Ibid., prepared statement, 2–3.

69. Ibid., prepared statement, 3–4. Another supporter of the line-item veto, Representative Mark E. Souder (R-IN) commented that "putting Congress in charge of spending is like putting Connie Chung in charge of the CIA," prepared statement, ibid., 4.

70. Ibid., prepared statement, 6.

71. Ibid. For more on the issue of the line-item veto and how appropriations reductions concerning the judicial branch would impact separation of powers arrangements, see comments by Representative Carrie P. Meek (D-FL), 26–27, Christopher Shays (R-CT), 41–42, and testimony and statement by Judge Gilbert S. Merritt, Chairman, Executive Committee of the Judicial Conference of the United States, and the Chief Judge of the 6th Circuit Court of Appeals, 85–97. For more on the general constitutional issues of delegation, see Congressional Research Service, American Law Division, on "Constitutionality of Granting President Power to Reduce Discretionary Budget Authority and to Revoke Certain Targeted Tax Benefits," included in the Committees' hearing, 127–67. The memo concludes, "on the basis of textual analysis and precedent that it would be constitutionally permissible for Congress to delegate to the President the power to reduce or omit various items from appropriations acts under the terms set out in the draft bill."

72. Ibid., 16. Senator John McCain (R-AZ) made a very similar point that in case of presidential abuse of the line-item powers, "repercussions I think would be very severe, both from the view of the American people and the ability of Congress to react in many, many ways." He further argued that with the possible exception of Wisconsin (in which Governors can add legislation in addition to taking items out) he knows of no state in which the line-item power led to such kinds of threats and power over legislators. Ibid., 19.

73. Ibid., 47–61.

74. Ibid., 62. For full testimony and prepared statement, see 61–75.

75. Hearing before the Senate Committee on the Budget, *Concurrent Resolution on the Budget for FY96, Vol. II*, 2. Senator Exon made an additional pitch for his bill by arguing that McCain's bill had received between 40 and 44 votes in favor over the past five years but it was an insufficient number to overcome an almost certain filibuster. See opening statement, 3.

76. Ibid., 5–6.

77. Ibid., 7.

78. Ibid., prepared statement, 55.

79. Ibid., 9.

80. Ibid., 59. Senator Bradley also defended his line-item bill, S. 137, which authorized presidential rescissions for discretionary spending and targeted tax expenditures passed under separate enrollment. Senator Ernest Hollings (D-SC) also proposed a separate enrollment bill.

81. Ibid., 10.

82. Ibid., 12.

83. Ibid., 14–15.

84. S.J. Res. 2, sponsored by Senators Strom Thurmond (R-SC), Bob Dole (R-KS), and Alan K. Simpson (R-WY), which provided for an item veto for ap-

propriations bills with a normal congressional override process. S.J. Res. 16, sponsored by Senator Hank Brown (R-CO) provided for an item veto for any kind of legislation concerning spending authority with a normal congressional override process for each item reduced or disapproved. The hearing did not examine all item veto amendment proposals introduced in the 104th Congress by that time.

85. Hearing before the Senate Subcommittee on the Constitution, Federalism, and Property Rights of the Judiciary Committee, *Line-Item Veto: A Constitutional Approach*, 104th Cong., 1st sess., 24 January 1995, 2.

86. Ibid., 6. Biden also said he supported Bradley's separate enrollment bill, S. 137, as his preferred statutory approach.

87. Ibid., 4–21.

88. House Committee on Government Reform, *Line Item Veto Act*, 104th Cong., 1st sess., 1995, H. Rept. 11, 5, Part 1, to accompany H.R. 2, Rules Committee. The Rules Committee's reported amendments clarified that Congress must vote to disapprove the president's entire rescission package to prevent "unrelated matter" being incorporated into the bill and disallowing any congressional "cherry picking" from the president's special message. In addition, the term "targeted tax benefit" was defined as benefiting five or fewer taxpayers and the Rules Committee specified expedited procedures to ensure a vote on any disapproval bill, if members seek to have one. See 6–7.

89. Ibid., 17–18.

90. House Committee, *Line Item Veto Act*, 7, Part 2, to accompany H.R. 2.

91. Ibid., 10–11.

92. Ibid., 33–35. The ten minority members were Cardiss Collins, Edolphus Towns, Louise Slaughter, Eleanor Holmes Norton, Bob Wise, Henry A. Waxman, Barbara-Rose Collins, Paul E. Kanjorski, Chaka Fattah, and Carolyn Maloney.

93. In his remarks in favor of the item veto, Speaker Newt Gingrich commended Majority Leader Richard Armey for arranging line–item veto debates to coincide with Ronald Reagan's 84th birthday on February 6. See *Congressional Record*, 104th Cong., 1st sess., 1995, 141: H1262.

94. Ibid., H1081.

95. Ibid., H1113. For more debates and related votes, see also H1168 and H1225.

96. See Additional Views, Senate Budget Committee, *Legislative Line Item Veto Act of 1995*, 104th Cong., 1st sess., 1995, S. Rept. 9, 14, to accompany S. 4, (legislative day, February 22). For more on S. 14, see Senate Committee on the Budget, *Legislative Line Item Veto Act*, 104th Cong., 1st sess., 1995, S. Rept. 10 printed the same day. Amendments to S. 14 included provisions for targeted tax benefits and codifying certain pay-as-you-go rules.

97. Hearing before the Committee on Governmental Affairs, *S. 4 and S. 14, Line-Item Veto*, 104th Cong., 1st sess., 23 February 1995, 4. Senator Glenn re-

quested the additional hearing (perhaps because he missed the January 12 one), and Senator McCain criticized him for doing so and holding up the Committee's reporting on the bills. See 19–20 and 21 for Glenn's defense of his request.

98. Ibid., 8.

99. Ibid., 31–32.

100. Ibid., 33. Schick still recommended three changes to S. 14; the president should be able to submit a rescission bill and have it fast-tracked throughout the legislative year, Congress should be able to reduce the president's proposed program eliminations, not just approve or disapprove them, and eliminate the possible veto for tax expenditures, which can be curtailed by legislative votes.

101. Senate Committee on Governmental Affairs, *Legislative Line Item Veto Act of 1995*, 104th Cong., 1st sess., 1995, S. Rept. 13, 11–13, to accompany S. 4, (legislative day, March 6). See also Senate Committee on Governmental Affairs, *Legislative Line Item Veto Act*, 104th Cong., 1st sess., 1995, S. Rept. 14, 14–15 to accompany S. 14. The amendment allowed for S. 14 protected Social Security from any potential veto.

102. The Senate bill mandated that appropriations bills contain the same level of detail as their accompanying reports, which would ensure that large lump sums be disaggregated. In addition, authorization bills containing new direct spending or targeted tax benefits must contain such provisions in a separate section and identify these items in the accompanying report. Any appropriation or authorization bill not complying with these requirements would be subject to a point of order in both chambers. After passage of an appropriations or authorization bill, the enrolling clerk of the originating chamber would separate the items into individual bills and both chambers would vote again to approve or disapprove the separated items en bloc before submission to the president. See Conference Report, House Committee on Government Reform, *Line Item Veto Act*, 104th Cong., 2nd sess., 1996, H. Rept. 491, 16–17.

103. *Congressional Record*, 104th Cong., 1st sess., 1995, 141, Pt. 51: S 4190.

104. Ibid., Pt. 54, 23 March 1995, S 4412.

105. Ibid., S 4443.

106. See Elizabeth A. Palmer and Andrew Taylor, "House Pushes Negotiations on Line-Item Veto," *Congressional Quarterly Weekly Report* 53, no. 20 (1995): 1409; Andrew Taylor, "Clinton Criticizes Republicans for Line-Item Veto Delay," *Congressional Quarterly Weekly Report* 53, no. 23 (1995): 1627; and Mark T. Kehoe, "History of Line-Item Veto Effort," *Congressional Quarterly Weekly Report* 54, no. 13 (1996): 867.

107. See Andrew Taylor, "Republicans Break Logjam on Line-Item Veto Bill," *Congressional Quarterly Weekly Report* 54, no. 11 (1996): 687, and "GOP Negotiators Agree On Line-Item Veto," *Congressional Quarterly Weekly Report* 54, no. 12 (1996): 779.

108. Ibid., 19.

109. For more on the Byrd-expedited rescission substitute, see *Congressional Record*, 104th Cong., 2nd sess., 1996, 142: S 2949–54. Despite threats to do so, Senator Byrd did not filibuster. See Andrew Taylor, "Congress Hands President a Budgetary Scalpel," *Congressional Quarterly Weekly Report* 54, no. 13 (1996): 865. The party vote breakdown in the Senate on the conference report was: Republicans 50 to 3 and Democrats 19 to 28 (Northern Democrats 16 to 21 and Southern Democrats 3 to 7). The party breakdown in the House was Republicans 221 to 3 and Democrats 11 to 173 (Northern Democrats 5 to 123, Southern Democrats 6 to 50).

110. *Congressional Record*, 104th Cong., 2nd sess., 1996, 142, Pt. 44: S 2932.

111. Ibid., S 2954.

112. Ibid., S 2963.

113. House Committee, *Line Item Veto Act*, 15, to accompany S. 4.

114. Ibid., 16.

115. Public Law 130, 104th Cong., 2nd sess. (9 April 1996), section 1021 (a). See Secs. 1026 and 1027 for details on definitions.

116. Ibid., Sec. 1022 (a)–(b).

117. Ibid., Sec. 1025 (a)–(d). If Congress adjourns before the thirty-day deadline is reached, the bill begins the process again when Congress reconvenes.

118. Ibid., Sec. 1025 (e)–(f).

119. Ibid., Sec. 3.

120. Ibid., Sec. 5.

121. See Syllabus, *Raines v. Byrd*, U.S. Supreme Court 96–1671, 117 S. Ct. 2312 (1997), 1. The Chief Justice delivered the opinion of the Court and was joined by Justices O'Connor, Scalia, Kennedy, Thomas, and Ginsburg in part. Justice Souter filed a concurring opinion joined by Ginsburg in part. Justices Stevens and Breyer filed dissenting opinions.

122. *Byrd v. Raines*, 956 F. Supp. 25 (DDC 1997), 521 U.S. 811 (1997). U.S. District Judge Thomas Penfield Jackson wrote the judgment.

123. See Syllabus, ibid., 2, and case 6–8 for more on the standing question relating to legislators. "Some importance must be attached to the fact that appellants have not been authorized to represent their respective Houses in this action, and indeed both Houses actively oppose their suit. In addition, the conclusion reached here neither deprives Members of Congress of an adequate remedy—since they may repeal the Act or exempt appropriations bills from its reach—nor forecloses the Act from constitutional challenge by someone who suffers judicially cognizable injury resulting from it." Syllabus 2 and case 18.

124. Clinton canceled both a new direct spending law, Sec. 4722 (c) of the Balanced Budget Act of 1997, which waived the federal government's statutory right to up to $2.6 billion of funds levied by the City of New York against Medic-

aid providers, and a limited tax benefit law, Sec. 968 of the Taxpayer Relief Act of 1997, which permitted owners of certain food processors and refiners to defer recognition of capital gains if they sold their stock to eligible farmers' cooperatives. See *Clinton v. City of New York*, 97–1374 (1998), Syllabus, 1 and case Part I.

125. For more on constitutional issues related to *Raines* and *Clinton v. City of New York*, see Case Note, "Standing in the Way of Separation of Powers: The Consequences of Raines v. Byrd," *Harvard Law Review* 112, no. 7 (May 1999): 1741–58; Symposium entitled "The Phoenix Rises Again: The Nondelegation Doctrine from Constitutional and Policy Perspectives," *Cardozo Law Review* 20, no. 3 (January 1999); Bernard W. Bell, "Dead Again: The Nondelegation Doctrine, the Rules/Standards Dilemma and the Line Item Veto," *Villanova Law Review* 44, no. 2 (March 1999): 189–226; Courtney Worchester, "An Abdication of Responsibility and Violation of Finely Wrought Procedure: The Supreme Court Vetoes the Line Item Veto Act of 1996," *Boston University Law Review* 78, no. 5 (December 1998): 1583–1608; Saikrishna Bangalore Prakash, "Deviant Executive Lawmaking," *George Washington Law Review* 67, no. 1 (November 1998): 1–50.

126. U.S. Supreme Court, no. 97–1374, Part IV, 19.

127. Ibid., Part V, 25–26.

128. Ibid., Part VI, 31.

129. Ibid., Part III of Scalia's opinion, 15. Justice Scalia concludes Part III by saying that the title of the Line–Item Veto Act, chosen perhaps to allow public comprehension or to fulfill a campaign pledge, "has succeeded in faking out the Supreme Court. The President's action it authorizes in fact is not a line-item veto." Justice Breyer makes a similar conclusion in Part III of his dissent, which Justices O'Connor and Scalia join. Justice Scalia also concludes in Part IV that some of the parties lacked standing in the first place, an issue that is also raised by Justice Kennedy in his concurring opinion.

130. Ibid., Part V. In his concurring opinion, Justice Kennedy criticizes Breyer's characterization that the act does not threaten individual liberties.

131. Hearings before the Joint Study Committee on Budget Control, *Improving Congressional Budget Control*, 30.

132. Patrick J. Fett and Jeffrey S. Hill, "Enhancing the Legislative Powers of the Presidency: The Unanticipated Potential of the Line-Item Veto," paper prepared for delivery at the 1997 Annual Meeting of the American Political Science Association, Washington, D.C., 28–31 August 1997, 8.

133. Louis Fisher and Neal Devins, "How Successfully Can the States' Item Veto be Transferred to the President?" *Georgetown Law Journal* 75, no. 1 (October 1986): 162. See also Fisher, "Line Item Veto Act of 1996: Heads-Up from the States," *Public Budgeting and Finance* 17, no. 2 (Summer 1997): 3–17. For studies on the mixed fiscal and partisan effectiveness of state item vetoes, see Glenn Abney and Thomas P. Lauth, "The Item Veto and Fiscal Responsibility," *Journal of Poli-*

tics 59, no. 3 (August 1997): 882–92; "Former Governors' Perceptions of a Presidential Line-Item Veto," *Presidential Studies Quarterly* 27, no. 4 (Fall 1997): 745–59; Glenn Abney and Thomas P. Lauth, "The Line Item Veto in the States: An Instrument for Fiscal Restraint or an Instument for Partisanship?" *Public Administration Review* 45 (1985): 372–79; James J. Gosling, "Wisconsin Item Veto Lessons," *Public Administration Review* 46 (1986): 292–300; Barton Abrams and William R. Dougan, "The Effects of Constitutional Restraints on Governmental Spending," *Public Choice* 49 (1986): 101–16; Douglas Holtz-Eakin, "The Line Item Veto and Public Sector Budgets: Evidence from the States," *Journal of Public Economics* 36 (1988): 269–92; David C. Nice, "The Item Veto Expenditure Restraint," *Journal of Politics* 50 (1988): 487–99; W. Mark Crain and James C. Miller III, "Budget Process and Spending Growth," *William and Mary Law Review* 31 (1990): 1021–46; Alan J. Dixon, "The Case for the Line Item Veto," *Journal of Law, Ethics, and Public Policy* 1 (1985): 207–26.

134. Fisher, *Congressional Abdication*, 149–50.

135. Ibid., 150–51.

Conclusion

1. *Congressional Record*, 104th Cong., 1st sess., 1995, 14: S 4308.

2. Hearings before the Joint Study Committee on Budget Control, *Improving Congressional Budget Control*, 37.

3. Prepared statement, Hearing before the Task Force on Budget Process, Reconciliation and Enforcement of the House Committee on the Budget, *Budget Process Reform*, 34.

4. *Congressional Record*, 101st Cong., 2nd sess., 1990, 135, Pt. 150: S 17568.

5. George Will, "Bush's Winter of Discontent," repr. *The Courier-Journal* (Louisville, KY), Forum sec., D3, 8 February 2004.

6. See Brian M. Riedel, "$20,000 per Household: The Highest Level of Federal Spending Since World War II," http://www.heritage.org/Research/Budget/BG1710.cfm, 3 December 2003; Richard Kogan, "Swelling Deficits: Increased Spending is not the Principal Culprit," http://www.cbpp.org/10-27-03bud.htm (27 October 2003); and "The Concord Coalition's Report on Fiscal Responsibility," 5, no. 1 (July 2003), accessible through www.concordcoalition.org.

BIBLIOGRAPHY

Aldrich, John H., and David W. Rhode. "The Logic of Conditional Party Government: Revisiting the Electoral Connection." In *Congress Reconsidered*, edited by Lawrence C. Dodd and Bruce I. Oppenheimer, 269–92. 7th ed. Washington: CQ Press, 2001.

Arnold, Douglas R. *The Logic of Congressional Action*. New Haven: Yale University Press, 1990.

Barber, Sotirios A. *The Constitution and the Delegation of Congressional Power*. Chicago: University of Chicago Press, 1975.

Berman, Larry. *The Office of Management and Budget and the Presidency, 1921–1979*. Princeton, NJ: Princeton University Press, 1979.

Bessette, Joseph M. *The Mild Voice of Reason: Deliberative Democracy and American National Government*. Chicago: University of Chicago Press, 1994.

Binder, Sarah. "Congress, the Executive, and the Production of Public Policy: United We Govern?" In *Congress Reconsidered*, edited by Lawrence C. Dodd and Bruce I. Oppenheimer, 293–313. 7th ed. Washington: CQ Press, 2001.

Brady, David, and Mark A. Morgan. "Reforming the Structure of the House Appropriations Process: The Effects of the 1885 and 1919-20 Reforms on Money Decisions." In *Congress: Structure and Policy*, edited by Matthew D. McCubbins and Terry Sullivan, 207–34. New York: Cambridge University Press, 1987.

Byrd, Robert. "The Control of the Purse and the Line Item Veto Act." *Harvard Journal on Legislation* 35, no. 2 (1998): 297–333.

Campbell, Colton C. *Discharging Congress: Government by Commission*. Westport, CT: Praeger Publishers, 2002.

Cooper, Joseph. *Congress and Its Committees*. New York: Garland Press, 1988.

_____. *The Origins of the Standing Committees and the Development of the Modern House*. Houston: Rice University Press, 1970.

Davidson, Roger H., and Walter J. Oleszek. "Adaptation and Consolidation: Structural Innovation in the U.S. House of Representatives." *Legislative Studies Quarterly* 1 (1976): 37–65.

Dodd, Lawrence C. "Congress and the Cycles of Power." In *The Presidency and the Congress: A Shifting Balance of Power?*, edited by William S. Livingston, Lawrence C. Dodd, and Richard L. Schott, 46–69. Austin: LBJ School of Public Affairs, 1979.

———. "Congress and the Quest for Power." In *Congress Reconsidered*, edited by Lawrence C. Dodd and Bruce I. Oppenheimer, 269–307. 1st ed. New York: Praeger Publishers, 1977.

———. "Congress, the Constitution, and the Crisis of Legitimation." In *Congress Reconsidered*, edited by Lawrence C. Dodd and Bruce I. Oppenheimer, 390–420. 2nd ed. Washington: CQ Press, 1981.

———. "Congress, the Presidency, and the American Experience: A Transformational Perspective." In *Divided Democracy*, edited by James A. Thurber, 275–302. Washington: CQ Press, 1991.

———. "The Rise of the Technocratic Congress: Congressional Reform in the 1970s." In *Remaking American Politics*, edited by Richard A. Harris and Sidney M. Milkis, 89–111. Boulder: Westview Press, 1989.

Epstein, David, and Sharyn O'Halloran. *Delegating Powers: A Transaction Cost Politics Approach to Policy Making under Separate Powers*. New York: Cambridge University Press, 2000.

Fenno, Richard F. *Congressmen in Committees*. Boston: Little, Brown, 1973.

———. *Home Style: House Members in Their Districts*. Boston: Little, Brown, 1978.

———. *The Power of the Purse: Appropriations Politics in Congress*. Boston: Little, Brown, 1966.

Fett, Patrick J., and Jeffrey S. Hill. "Enhancing the Legislative Powers of the Presidency: The Unanticipated Potential of the Line-Item Veto." Annual Meeting of the American Political Science Association, Washington, D.C., 29 August 1997.

Fiorina, Morris. "Legislative Choice of Regulatory Forms: Legal Process or Administrative Process?" *Public Choice* 39 (1982): 33–71.

Fisher, Louis. "Annual Authorizations: Durable Roadblocks to Biennial Budgeting." *Public Budgeting and Finance* 3, no. 1 (1983): 23–40.

———. *Congressional Abdication on War & Spending*. College Station, TX: Texas A&M University Press, 2000.

———. "Federal Budget Doldrums: The Vacuum in Presidential Leadership." *Public Administration Review* 50, no. 6 (1990): 693–700.

———. *The Politics of Shared Power: Congress and the Executive*. Washington: CQ Press, 1993.

_____. *Presidential Spending Power.* Princeton: Princeton University Press, 1975.

Harris, Joseph P. *Congressional Control of Administration.* Washington: Brookings Institution, 1964.

Havens, Harry S. "Gramm-Rudman-Hollings: Origins and Implementation." *Public Budgeting & Finance* 6, no. 3 (Autumn 1986): 4–24.

Hertzke, Allen D., and Ronald M. Peters, Jr., eds. *The Atomistic Congress: An Interpretation of Congressional Change.* Armonk, NY: M.E. Sharpe, 1992.

Hibbing, John R., and Elizabeth Theiss-Morse. *Congress as Public Enemy: Public Attitudes toward American Political Institutions.* New York: Cambridge University Press, 1995.

Huntington, Samuel P. "Congressional Reponses to the Twentieth Century." In *The Congress and America's Future*, edited by David Truman, 5–31. 2nd ed. Englewood Cliffs, NJ: Prentice Hall, 1975.

Jones, Charles O. *The Presidency in a Separated System.* Washington: Brookings Institution, 1994.

Kiewiet, D. Roderick, and Matthew D. McCubbins. *The Logic of Delegation: Congressional Parties and the Appropriations Process.* Chicago: University of Chicago Press, 1991.

Kosters, Marvin. *Fiscal Politics and the Budget Enforcement Act.* Washington: AEI Press, 1993.

Lowi, Theodore J. *The End of Liberalism: Ideology, Policy, and the Crisis of Public Authority.* New York: W.W. Norton, 1979.

Mayer, Kenneth R., and David T. Canon. *The Dysfunctional Congress? The Individual Root of an Institutional Dilemma.* Boulder, CO: Westview Press, 1999.

Mayhew, David R. *Congress: The Electoral Connection.* New Haven: Yale University Press, 1974.

McMurtry, Virginia A. "The Impoundment Control Act of 1974: Restraining or Reviving Presidential Power?" *Public Budgeting and Finance* 17 (1997): 39-61.

Mills, Gregory B., and John L. Palmer, eds. *Federal Budget Policy in the 1980s.* Washington: Urban Institute Press, 1984.

Nixon, Sondra. "Budget Amendments: An Idea that Never Goes Out of Style," *Congressional Quarterly Weekly Report* 53, no. 2 (January 1995): 14.

Oppenheimer, Bruce I. "Abdicating Congressional Power: The Paradox of Republican Control." In *Congress Reconsidered*, edited by Lawrence C. Dodd and Bruce I. Oppenheimer, 371–89. 6th ed. Washington: CQ Press, 1997.

Orren, Karen, and Stephen Skowronek. "Order and Time in Institutional Study." In *Political Science in History*, edited by James Farr, John S. Dryzek, and Stephen T. Leonard, 296–317. Cambridge: Cambridge University Press, 1994.

Palazzolo, Daniel J. *Done Deal? The Politics of the 1997 Budget Agreement.* New York: Chatham House, 1999.

_____. *The Speaker and the Budget*. Pittsburgh: University of Pittsburgh Press, 1992.

Pfiffner, James P. *The President, the Budget, and Congress: Impoundment and the 1974 Budget Act*. Boulder, CO: Westview Press, 1979.

Pitkin, Hanna F. *The Concept of Representation*. Berkeley: University of California Press, 1967.

Polsby, Nelson W. "The Institutionalization of the House of Representatives." *American Political Science Review* 62 (1968): 144–68.

Rhode, David W. *Parties and Leaders in the Postreform House*. Chicago: University of Chicago Press, 1991.

Rossiter, Clinton. *The Federalist Papers*. New York: Mentor/Penguin, 1961.

Savage, James. *Balanced Budgets & American Politics*. Ithaca, NY: Cornell University Press, 1988.

Schick, Allen. *The Capacity to Budget*. Washington: Urban Institute, 1990.

_____. *Congress and Money: Budgeting, Spending, and Taxing*. Washington: Urban Institute, 1980.

_____. *The Federal Budget: Politics, Policy, Process*. Washington: Brookings Institution, 1995.

_____, ed. *Crisis in the Budget Process: Exercising Political Choice*. Washington: American Enterprise Institute, 1986.

Schickler, Eric. *Disjointed Pluralism: Institutional Innovation and the Development of the U.S. Congress*. Princeton, NJ: Princeton University Press, 2001.

Schoenbrod, David. *Power Without Responsibility: How Congress Abuses the People through Delegation*. New Haven: Yale University Press, 1993.

Sellers, Patrick J. "Fiscal Consistency and Federal District Spending in Congressional Elections." *American Journal of Political Science* 41, no. 3 (1997): 1024–41.

Shuman, Howard E. *Politics and the Budget: The Struggle between the President and Congress*. 3rd ed. Englewood Cliffs, NJ: Prentice Hall, 1992.

Silverstein, Gordon. *Imbalance of Powers: Constitutional Interpretation and the Making of American Foreign Policy*. New York: Oxford University Press, 1997.

Sinclair, Barbara. *Unorthodox Lawmaking: New Legislative Processes in the U.S. Congress*. Washington: CQ Press, 1997.

Smith, Steven S., and Gerald Gamm. "The Dynamics of Party Government in Congress." In *Congress Reconsidered*, edited by Lawrence C. Dodd and Bruce I. Oppenheimer, 245–68. 7th ed. Washington: CQ Press, 2001.

Spitzer, Robert J. "The Constitutionality of the Presidential Line-Item Veto." *Political Science Quarterly* 112 (Summer 1997): 261–83.

Stewart, Charles H., III. *Budget Reform Politics: The Design of the Appropriations Process in the House of Representatives, 1865-1921*. New York: Cambridge University Press, 1989.

Stith, Kate. "Congress's Power of the Purse." *Yale Law Journal* 97 (1990): 1343–97.

Swift, Elaine K. *The Making of an American Senate: Reconstitutive Change in Congress, 1789-1841.* Ann Arbor: University of Michigan Press, 1996.

Sundquist, James L. *The Decline and Resurgence of Congress.* Washington: Brookings Institution, 1981.

Taylor, Andrew. "Senate Again One Vote Short; GOP Says House Will Act." *Congressional Quarterly Weekly Report* 55, no. 10 (8 March 1997): 577–79.

Thurber, James A. "Centralization, Devolution, and Turf Protection in the Congressional Budget Process." In *Congress Reconsidered,* edited by Lawrence C. Dodd and Bruce I. Oppenheimer, 325–46. 6th ed. Washington: CQ Press, 1997.

Thurber, James A., and Samantha L. Durst. "The 1990 Budget Enforcement Act: The Decline of Congressional Accountability." In *Congress Reconsidered,* edited by Lawrence C. Dodd and Bruce I. Oppenheimer, 375–97. 5th ed. Washington: CQ Press, 1993.

Tulis, Jeffrey K. *The Rhetorical Presidency.* Princeton, NJ: Princeton University Press, 1987.

Uslander, Eric M. *The Decline of Comity in Congress.* Ann Arbor: University of Michigan Press, 1993.

Weaver, R. Kent. "The Politics of Blame Avoidance." *Journal of Public Policy* 6, no. 4 (1986): 371–98.

Weissman, Stephen R. *A Culture of Deference: Congress's Failure of Leadership in Foreign Policy.* New York: Basic Books, 1995.

White, Joseph, and Aaron Wildavsky. *The Deficit and the Public Interest: The Search for Responsible Budgeting in the 1980s.* Berkeley: University of California Press; New York: Russell Sage Foundation, 1989.

Wildavsky, Aaron. *The New Politics of the Budgetary Process.* Glenview, IL: Scott-Foresman, 1988.

———. The *Politics of the Budgetary Process.* 4th ed. Glenview, IL: Scott-Foresman, 1984.

Wildavsky, Aaron, and Naomi Caiden. *The New Politics of the Budgetary Process.* 3rd ed. New York: Longman, 1997.

Wilkinson, Vernon L. "Federal Legislation: The Item Veto in the American Constitutional System." *Georgetown Law Journal* 25 (1936): 106–12.

Wilson, Woodrow. *Congressional Government.* New York: World Publishers, 1954. First published 1885.

INDEX

District of Columbia, 113, 115 115,
116, 205, 206, 207

vetoes, 122, 168, 189, 194–195, 199,
212; overrides, 168; power, 38–39,
99, 108, 178–179, 180, 202, 207
Vietnam War, 34, 52, 63

War Powers Resolution (1974), 52
Warner, Senator John, 181
Watergate, 52, 57

Weinberger, Casper W., 59, 122–123
White, Justice Byron, 116
Whitten, Representative Jamie L., 1,
93–94
Wildavsky, Aaron, 26, 79, 162
Wilkinson, Vernon L., 177–178
Will, George, 223
Williams, Representative Pat, 100–101
Wilson, President Woodrow, 30
World War I, 30
World War II, 1, 32, 55